WINDOWS 11
MADE EASY

Take Control of Your Computer

By James Bernstein

Copyright © 2022 by James Bernstein. All rights reserved.

All rights reserved. This book or any portion thereof
may not be reproduced or used in any manner whatsoever
without the express written permission of the publisher
except for the use of brief quotations in a book review.

Printed in the United States of America

Bernstein, James
Windows 11 Made Easy
Part of the Windows Made Easy series

For more information on reproducing sections of this book or sales of this book,
go to **www.madeeasybookseries.com**

Contents

Introduction 7

Chapter 1 - Introducing Windows 11 8
Windows History and Versions 8
Windows Hardware Requirements 15

Chapter 2 – Installing Windows 17
Clean Installation vs. Upgrade Installation 17
How to Install Windows 18
Windows Update 30

Chapter 3 – Configuring and Customizing Windows 34
Initial Look and Feel Compared to Windows 10 34
Using Windows – Programs and the Start Menu 41
Customizing the Windows Start Menu and Taskbar 44
Changing the Date and Time 53
Cortana 55
Windows Desktop 58
Changing Your Desktop Background 61
Changing Your Display Settings 64
Changing Themes, Colors, and Sounds 66
Screen Savers 68
Windows Power Settings 69
Windows Control Panel 73

Chapter 4 – Installing Devices 78
Installing Printers\Scanners 78

Connecting a Smartphone to Your Computer 82

Mouse Settings 83

Installing USB Devices 86

Dual Monitor Setup 86

Chapter 5 – Windows Apps 88

Apps vs. Programs 88

Microsoft Store Apps 90

Uninstalling Apps 92

Chapter 6 – File and Folder Management 95

Windows File Structure 95

Changing File and Folder Views 96

File Extensions 98

Moving, Copying, Renaming and Deleting Files 99

Creating a New Folder or File 105

Default Windows Folders 106

Searching for Files and Folders 107

Chapter 7 – User Accounts 111

User Account Types 111

Creating User Accounts 112

Changing Passwords 122

Switching Users 125

Creating a Password Reset Disk 126

Chapter 8 – Microsoft Edge Web Browser 129

Introducing Microsoft Edge 129

Using Microsoft Edge	130
Using Multiple Tabs	132
Using Favorites	133
Customizing Edge Settings	135

Chapter 9 – Windows 11 Settings 143

Windows 11 Settings App	143
System Settings	145
Bluetooth & Devices	149
Network & Internet	150
Personalization	152
Apps	154
Accounts	156
Time & Language	157
Gaming	158
Accessibility	159
Privacy & security	160
Windows Update	162

Chapter 10 – Networking 165

Workgroups	165
Domains	165
IP Addresses and Configuration	167
Dynamic and Static IP Addresses	170
DHCP	170
Wireless Setup	171

Chapter 11 – Basic Troubleshooting 174

Printer Troubleshooting	174

Wireless and Internet Troubleshooting 176

Error Messages, Crashes, and Freezing Issues 182

Error Types 182

Windows Blue Screen of Death (BSOD) 183

Using Task Manager and Ctrl-Alt-Del 184

System Configuration Utility (MSconfig) 185

Booting with the Windows DVD to Run Repair Utilities 187

What's Next? 192

About the Author 194

Introduction

These days everyone has a desktop computer, laptop, or at least a device such as a smartphone or a tablet that they use to do things such as go online, send emails, and so on. And for the people who use a personal computer at home or at work, then there is a very good chance that it is running Microsoft Windows, especially at the office where Windows has a much larger market share than other operating systems such as Apple's Mac OS.

When Windows 10 first came out, Microsoft has said that it would be the last version of their desktop operating system and that they would just continue to update it and add new features rather than come out with new versions. But now that Windows 11 is out, that proves what many of us always believed, that there would eventually be a replacement for Windows 10.

The goal of this book is to help you get the most out of your Windows 11 computer and make you a more proficient computer user. I will cover the basics (in detail) to better help you understand how to do things like configure and customize Windows, use the great built-in features and software as well troubleshoot issues that you may run into while using your computer. A lot of this content will apply to previous versions of Windows, so you will be able to apply your newfound knowledge to older computers as well. Also keep in mind that since Microsoft is constantly updating Windows that if you come across something in this book that doesn't match up with what your computer shows, it's most likely that Microsoft has changed how you do that procedure, so be warned.

So, on that note, let's get things started and turn you into a Windows 11 expert, or at least get you a few steps closer!

Chapter 1 - Introducing Windows 11

Microsoft Windows is what is known as an operating system. An operating system is what allows your software, such as Microsoft Word or Google Chrome, to work with your computer, and therefore let you use the software itself. A computer consists of various hardware components, such as video cards and network adapters, and the operating system is what allows the user (which is you) to make use of that hardware so you can do things like check your email, edit photos, play games, etc.

Windows History and Versions
Windows has been around for a long time, and there have been many versions. So, let's start with a history of the different versions and features that have taken us to where we are today (Windows 10).

Windows 3.1
Windows 3.1 was released in April 1992 and became the best-selling GUI in the history of computing. It added multimedia functionality, which included support for connecting to external musical instruments and MIDI devices. TrueType font support was added to provide Windows with a WYSIWYG or What You See Is What You Get interface. Windows 3.1 added the ability to close applications by pressing Ctrl+Alt+Del and terminating hung applications from the list of running programs. Drag and drop functionality provided a new way to use the GUI, and support for Object Linking and Embedding (OLE) was added. OLE allowed embedding elements from different applications into one document.

Windows 3.11
Windows 3.11 was released in November 1993. It did not add any feature improvements over Windows 3.1 but corrected problems (most of which were network problems). Microsoft replaced all new retail versions of Windows 3.1 with Windows 3.11 and provided a free upgrade via their Web site to anyone who currently owned Windows 3.1.

Windows for Workgroups 3.1
Windows for Workgroups (WFW) 3.1 was released in April 1992. It was the first Microsoft OS to provide native support for peer-to-peer networks. It supported file and printer sharing and made it easy to specify which files should be shared with other computers running DOS or Windows. WFW also included Microsoft Mail (an e-mail client) and Schedule+ (a workgroup scheduler).

Windows for Workgroups 3.11

Windows for Workgroups (WFW) 3.11 was released in February 1994 and was geared toward local area networking. This made it a hit for corporations wanting to increase productivity by sharing information. The default networking protocol was NetBEUI, and TCP/IP or IPX/SPX could be added. WFW 3.11 clients could connect to both workgroups and domains, and it provided built-in support for Novell NetWare Networks. WFW 3.11 also improved support for remote access services.

Windows 95

Windows 95 was released in August 1995, and it changed the face of Windows forever. Windows 95 had features such as Plug-and-Play to make hardware installations easier, and dial-up networking for connecting to the Internet or another network via a modem. Windows 95 was the first Microsoft operating system that supported long filenames. Windows 95 also supported preemptive multitasking. Perhaps the most drastic change was that Windows 95 was a "real" OS. Unlike its predecessors, it did not require DOS to be installed first. Windows 95b (OSR2) was an improved version that was never offered for sale to the public and was only available to Original Equipment Manufacturers (OEMs) to install on new computers that they were offering for sale. Windows 95b added support for universal serial bus (USB) devices and the FAT32 file system that allowed for larger partitions, better disk space usage, and better performance.

Windows 98

Windows 98 was released on June 25, 1998. It was the retail upgrade to Windows 95 that provided support for reading DVDs and using USB devices. Applications in Windows 98 opened and closed more quickly. Like 95b, Windows 98 included a FAT32 converter, which allowed you to use hard drives over the 2GB limit imposed by DOS. The backup program was revamped to support more backup devices (including SCSI), and Microsoft added the Disk Cleanup utility to help find and delete old unused files. Windows 98 also included Internet Explorer 4.0 and the Active Desktop.

Windows 98 Second Edition

Windows 98 Second Edition (SE) was released in June 1998 as an incremental update to Windows 98. Windows 98 SE improved the home multimedia experience, home networking, and Internet browsing. Windows 98 SE introduced Internet Connection Sharing (ICS), which allowed a Windows 98 SE machine to function as a Network Address Translation (NAT) server for other machines on the home network. In other words, you could have multiple machines connected to the Internet at the same time using only a single ISP account and a single public IP address and all Internet traffic would go through the Windows 98 SE machine running ICS. Windows 98 SE also included NetMeeting and Internet Explorer 5.0. Windows 98 SE was the first consumer operating system capable of using the same drivers as Windows NT 4.0.

Windows ME
Windows Millennium Edition (ME) was the last OS built on the MS-DOS kernel. It was released in September 2000 and added improved support for digital media through applications such as Image Acquisition, Movie Maker, and Windows Media Player. Image Acquisition was added to simplify downloading images from digital cameras. Movie Maker was included to ease editing and recording digital video media files. Media Player was used to organize and play music and video files. To enhance reliability, Windows ME added the "system restore" feature, which could be used to restore any deleted system files to fix problems. Another important feature was system file protection, which prevented important OS files from being changed by applications. Windows ME also included a new home networking wizard to make adding peripherals and computers to a home network easier.

Windows 2000
Windows 2000 was released in February 2000 and put an end to the NT name. Even though it was built on the same NT kernel, it no longer used the name. Windows 2000 shipped with four versions: Professional, Server, Advanced Server, and Datacenter Server. Windows 2000 Professional was the replacement for NT 4.0 Workstation and was used as a desktop/client OS. Windows 2000 added many of the features that NT 4.0 didn't have, such as a disk defragmenter, device manager, and Plug and Play support.

Windows XP Home Edition
Windows XP Home Edition was released in 2001. It was the first consumer OS based on the NT code, which makes it the most stable and secure Microsoft consumer OS to date. Home Edition supports the Internet Connection Firewall (ICF), which protects your computer while you are connected to the Internet. It also features Fast User Switching, which allows you to switch between users' desktops without having to log off first. Home networking and multimedia capabilities have also been enhanced. Remote Assistance is a new feature that lets you ask someone for help. The helper can then remotely control your desktop and chat with you online. Also included are features such as Task Manager and System Monitor, and brand new features such as the Desktop Cleanup Wizard and taskbar grouping were introduced.

Windows XP Professional

Windows XP Professional includes all the features of Home Edition, and many new features geared toward business uses. Some of the new features include:

- Remote desktop, which allows XP Pro to act as a mini Terminal Server, hosting one remote session.
- Encrypting File System (EFS), which allows you to encrypt files stored on disk. EFS was included with Windows 2000 Professional, but XP Professional adds the ability to share encrypted files with other users.
- Internet Protocol Security (IPSec), which allows you to encrypt data that travels across the network.
- Integrated smart card support, which allows you to use smart card authentication to log on to the network, including Windows Server 2003 terminal sessions.
- Recovery console, which provides a command-line interface that administrators can use to perform repair tasks if the computer won't boot.
- The ability to join a Windows domain. While users who have a domain account can log onto the domain from an XP Home computer, the Home computer cannot have a computer account in the domain. XP Professional computers have computer accounts, allowing the administrator to manage them centrally.

Windows XP Media Center Edition

Windows XP Media Center Edition is built on Windows XP technology and comes preinstalled on Media Center PCs. Media Center Edition combines home entertainment and personal computing. It puts all of your media in one place and allows you to control it via remote control. Some of the features of Windows XP Media Center Edition include:

- Watching live TV
- Personal Video Recording (PVR)
- Electronic Program Guide (Guide)
- Playing DVDs
- Listening to music
- Watching videos
- The Media Center Remote Control

Windows Vista

Microsoft Windows Vista was released in January 2007. It included many changes and added new features such as the updated graphical user interface\visual style called Windows Aero. It also featured redesigned print, audio, networking, and display subsystems. It offers improved security, easier networking, better organization, and new multimedia capabilities. Criticism of Windows Vista was based on its high system requirements, lack of driver and hardware support, as well as other problems, such as crashing and locking up.

Windows Vista comes in a variety of editions, including Home Basic, Home Premium, Ultimate, Business, and Enterprise, each with its own set of features which allows you to choose the edition you need based on pricing and what you plan to do with the operating system.

Windows 7
Microsoft Windows Vista was released in October 2009 and is the successor to Windows Vista. It features the same look and interface as Vista but offers better performance and reliability. Windows 7 has more efficient ways to manage files and improved taskbar previews. It also has faster startup time and runs programs faster than Vista, although it still requires higher end hardware to run up to its potential.

Windows 7 comes in many editions, including Starter, Home Premium, Professional, Ultimate, and Enterprise, each with its own set of features which allows you to choose the edition you need based on pricing and what you plan to do with the operating system.

Windows 8
Windows 8 was released in October of 2012 and is Microsoft's first attempt to combine the desktop PC and smartphone\tablet operating system into one OS. With this new OS came new devices, such as tablets, which could easily be converted into laptops and desktops with tablet-like interfaces and features.

Windows 8 is a big change from Windows 7 and the standard interface that everyone was used to. Many people were turned off by this new interface while others embraced it. Windows 8.1 fixed some of the things people didn't like, but the OS never gained the popularity Microsoft wanted.

Windows 10
Microsoft originally claimed that Windows 10 would be the last desktop version of Windows, and it will be continually updated and improved upon so there won't be a need for a replacement. Windows 10 brings back some of the look and feel we all loved about Windows 7 but also retains that tablet-type feel that Windows 8 had. The Start menu was brought back, but this time it has Live Tiles that change

Chapter 1 - Introducing Windows 11

information for things like current events and weather. It also comes with a built-in personal assistant named Cortana, which is similar to Apple's Siri.

Windows 11

Now that we know Windows 10 was not the last version of Windows, we can all move on and start learning how to use Windows 11. As you will see throughout this book, Windows 11 has many of the same features as Windows 10 plus some new features of course. Otherwise, there would be no point in releasing it!

The main thing you will notice is that the look and feel is different with a more "cartoonish" look to things as well as some brighter colors. Windows 11 will also come in several versions just like previous versions of Windows have for many years. To find out which edition of Windows 11 you are running, simply click on the *Start* button (window icon in the middle of the taskbar) and then click on the *Settings* gear icon. Finally, click on *About* at the bottom of the list and it will tell you your Windows version, as well as other useful information such as your computer name (Win11-PC), what processor your computer is using and how much RAM your computer has installed (figure 1.1).

Some key things to take note of are the version and OS build numbers. This will tell you how "updated" your copy of Windows is and can come in handy for troubleshooting and finding out what features your version of Windows will have.

Chapter 1 - Introducing Windows 11

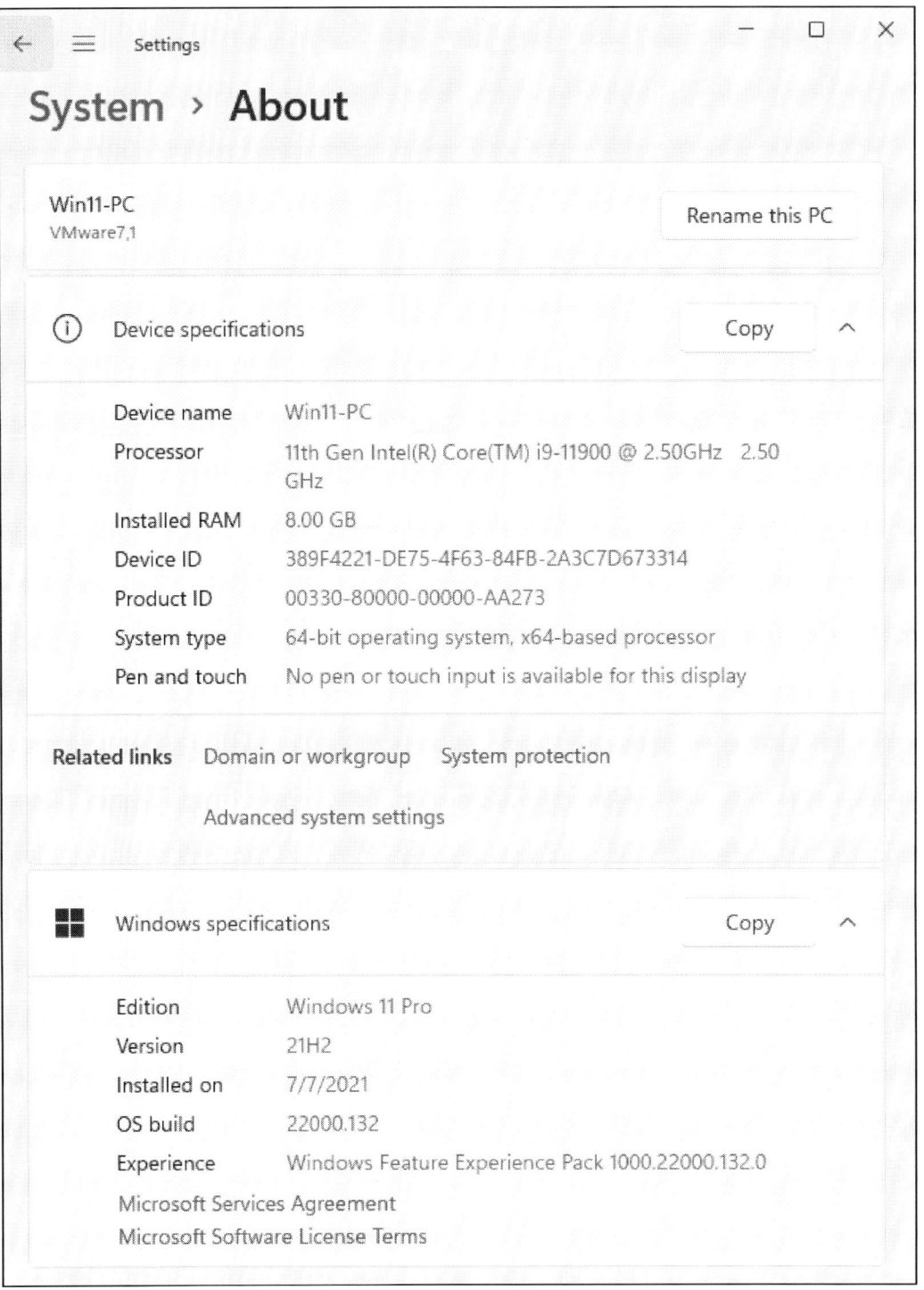

Figure 1.1

Windows 11 comes in several editions, including Home, Professional, and Enterprise. For most computers that you will buy from retail stores for home use, you will get the Home edition or maybe the Professional edition if you need the extra features (let's say for a home office). The Enterprise edition will be used in larger corporations that need the advanced security and management capabilities that it provides. The Professional and Enterprise are also used for joining Active Directory domains etc.

When you have Windows preinstalled on your computer it's called an OEM version (Original Equipment Manufacturer), and it means it's not a retail version but rather a bulk licensed version that the computer manufacturer has purchased. If you were to purchase a retail version of Windows 11 Home Edition, it would run you around $139. The only reason to buy your own copy would be if you planned on installing Windows yourself on your computer or wanted a copy to use for troubleshooting since you can boot your computer with the Windows DVD and perform various troubleshooting tasks. If you have a valid Windows 11 license you can also download the installation media from Microsoft for free.

If you ever need to reinstall Windows 11 on your computer from scratch and your computer originally came with Windows 11, you can use the license key that should be on a sticker on the side of your computer's case.

Windows Hardware Requirements

All software comes with what they call "hardware requirements," which is basically a guideline that you can use to see if your computer can handle running the software. Windows 11 also comes with its own set of hardware requirements, so if you have an older computer from 5 years ago, it most likely won't be able to run Windows 11. Of course, you can *try* to install it on the old clunker, but it would probably be so slow that you would be able to do things faster in your head!

Here are the minimum hardware requirements from Microsoft. And when I say minimum, I mean *just enough* to run Windows, but probably not enough to make it run fast enough to tolerate.

- **Processor\CPU** – 1 GHz or faster (many older processors aren't supported)
- **RAM** – 4GB
- **Hard drive space** – 64GB

- **Graphics card** - Compatible with DirectX 12 or later, with a WDDM 2.0 driver
- **Display** – 720p capable monitor
- **TPM (Trusted Platform Module)** - Version 1.2 with version 2.0 recommended.

In reality, you should really have a 3.x GHz processor with 2 or more cores, 8GB of RAM or more, and 100GB of free hard drive space. All newer monitors should support 720p, so this number will be based on the size of your monitor and the video card installed in your computer.

A Trusted Platform Module is used to provide hardware based security features so if your computer does not have this chip, then you won't be able to run Windows 11. Newer computers should have one and sometimes you can even add one but if your computer is so old that it doesn't, it might be time for an upgrade.

To see your hardware specifications regarding your processor and RAM refer to figure 1.1 under *Device specifications*.

If your computer does not meet the minimum requirements to run Windows 11 then you will be able to stay with Windows 10 and have it supported for updates through October 2025.

Chapter 2 – Installing Windows

If you are the adventurous type and want to try installing Windows yourself on a new computer, or even as an upgrade on your existing computer, then you should know it's a fairly simple process, and once you do it a few times you can pretty much do it in your sleep. It's actually pretty hard to mess up a Windows installation unless you do something like install it on the wrong hard drive!

Some people like to build their own computers, and when you do this then you will need to install your operating system (Windows) yourself, otherwise you just have yourself an expensive paperweight. The key thing to remember before you begin the installation process is to make sure you don't have any files on your hard drive that you want to keep because they will most likely be erased depending on if you are doing a clean (new) installation or an upgrade. If you do have files you want to keep, make sure to back them up onto something like an external hard drive, USB flash drive, or burn them to a DVD.

Clean Installation vs. Upgrade Installation
There are two main ways to install Windows on your computer, and which one you choose will depend on what you are trying to accomplish. A clean installation will wipe out any existing copy of Windows you have installed on your hard drive and install a new copy of Windows with the default settings. This is your only option when you have a blank hard drive or built your own computer with new parts.

During a clean installation, you will tell Windows what drive to install itself on, if you have more than one, otherwise you will install it on the one drive installed in your computer. You can decide if you want Windows to use the entire drive for the installation, or if you want some space left over for a second partition that you can use later. This is common if you want to have a separate drive with its own drive letter that you can use for things such as file storage etc. (I will go over the installation process later in this chapter.)

An upgrade installation will replace your older version of Windows such as Windows 10 with Windows 11 and keep all of your files, programs, installed printers, and other settings intact. It's still a good idea to back up your important files before doing an upgrade installation because there is always the chance that something can go wrong, and you will end up with a corrupt version of Windows and then end up having to do a clean installation regardless.

I prefer clean installations of Windows compared to doing upgrades, because when you do an upgrade there is a chance you may keep any existing problems you might have had with your previous version of Windows.

How to Install Windows

Like I mentioned before, the process for installing Windows is pretty simple, and I will now go over the steps to perform a clean installation of Windows 11 Home Edition. You can perform an upgrade from within Windows or from booting to the Windows DVD, but for a clean installation you will want to boot from the Windows DVD to start the installation process. If your computer is not set to read from your CD\DVD drive first, then you will need to either go into the BIOS (or UEFI for newer computers) and change the boot order or look for the key that needs to be pressed on startup that will let you choose the boot device. Some computers make it obvious while others don't give you that information. Many times, it's the F12, F2 or Esc key.

If your computer didn't come with a Windows DVD then you should be able to download what they call an ISO file from the Microsoft website and then use your DVD burning software to convert\burn it to a bootable DVD, or even a bootable flash drive.

Once you have booted your computer with your Windows DVD and pressed any key on your keyboard to boot from the DVD, you will be asked to choose your language, time and currency format, and keyboard input (figure 2.1). Normally the defaults will be correct, and you can then click on *Next* and then on the *Install now* button.

Chapter 2 – Installing Windows

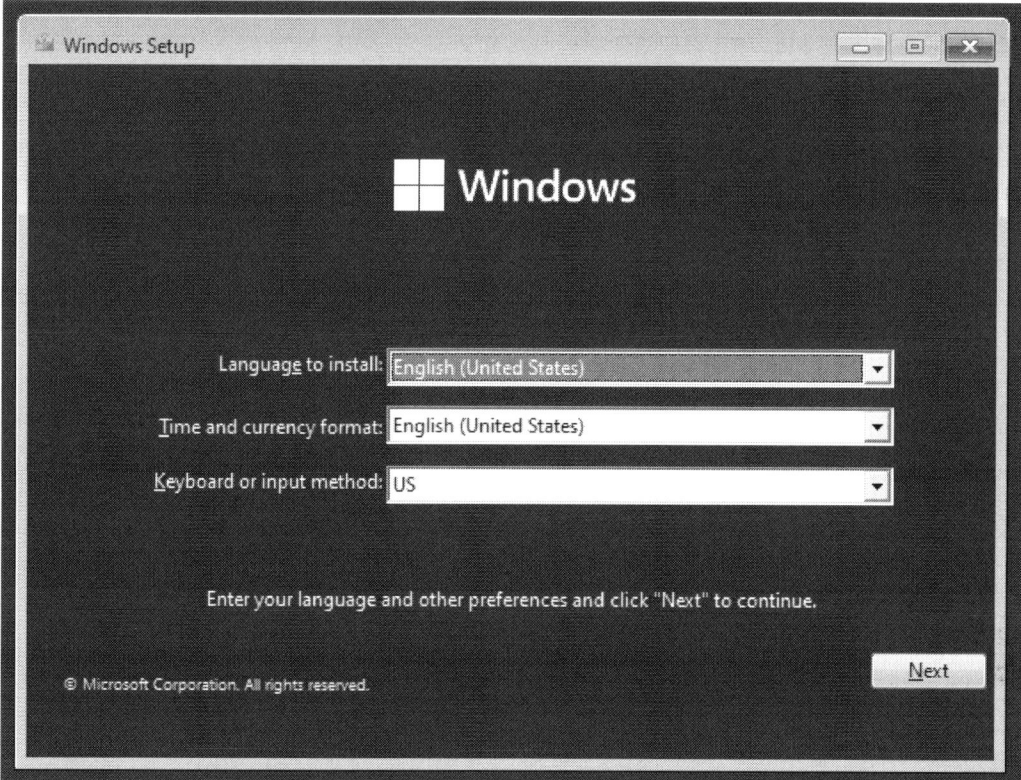

Figure 2.1

On the next screen you will be asked to type in your Windows product key, which will be included with the Windows 11 DVD. If you are using a DVD that you borrowed from someone and your computer originally came with Windows 11, then you can enter the product key from the sticker that should be someplace on your computer's case. If you don't have a key, you can still install Windows by clicking on *I don't have a product key* and then enter one later or use it in trial mode.

Chapter 2 – Installing Windows

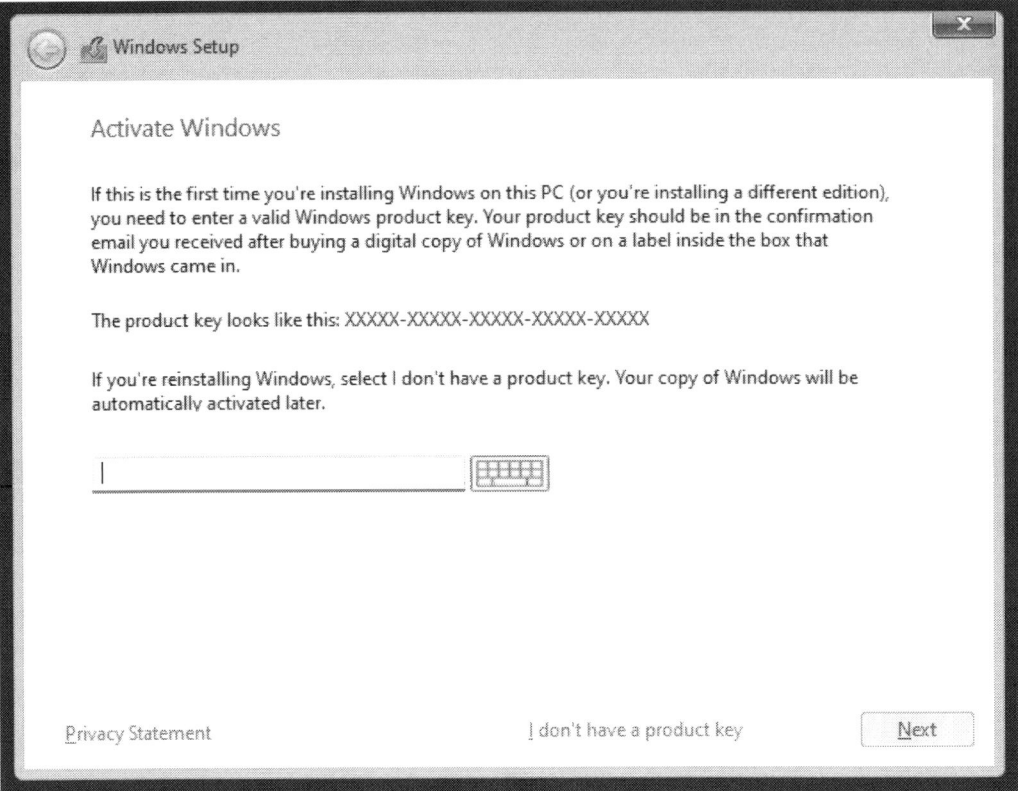

Figure 2.2

Next, you will be able to choose which edition of Windows you want to install. The choices you see here will vary depending on your installation media. Just make sure to choose the one that matches your product key. If you entered the product key, then you might not see this screen because it will choose the edition for you based on that key.

Chapter 2 – Installing Windows

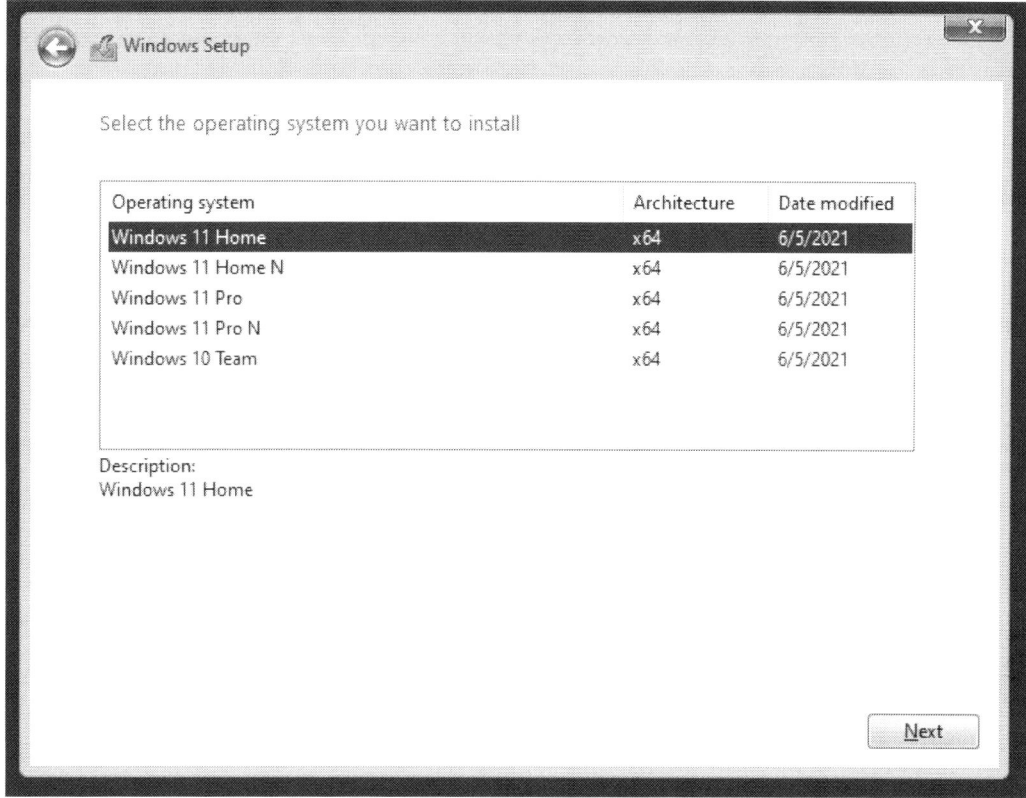

Figure 2.3

Next, you will check the box that says you accept the license terms that are listed. Most people don't read them, but you can if you are feeling up to it!

The next window is where you will have to make a choice based on what type of installation you are doing. Since we are doing a clean installation, we will pick the second option that says *Custom: Install Windows only (advanced)*. You will notice in the description that it says that your files, settings, and applications will not be moved to Windows with this option, so make sure you back up your files!

 When installing a clean version of Windows on your existing computer another thing to remember is that you will need to reinstall any programs that don't come with Windows, so make sure you have your installation media for your software.

Chapter 2 – Installing Windows

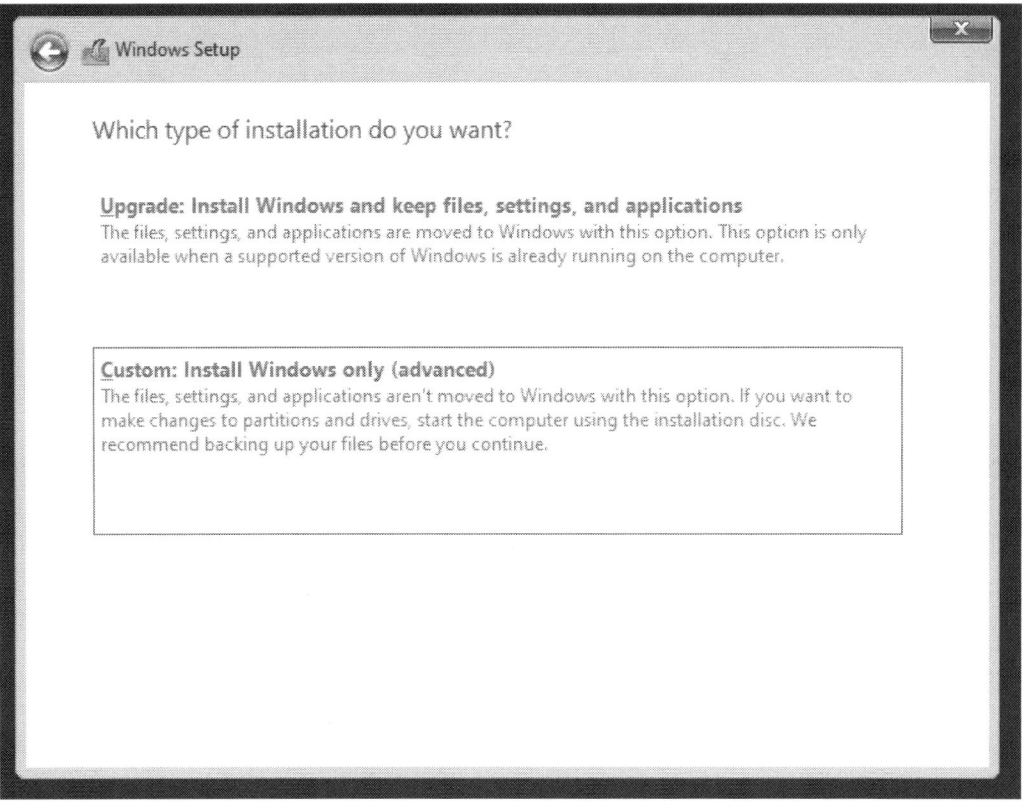

Figure 2.4

The next section is where you will need to choose what hard drive you are going to install Windows 11 on, as well as how much of the hard drive you are going to use. If you click on *Next*, it will use the selected hard drive and create a partition using all the space on the drive. Then it will format the drive to get it ready to install Windows on.

If you click on *New*, then you can decide how much of the total drive capacity will be used for Windows. Then the rest will be listed as "unused", and you can create additional drives with it after Windows is installed.

Chapter 2 – Installing Windows

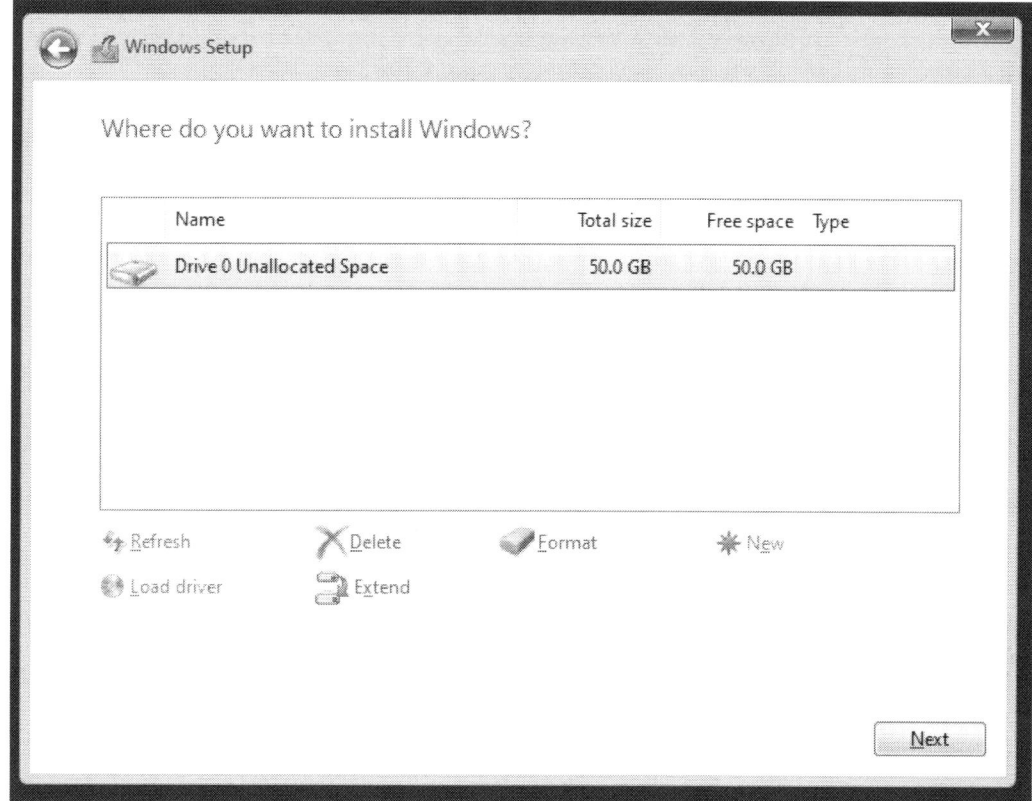

Figure 2.5

Now you can see in figure 2.6 that the installation is running. This process will take a bit of time depending on the performance of the hardware installed in your computer such as processor speed, hard drive type, and the amount of RAM installed.

Chapter 2 – Installing Windows

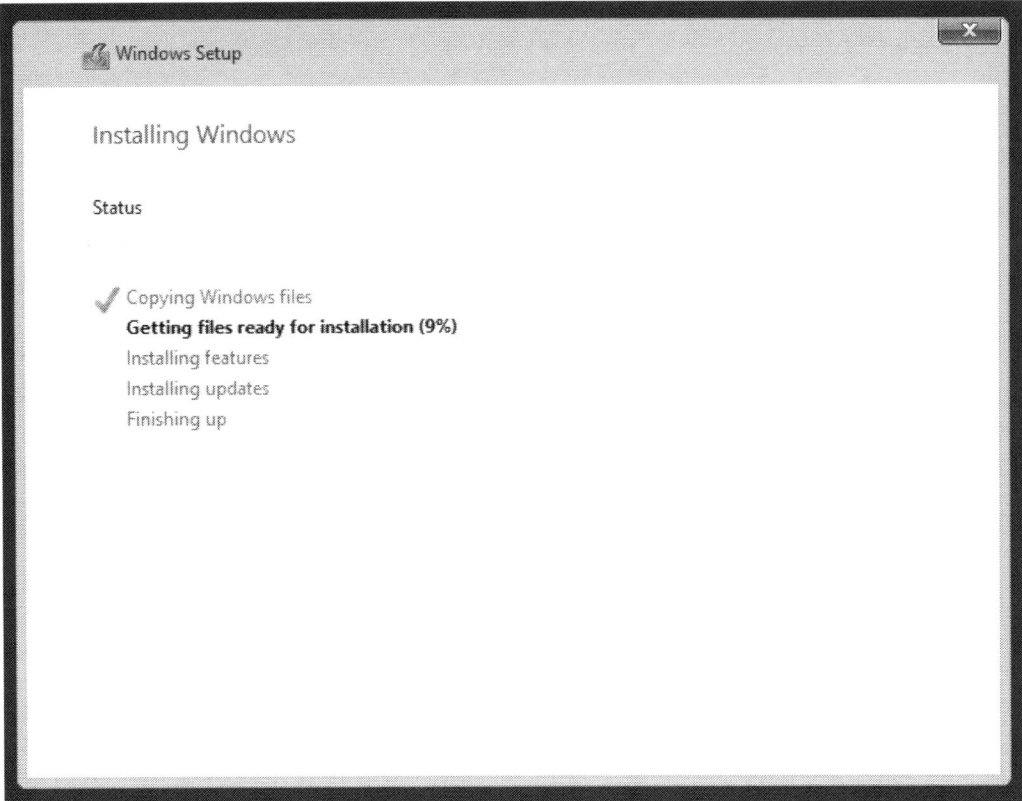

Figure 2.6

After the installation is complete, Windows will restart the computer and prepare your hardware for use with Windows. Then Windows will start up and begin its basic configuration where it will ask you to specify your region, keyboard layout, network (Internet\wireless) connection settings, and will then check for updates.

Chapter 2 – Installing Windows

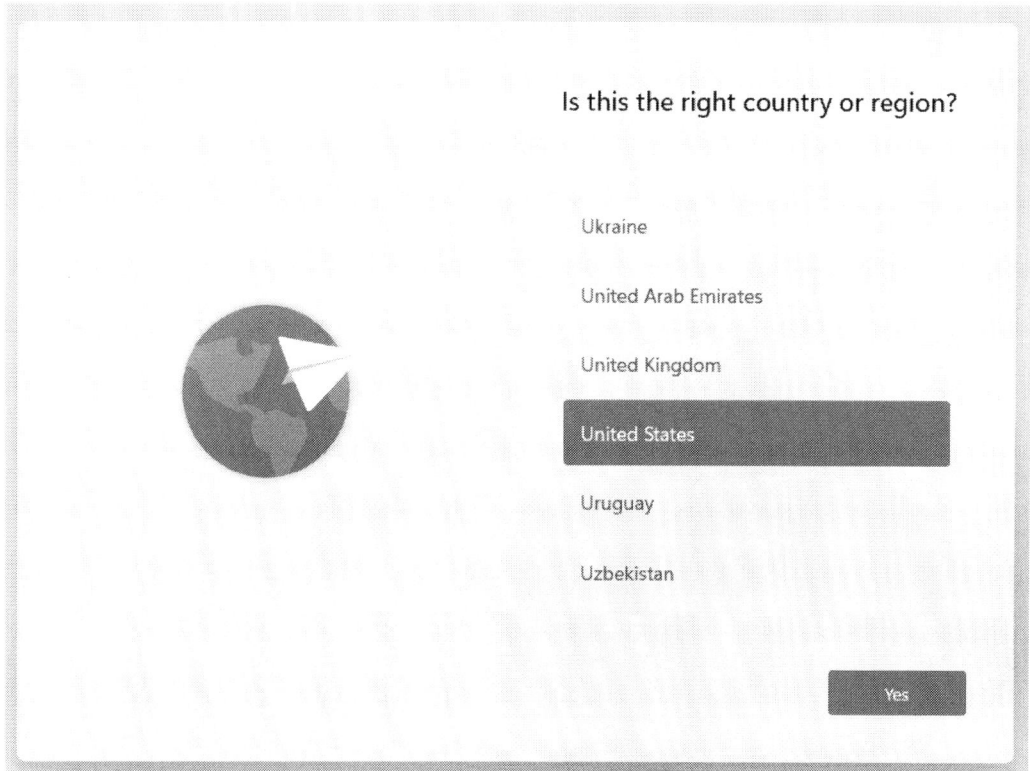

Figure 2.7

At the end will ask you to add your Microsoft account information to your new Windows installation to be used for login purposes. (I will be going into user accounts in more detail in Chapter 7.) If you don't have a Microsoft account, you can create one from this screen by clicking on the *Create one* link. If you forgot your Microsoft account email or password, you can click on the *Sign-in options* link to go through the reset process.

Chapter 2 – Installing Windows

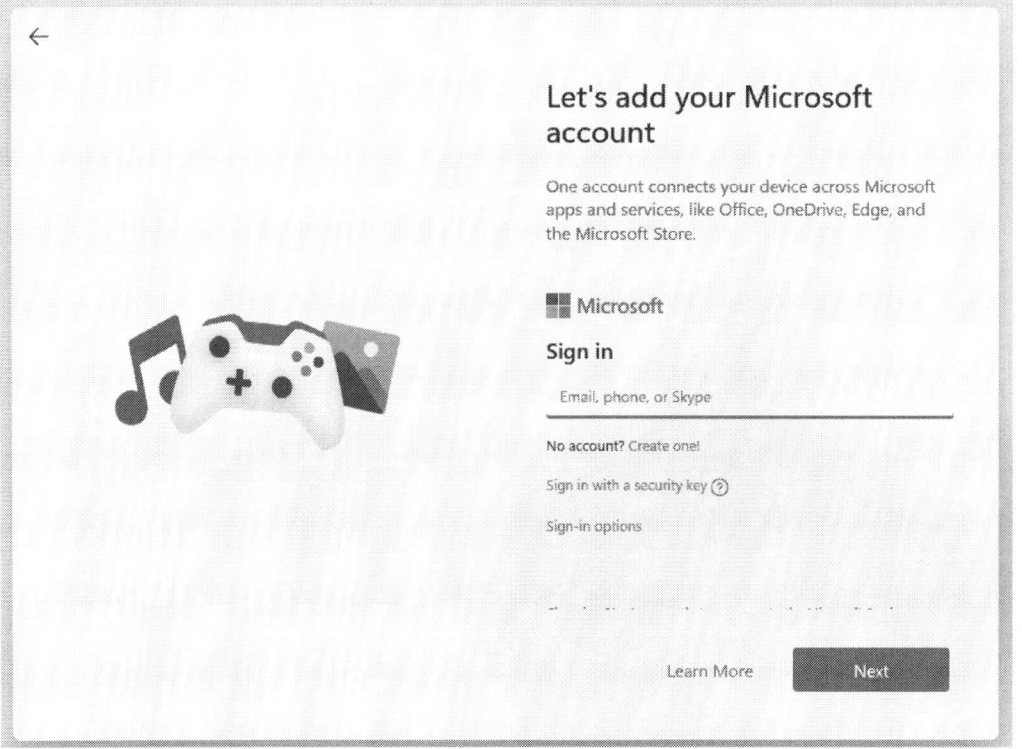

Figure 2.8

Next, you will be prompted to create a PIN that will be used to log into your computer, so you don't need to enter your Microsoft account email address and password each time. This PIN can be something simple such as 4 numbers or you can even add text to make it more like an actual password.

Chapter 2 – Installing Windows

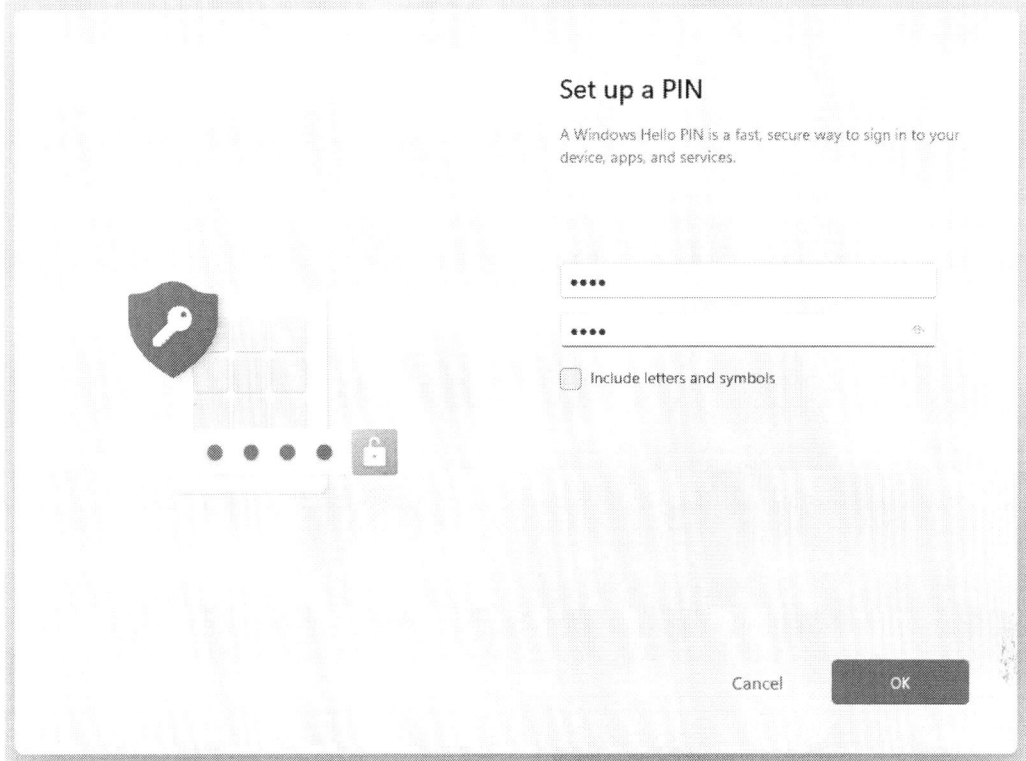

Figure 2.9

Once you are logged in, Windows might ask you if you wish to copy your files and settings from your old computer to your new one, assuming your old computer is not too old and was configured to use OneDrive etc. (figure 2.10).

OneDrive is Microsoft's online cloud storage service that you get for free with Windows. You get a limited amount of online storage space and if you want to get extra then you will have to sign up for one of their subscription plans.

 If you are interested in learning more about Microsoft OneDrive and other online cloud platforms such as DropBox and Google Drive, then check out my book titled **Cloud Storage Made Easy**.
https://www.amazon.com/dp/1730838359

Chapter 2 – Installing Windows

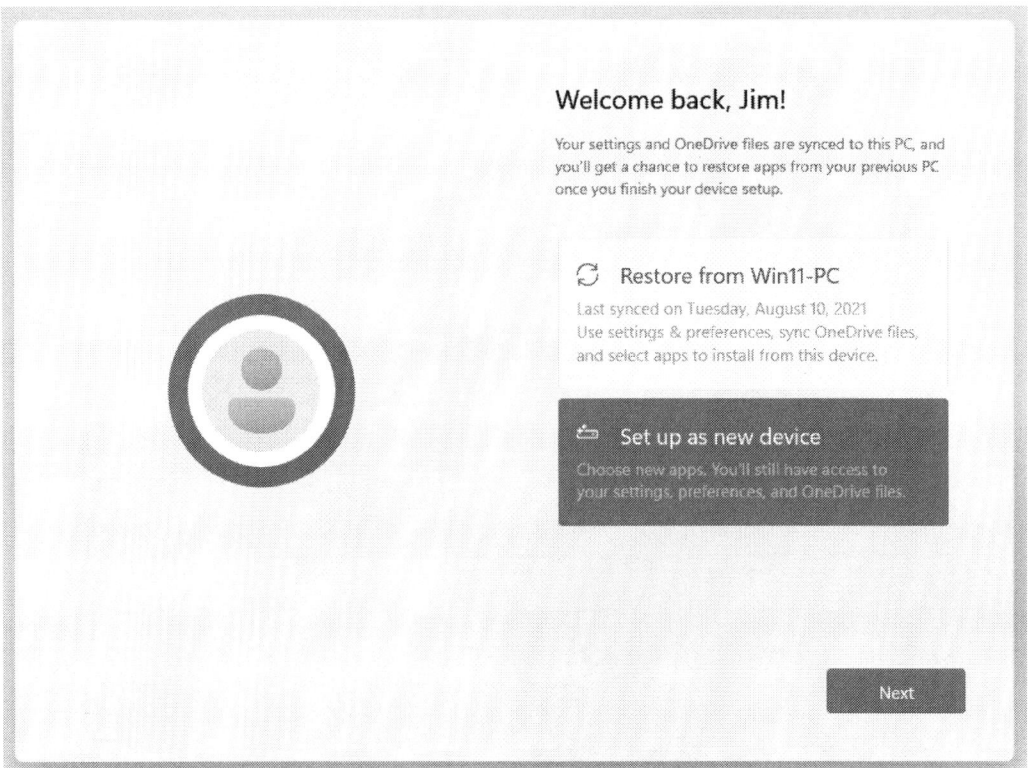

Figure 2.10

I'm going to choose the *Setup as a new device* option and click on the *Next* button. Then you will be prompted to choose your privacy settings and then disable any settings you don't agree with. Generally, I disable all of these settings since Microsoft doesn't need to know what I'm doing on my computer.

After clicking on *Accept* I will then be prompted to let Windows know what I will be doing with my computer so it can "customize my experience". I can also choose the *Skip* button if I don't want Windows to apply any customization.

Chapter 2 – Installing Windows

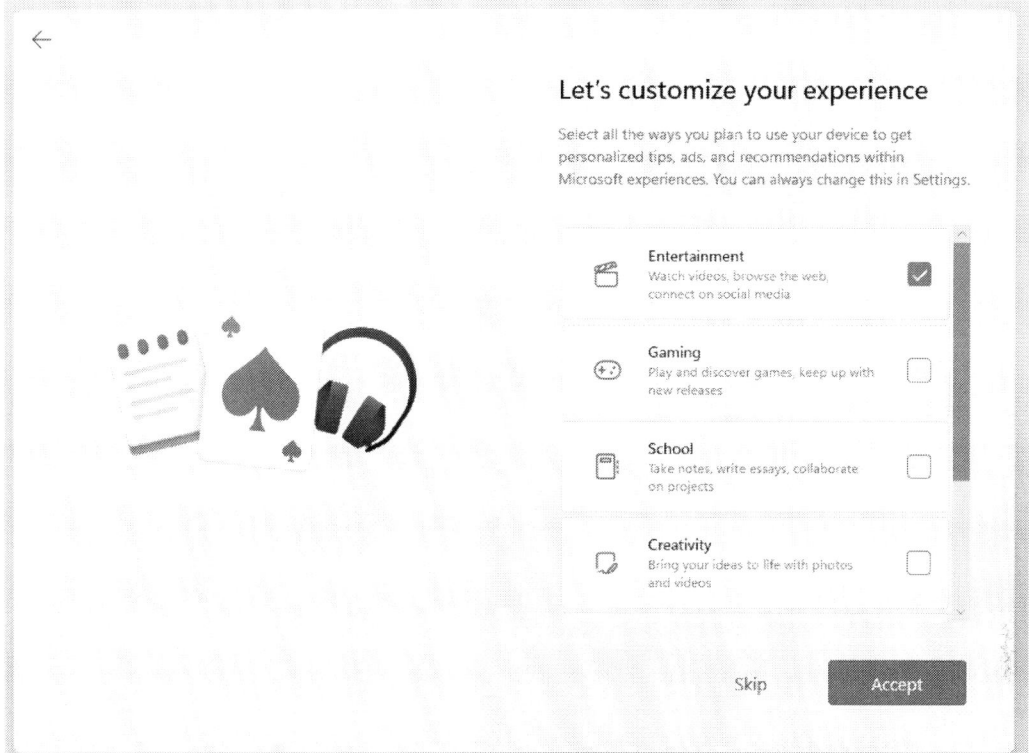

Figure 2.11

Now I will be asked if I want to use OneDrive to back up my files automatically or whether I would like it to be disabled. OneDrive will back up my desktop, documents and pictures folders by default. You can always go back and enable OneDrive if you don't want to use it right away.

Chapter 2 – Installing Windows

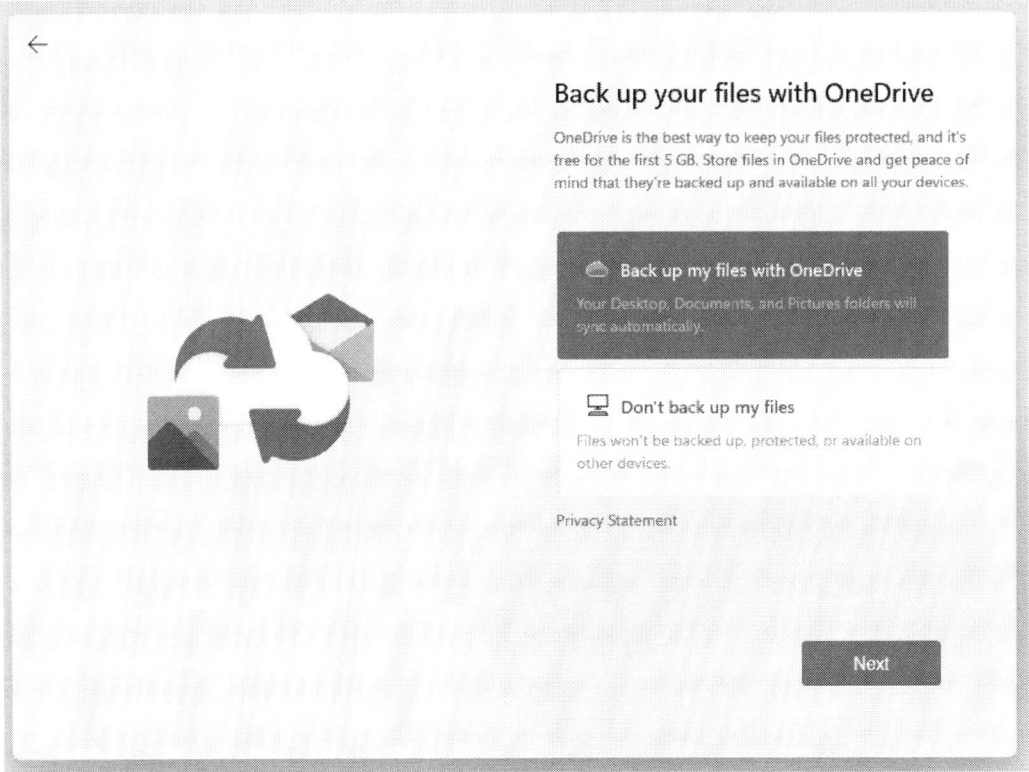

Figure 2.12

After you click on Next, Windows will check for some updates once again and this process can take quite a bit of time to complete. It will also reboot your computer once the updates are complete.

Then you will be asked to enter the PIN you created during the installation process and then Windows will go through a few more setup steps. After that, you will be presented with your new Windows 11 desktop and you will be ready to start using your new operating system.

Windows Update
One last thing I want to mention in this chapter is Windows Update and what these updates do to your computer. Windows Updates consist of fixes, patches, and upgrades that are applied to your computer to fix bugs, patch security holes, and add new features to Windows. If your computer is connected to the Internet, then these updates are downloaded and installed automatically.

One downside to the way Windows does its updates is that you can't stop them from being installed like you could with previous versions of Windows. Also, if you are not in front of your computer to stop the reboots that are required after many of these updates, then you might lose any unsaved documents that you have open during the reboot. It's always a good idea to save your work before walking away from your computer for any extended period of time.

You can view the Windows Update settings and update history from the Windows settings (discussed in detail in Chapter 9), then *Windows Update*. You can pause updates for up to 5 weeks if you do not want to have any updates applied that might cause an issue with something you are working on.

Chapter 2 – Installing Windows

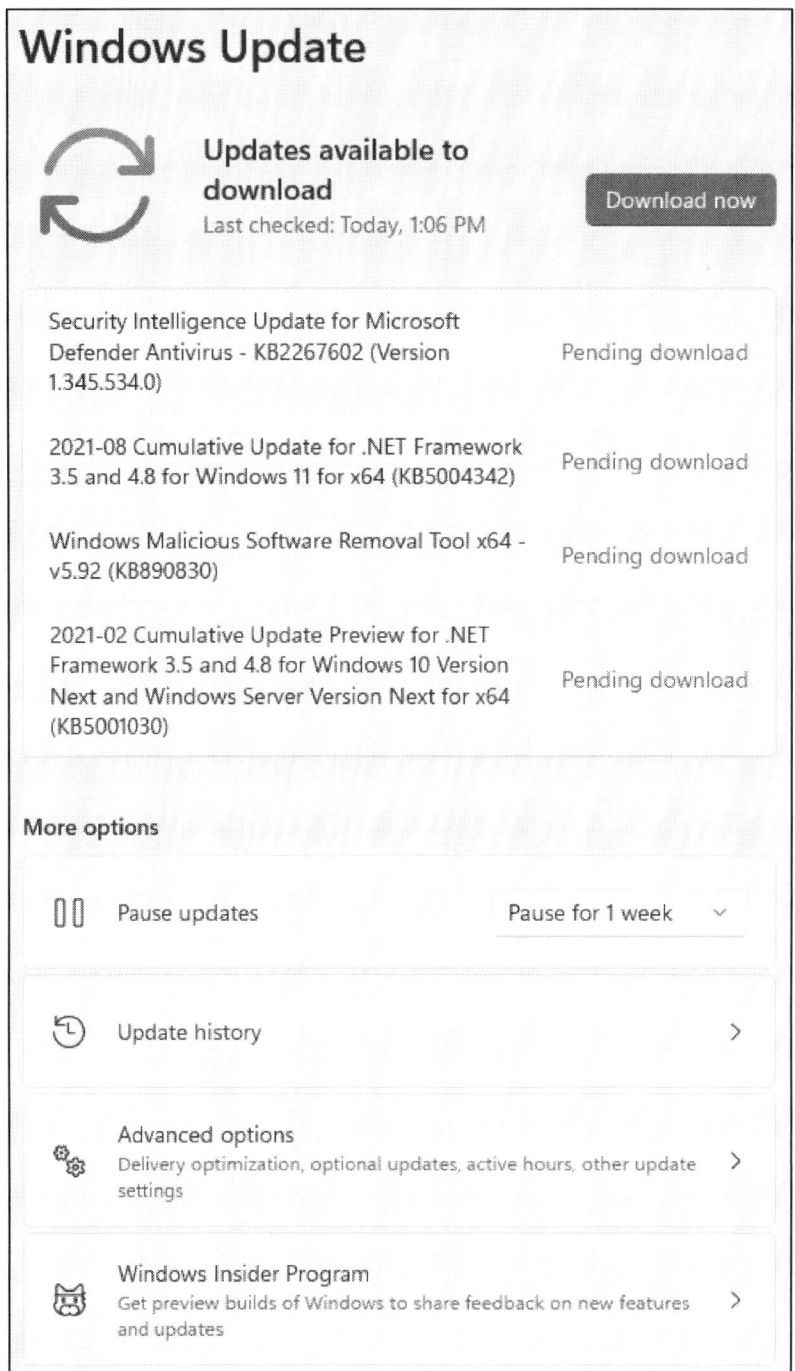

Figure 2.13

Clicking on *Advanced options* will allow you to fine tune your Windows Update settings and do things such as have Windows update other products such as Microsoft Office software and set your working hours so Windows won't try and update or reboot your computer during that time.

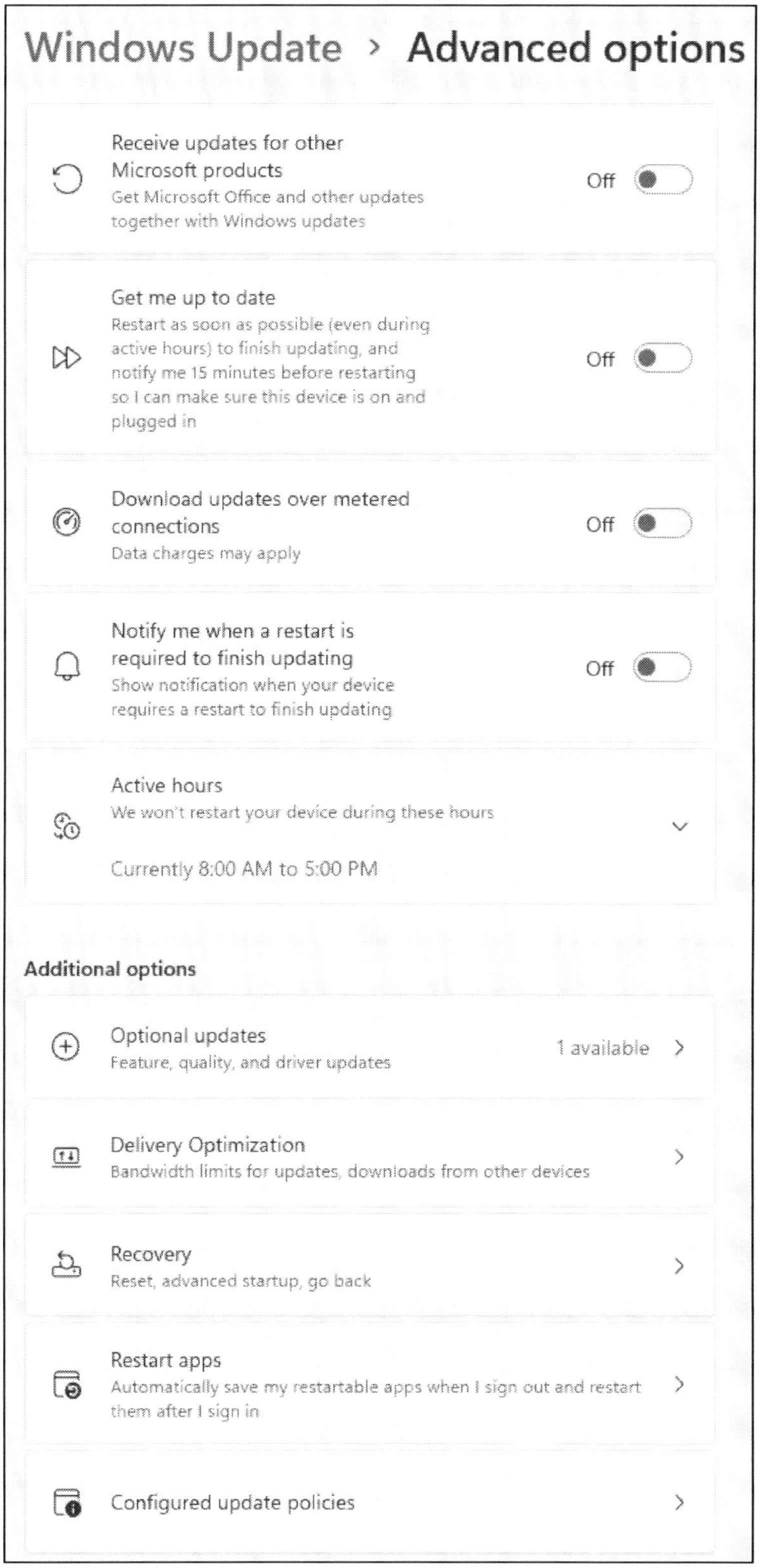

Chapter 2 – Installing Windows

Windows Update > Advanced options

Receive updates for other Microsoft products
Get Microsoft Office and other updates together with Windows updates
Off

Get me up to date
Restart as soon as possible (even during active hours) to finish updating, and notify me 15 minutes before restarting so I can make sure this device is on and plugged in
Off

Download updates over metered connections
Data charges may apply
Off

Notify me when a restart is required to finish updating
Show notification when your device requires a restart to finish updating
Off

Active hours
We won't restart your device during these hours
Currently 8:00 AM to 5:00 PM

Additional options

Optional updates
Feature, quality, and driver updates
1 available >

Delivery Optimization
Bandwidth limits for updates, downloads from other devices
>

Recovery
Reset, advanced startup, go back
>

Restart apps
Automatically save my restartable apps when I sign out and restart them after I sign in
>

Configured update policies
>

Figure 2.14

Chapter 3 – Configuring and Customizing Windows

This chapter will cover a lot of information because in order to get the most out of Windows 11, you will want to make it work the way you want it to work so your everyday tasks will be easy to do and you won't end up spending a bunch of time trying to figure out how to do things.

Initial Look and Feel Compared to Windows 10
Let's begin the chapter with a discussion of how Windows 11 has changed in regard to its look and feel compared to Windows 10 (in case you are coming from a Windows 10 computer). Microsoft likes to change how Windows works with new releases for some reason, so we have to learn how to do things all over again with each new version. Maybe they figure they need to make things look different enough, so you think you are getting a completely new operating system!S

One of the biggest changes between Windows 10 and 11 is the *Taskbar* and *Start Menu*. The Start Menu back in Windows 7 was great, super easy to use, and very intuitive (if you can remember back that far). As you can see in figure 3.1 it gets right to the point and things are easy to find. You have your programs listed on the left and your tools and utilities listed on the right.

Chapter 3 – Configuring and Customizing Windows

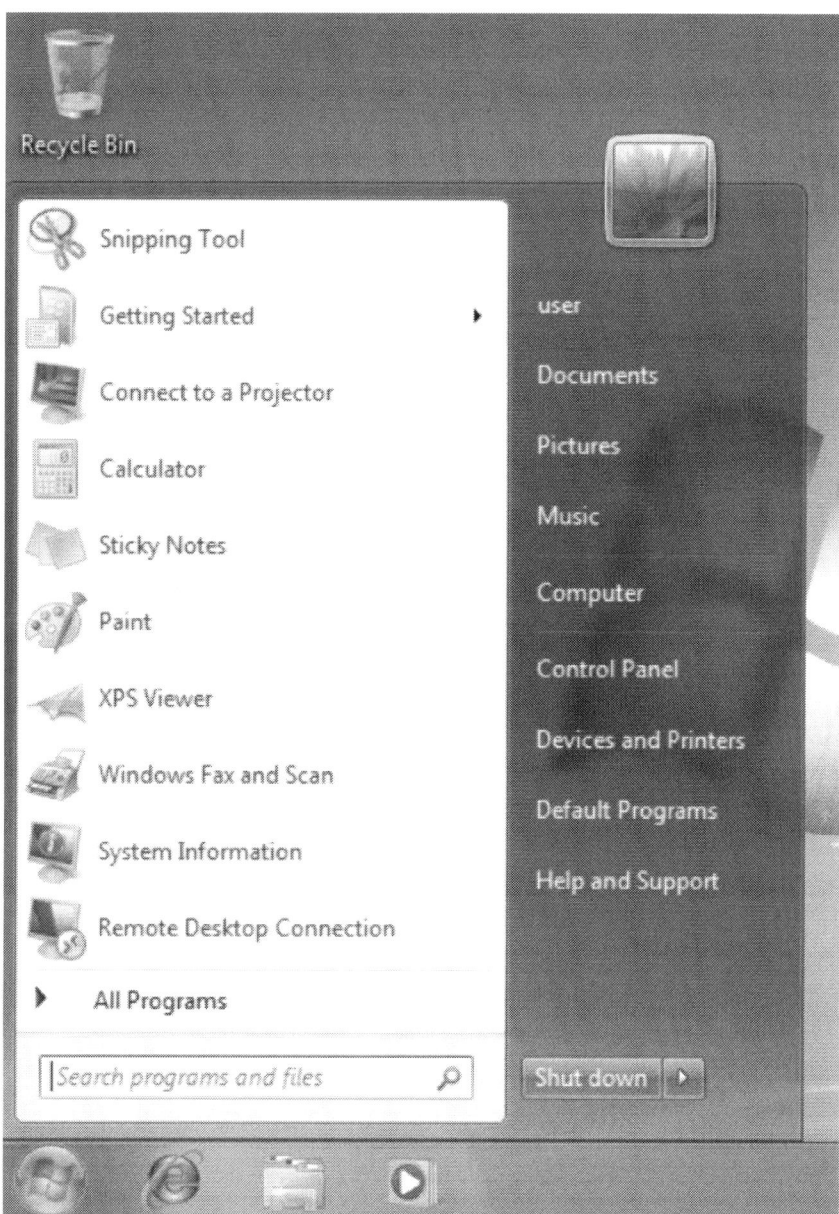

Figure 3.1

When Windows 8 came out they really messed things up with the Start Menu, and at first completely got rid of the Start button itself! Then in Windows 8.1 they brought back the Start button, but it still took you to the awful Start Menu (as shown in figure 3.2). They also implemented their "tile" interface that was meant to make Windows feel the same on a tablet and on a computer, but it didn't go over well at all with computer users.

Chapter 3 – Configuring and Customizing Windows

Figure 3.2

With Windows 10 they combined the Start Menus of Windows 7 and Windows 8 to come up with a hybrid menu that you can see in figure 3.3. There is a popup Start Menu on the left and then customizable tiles on the right.

Chapter 3 – Configuring and Customizing Windows

Figure 3.3

I still don't like the Windows 10 Start Menu and think it's too crowded with junk that you will never use and don't need to see. Plus it can be difficult to find your installed programs without having to search for them.

Chapter 3 – Configuring and Customizing Windows

To get around this problem I always install a free program called **Open Shell** on my computers that will give you a Windows 7 style Start Menu and make your computer much easy to use. Google it!

Windows 11 retains the same functionality as the Windows 10 Start Menu but when you click on it, you will initially be presented with your pinned apps and programs as well as recent documents you have opened (figure 3.4).

Chapter 3 – Configuring and Customizing Windows

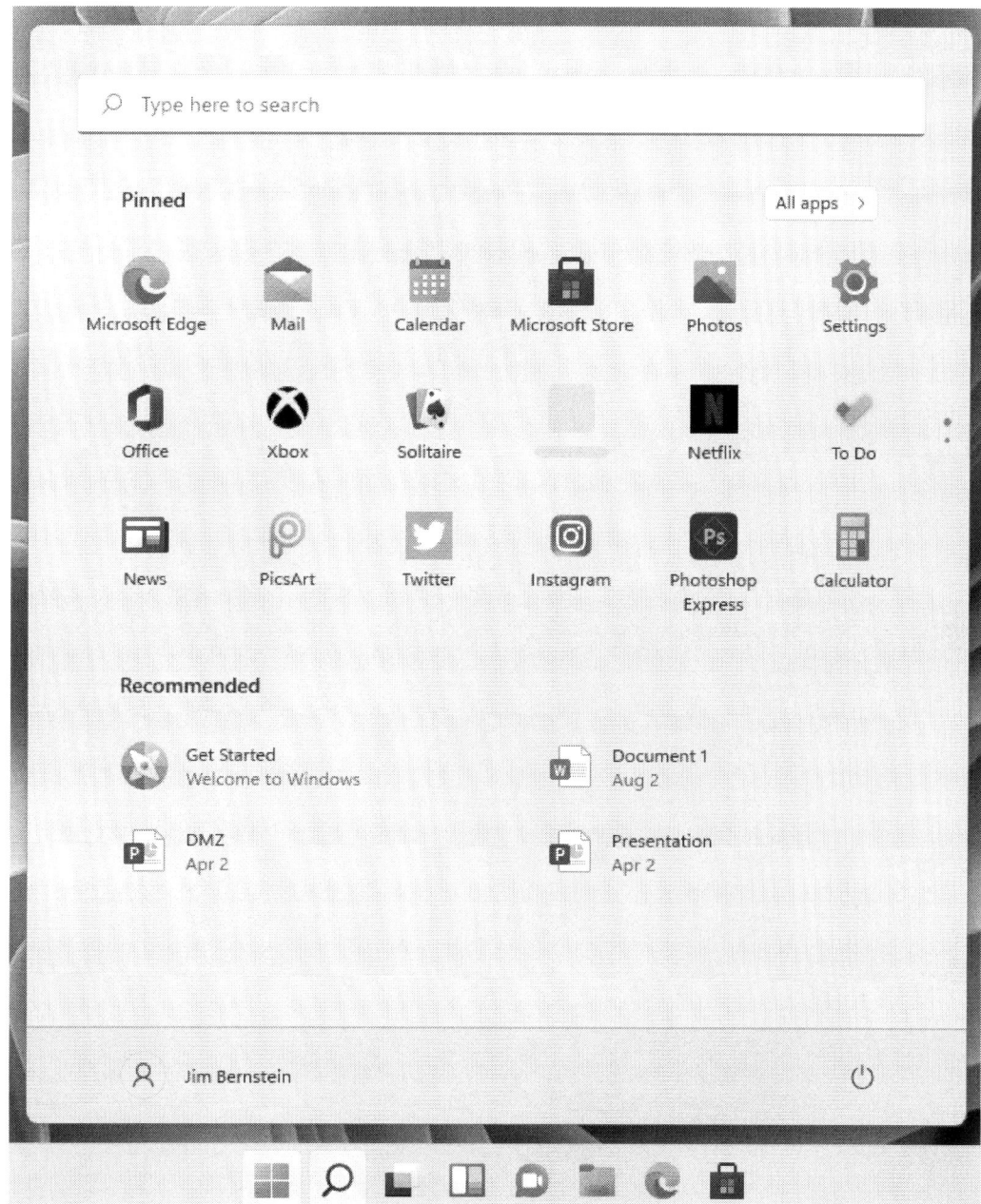

Figure 3.4

Clicking on *All apps* at the top right will show you a Windows 10 style listing of all the apps and software you have installed on your computer. It will be listed in alphabetical order, and you can scroll up and down the list until you find what you need. You can also use the search box at the top to help you find what you are looking for.

Chapter 3 – Configuring and Customizing Windows

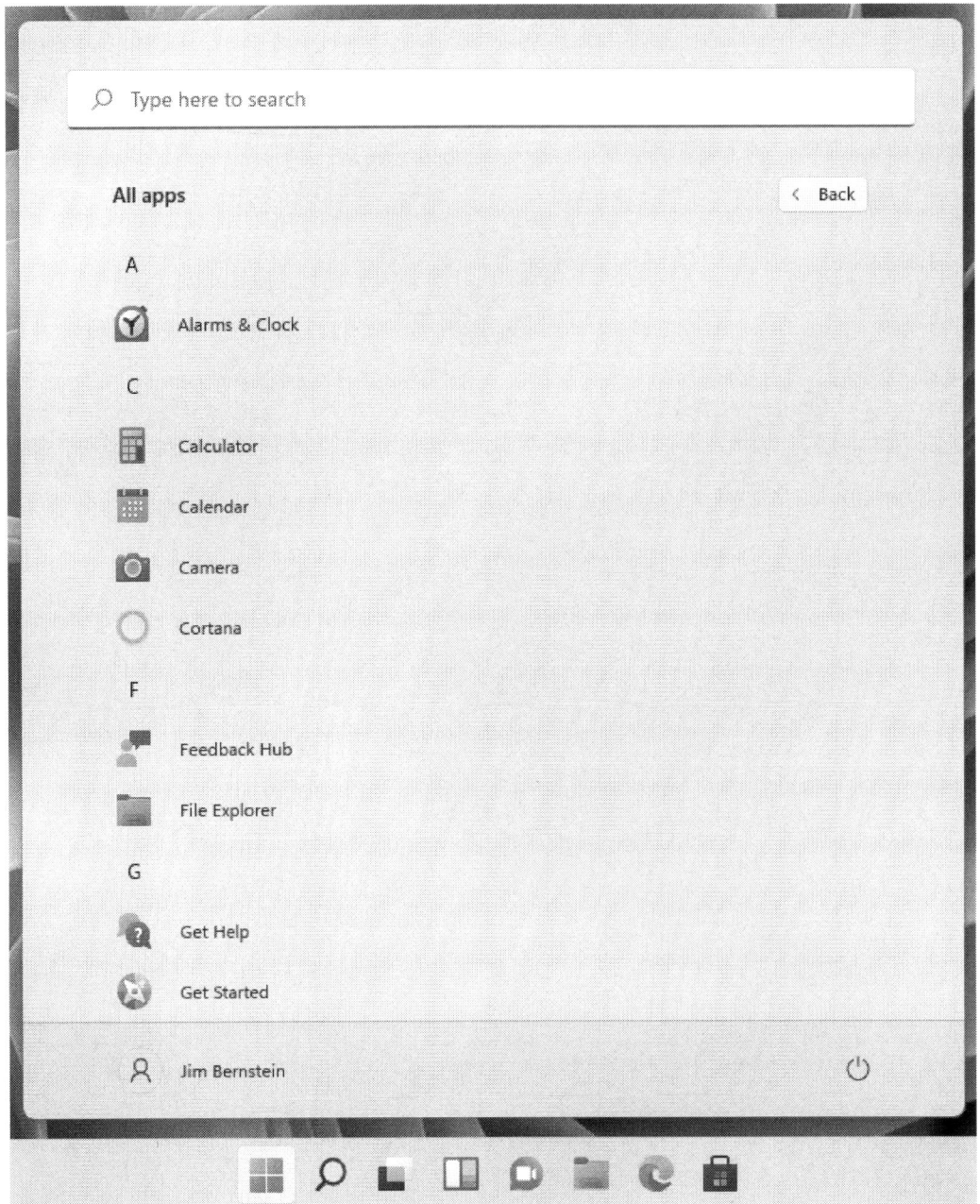

Figure 3.5

Of course, there are other differences between these versions of Windows, such as security improvements, Cortana which started in Windows 10 (discussed later), and the introduction of Windows Apps and the Microsoft Store which was implemented with Windows 8.

Chapter 3 – Configuring and Customizing Windows

Using Windows – Programs and the Start Menu

Now that you have your new PC with Windows 11 installed or have done your upgrade from an older version of Windows, it's time to figure out how all it all works! The key thing to remember with Windows is that there are usually multiple ways to do the same thing, so once you figure out what works the best for you, then you can stick with that method and not have to worry about the rest. Unfortunately, it seems Microsoft tends to change the way common tasks are performed just for the sake of changing things, so with each new version of Windows there will be at least some learning curve for everyone.

There are two main areas you need to get yourself acquainted with to be a reasonably functioning Windows user. The first thing you need to know how to do is to find your programs so you can open the ones you want to use to do what you need to do. Program shortcuts (or icons) can be located in several different places, such as on the desktop or on the taskbar, but they will still do the same thing when you click on them. Back with Windows 7 when you clicked on the Start button and then on *All Programs* you would actually see all the programs that were installed on your computer. With the Windows 11 Start Menu, that is not always the case. It tends to only show you certain programs and a bunch of Windows Apps (discussed in Chapter 5) that you might not care about.

If you are not seeing all of your installed programs on your Start Menu, then there is a method you can try to fix the issue. What you need to do is click on Start, and in the search box or Cortana box type in **%appdata%\Microsoft\Windows\Start Menu** and press enter. Then a window will pop up showing you a folder called *Programs*. What you need to do is right click on that Programs folder and choose *Properties* (figure 3.6). Then check the box that says *Hidden* and click on *Apply*. Choose the option for *Apply changes to this folder, subfolder and files* and click *OK* (figure 3.7).

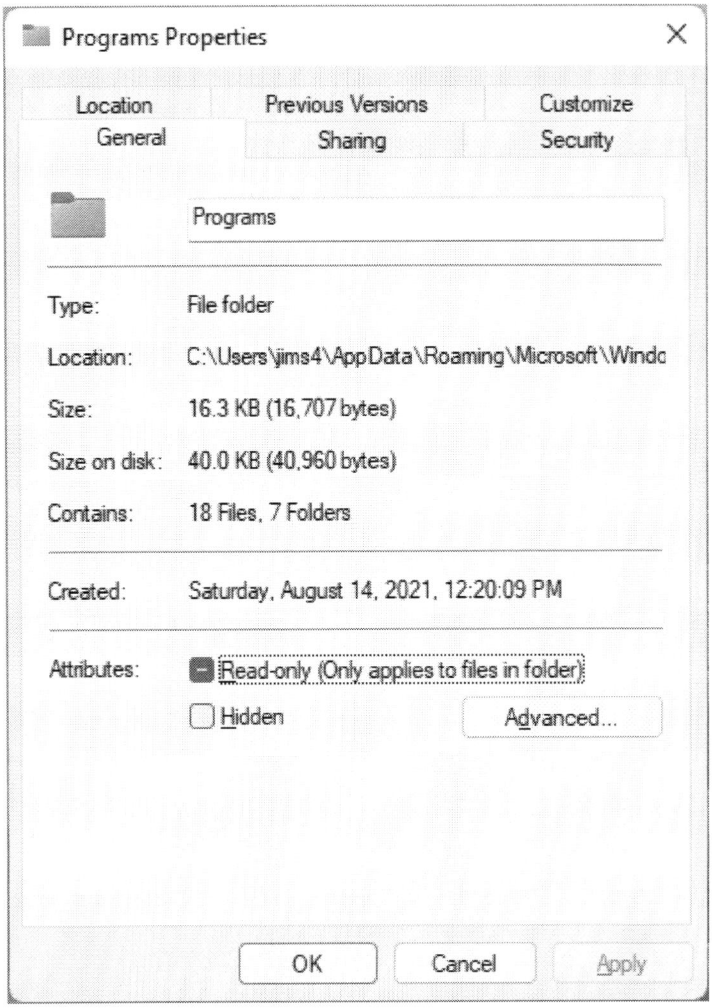

Chapter 3 – Configuring and Customizing Windows

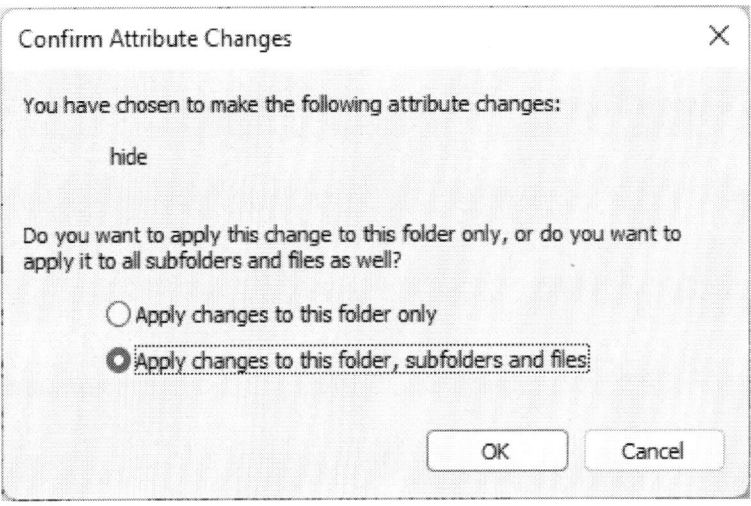

Figure 3.6

Figure 3.7

Then you will uncheck the *Hidden* box and click on *Apply* again and choose the *Apply changes to this folder, subfolder and files* option one more time and click *OK*. Now you should see all of your missing programs in your Start Menu when you click the Start button.

%appdata% is a system variable for the AppData folder on your computer. Think of it as a shortcut to AppData folder that uses the currently logged in user. So rather than having to type in C:\Users\frank\AppData\ it will take you right to the AppData folder for the user Frank, who is currently logged in.

Now that we have the Windows 11 Start Menu fixed, we can continue our discussion on finding your installed programs. All of your programs should be listed on your Start Menu, but you can also get to them via shortcuts on your desktop or your Taskbar, which is the area on the bottom of your screen that shows your open programs, the Start button, the clock, etc. It is possible to add and remove shortcuts from the desktop and Taskbar to suit your needs. I like to think that less is more when it comes to having items on either one because then it just makes things harder to find when you have a bunch of shortcuts and files scattered around that you don't use. You can also copy and paste shortcuts as needed to help you organize your programs so that everything you need is all in one place.

The other thing you really need to know how to do to be a successful Windows user is to be able to locate and manage your files. File management involves knowing where your files are located, how to find your files, and also how to manipulate them when needed. And by manipulate, I mean copy, paste, move, delete, and so on. I will cover file and folder management in Chapter 6, but for now it's important to understand that if you don't know how to get to the files you need, then it's going to be tough to do many of the common tasks that are performed on a daily basis.

Let's say you need to email your resume to a company for a job you are interested in. If you don't know where your resume is or how to search for it, then you won't be able to attach it to your email, and therefore won't be able to apply for the job. Or maybe you have some pictures on your smartphone that you want to copy to your computer. If you don't know how to browse your file system and copy

Chapter 3 – Configuring and Customizing Windows

pictures from your phone, then it will be difficult to get the job done, and you may end up copying the pictures somewhere that you didn't intend to, making them harder to find when you go to look for them later.

Once you get a handle on finding your programs and managing your files, you will find that most other computer tasks become a lot easier and less intimidating. So, take a moment and look over things like your desktop and start menu and see how things are organized when it comes to shortcuts for your programs. Then have a look at File Explorer and browse around the files and folders on your computer. You can get to File Explorer a few different ways, but I like to right click on the Start button and choose File Explorer if I'm on a computer that doesn't have an easy to access shortcut.

If you are interested in learning how to manage your Windows file system to become a Windows power user, then check out my book titled **Windows File Management Made Easy**.
https://www.amazon.com/dp/B085DTGM9Z

Customizing the Windows Start Menu and Taskbar
I have already discussed the Start Menu to some degree, and now I will talk about how to customize the Start Menu as well as the Windows Taskbar, which is the bar at the bottom of your screen that shows your open programs and allows you to do things such as switch between these running programs.

There are many ways to customize the Windows Start menu and Taskbar. As you can see back in figures 3.4 and 3.5, you have your pinned apps as well as an alphabetical listing of programs. If you right click an item from the alphabetical listing, you will have an option to have it pinned to the Start menu, as well as other options such as uninstalling the app depending on what type of app it is. You can also have it unpinned from the Start menu if it's already there.

If you go to the Windows 11 Settings (gear icon from the Start menu) and click on *Personalization* and then *Start*, you will have your Start menu options (figure 3.8). Here you can configure the Start menu to show recently added or your most commonly used apps, as well as recent files. There is also a section where you can

Chapter 3 – Configuring and Customizing Windows

choose which folders appear on the Start menu, such as Documents, Music, Pictures, Network, and so on.

One important thing to remember with Windows is that Microsoft is always changing things, so if you read about a way to change a setting, that option might not be there after a future upgrade release. It's very frustrating, and hopefully Microsoft stops doing this at some point!

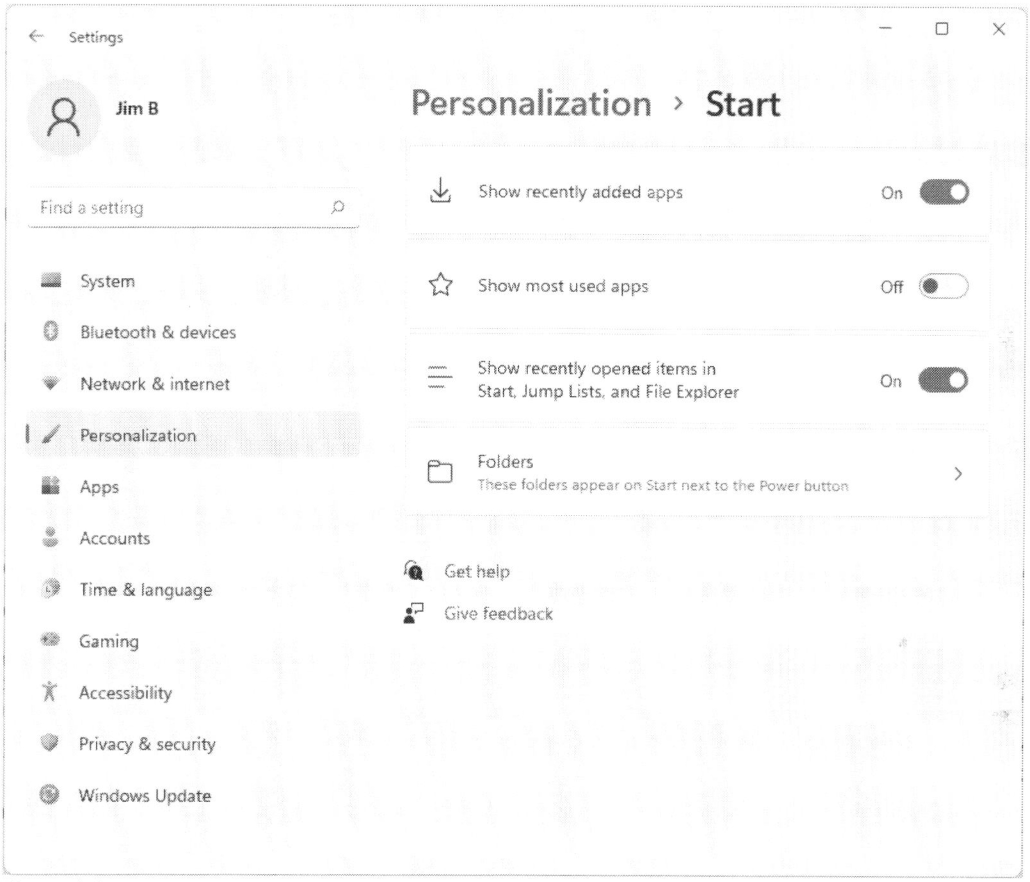

Figure 3.8

When it comes to using Windows, right clicking is your friend so if you do so on the on the Start button, you will get a whole other listing of things you can do or open, so give it a try.

Chapter 3 – Configuring and Customizing Windows

The Windows Taskbar is also very customizable, and you can fine tune how it looks and functions by changing some of the many settings that are available. Once you start opening programs and apps, they will be displayed next to your default Taskbar icons. Figure 3.9 shows the default Taskbar items and the last 3 on the right are apps that have been opened within Windows (Mail, Calculator and Photoshop). You can see that the last 3 items have small lines underneath them indicating that they are open programs rather than just pinned Taskbar items.

Figure 3.9

To customize how the Taskbar looks and functions, you can once again go to the Settings icon and then Personalization and finally Taskbar. There are four main categories that you can customize, and they are Taskbar items, corner icons, corner overflow and behaviors (figures 3.10 and 3.11).

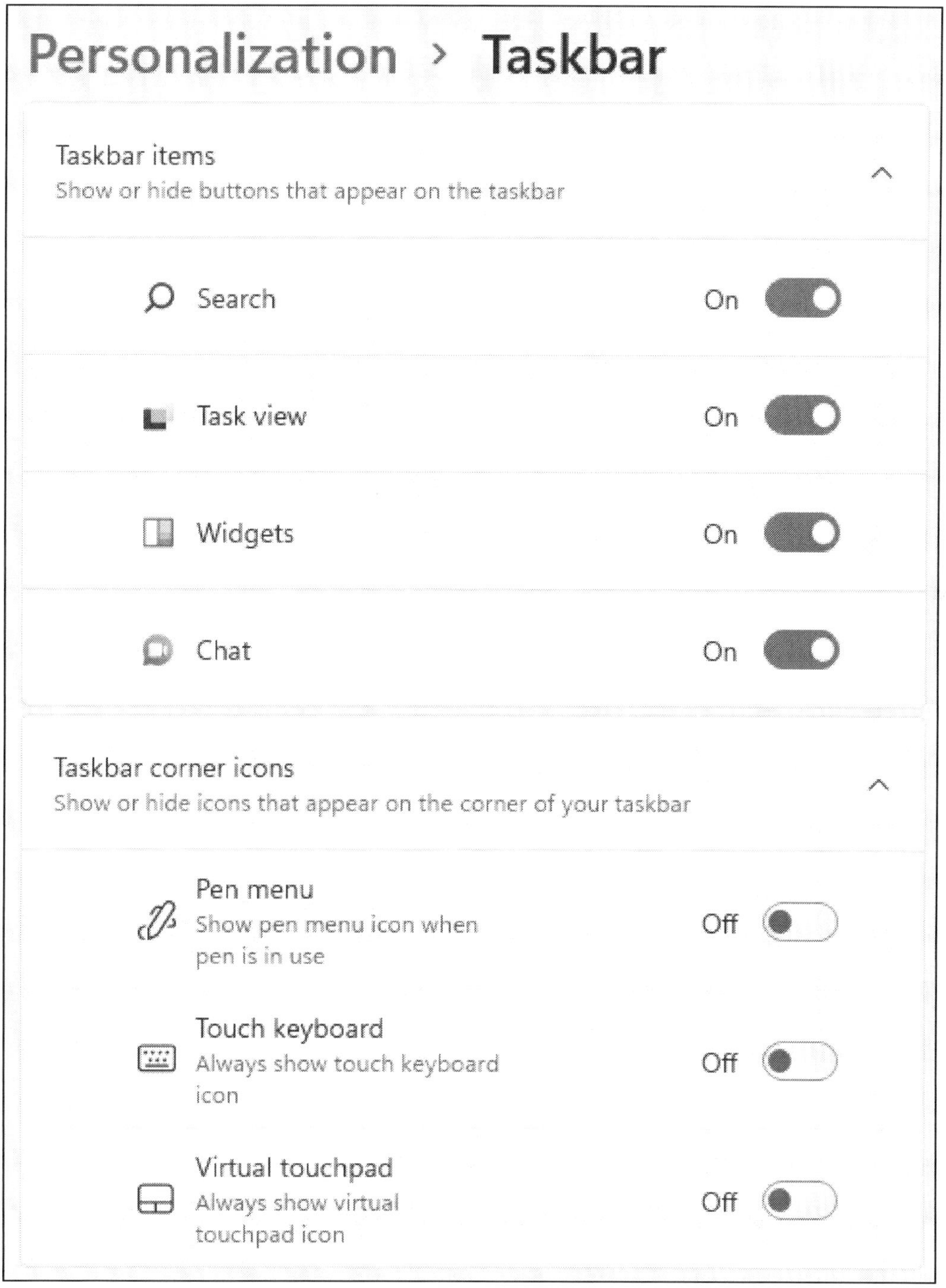

Chapter 3 – Configuring and Customizing Windows

Personalization > Taskbar

Taskbar items
Show or hide buttons that appear on the taskbar

- 🔍 Search — On
- ▭ Task view — On
- ▭ Widgets — On
- 💬 Chat — On

Taskbar corner icons
Show or hide icons that appear on the corner of your taskbar

- **Pen menu**
  Show pen menu icon when pen is in use — Off
- **Touch keyboard**
  Always show touch keyboard icon — Off
- **Virtual touchpad**
  Always show virtual touchpad icon — Off

Figure 3.10

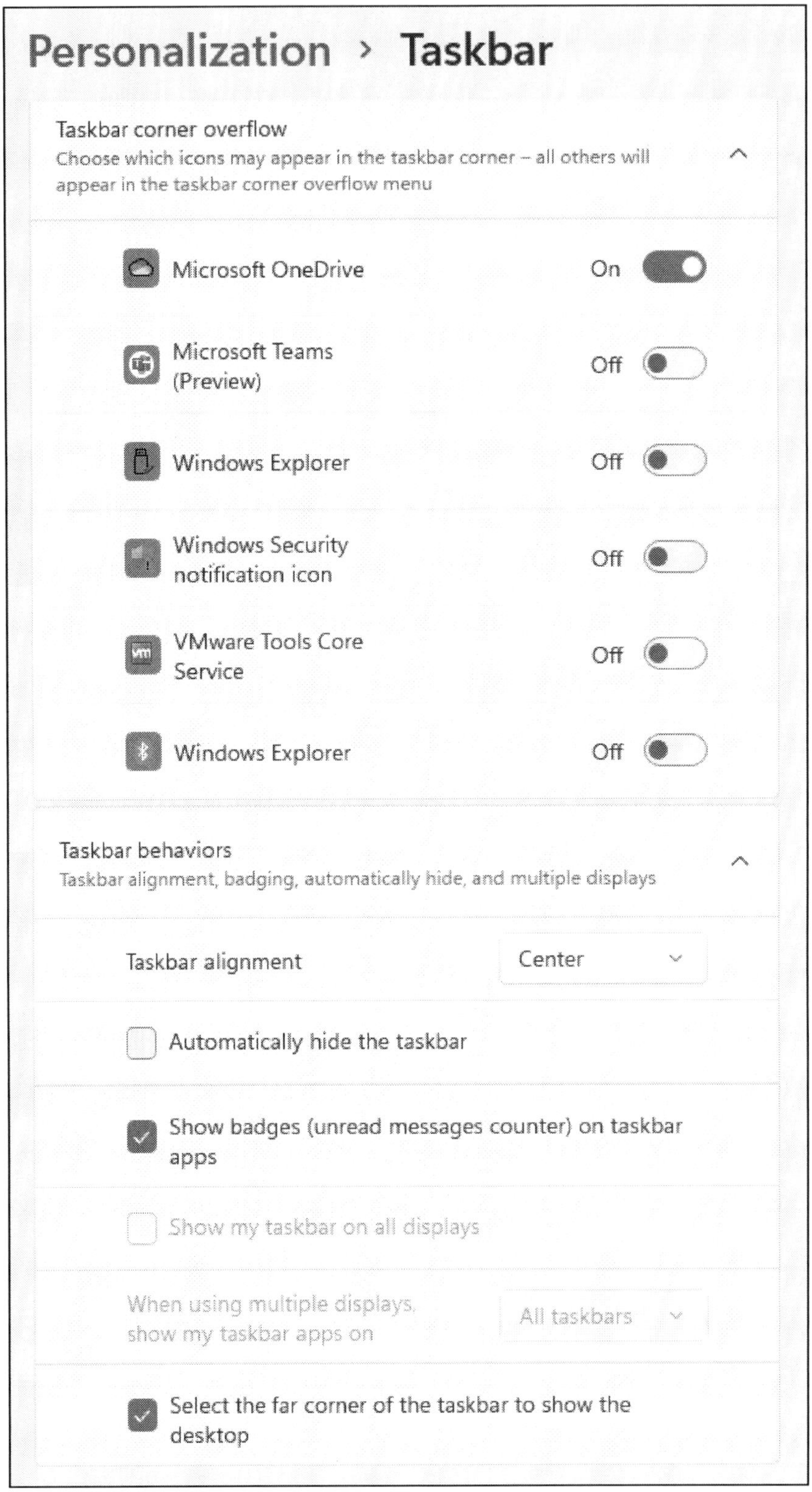

Chapter 3 – Configuring and Customizing Windows

Personalization › Taskbar

Taskbar corner overflow
Choose which icons may appear in the taskbar corner – all others will appear in the taskbar corner overflow menu

Microsoft OneDrive	On
Microsoft Teams (Preview)	Off
Windows Explorer	Off
Windows Security notification icon	Off
VMware Tools Core Service	Off
Windows Explorer	Off

Taskbar behaviors
Taskbar alignment, badging, automatically hide, and multiple displays

- Taskbar alignment — Center
- ☐ Automatically hide the taskbar
- ☑ Show badges (unread messages counter) on taskbar apps
- ☐ Show my taskbar on all displays
- When using multiple displays, show my taskbar apps on — All taskbars
- ☑ Select the far corner of the taskbar to show the desktop

Figure 3.11

Chapter 3 – Configuring and Customizing Windows

Taskbar Items

This section simply lets you decide which of the common Taskbar items will be displayed. If you decide to remove one of them from the Taskbar, that doesn't mean you can't get to it from somewhere else such as the Start menu.

- **Search** – You can use this feature to search for files, programs, apps etc.

- **Task view** – Clicking on this will show all your open apps as thumbnails on your screen and then you can click on whichever one you want to go to.

Figure 3.12

- **Widgets** – Widgets are used to display things such as the weather, stock quotes and current news events. Some of this information is pulled from your computer's location.

Chapter 3 – Configuring and Customizing Windows

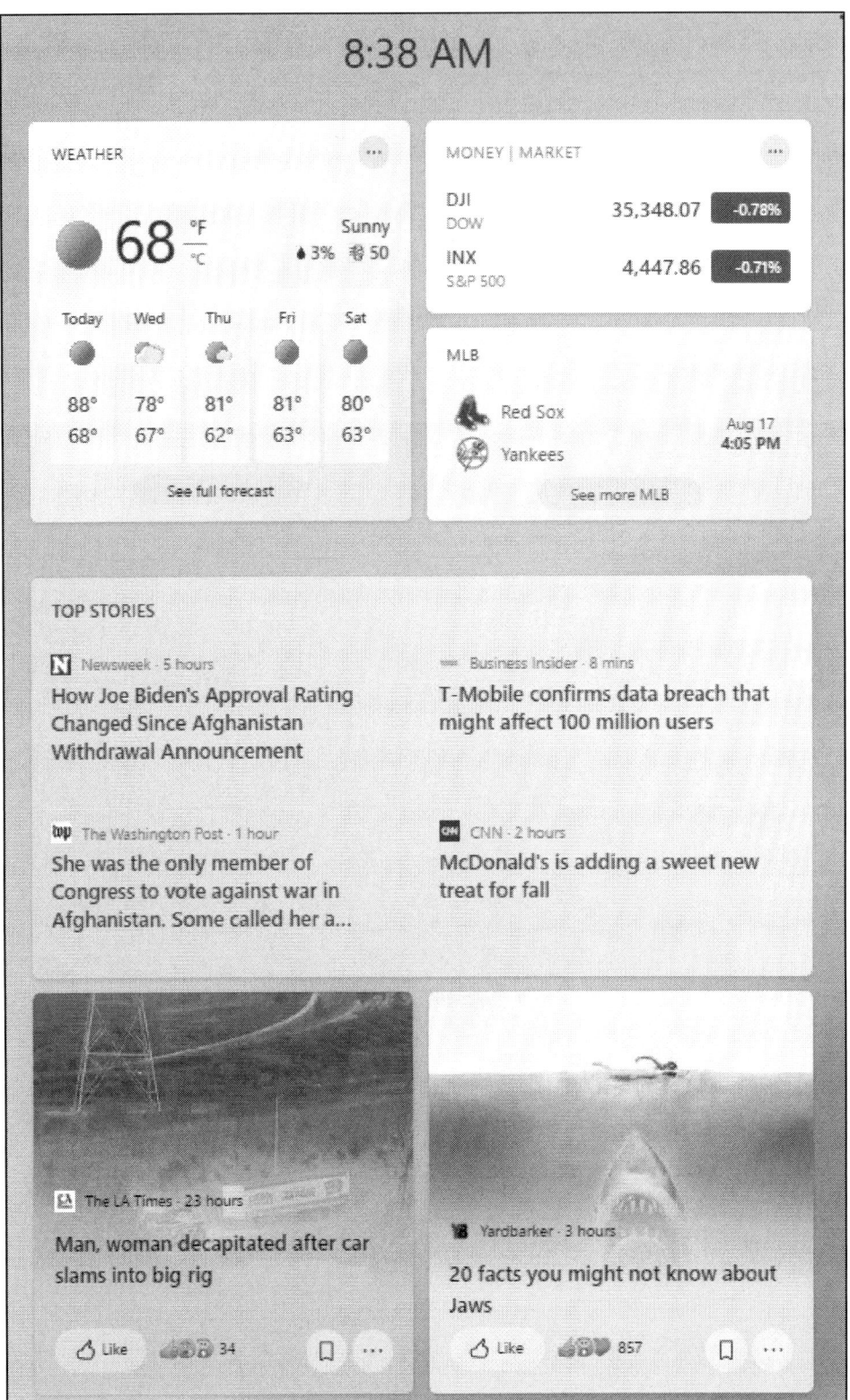

Figure 3.13

Chapter 3 – Configuring and Customizing Windows

- **Chat** – If you use Microsoft Teams which is Microsoft's collaboration software then you can start a chat with fellow team members from here.

Taskbar Corner Items

Here you can enable or disable various tools that are meant to be used with devices that have a touchscreen or some type of stylus writing device. These will appear at the lower right hand corner of your screen on the Taskbar.

- **Pen menu** – If you have a writing device that allows you to draw on your actual screen then you can enable this menu to see what options are available for this feature.

- **Touch keyboard** – This will display an on screen keyboard that you can use with your fingers or other touch device.

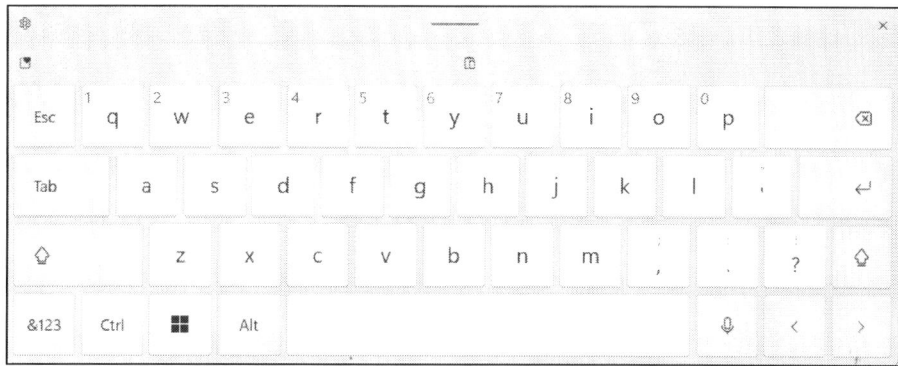

Figure 3.14

- **Virtual touchpad** – This option will let you have an on screen touch pad that you can use as if you were using the type that comes with laptops.

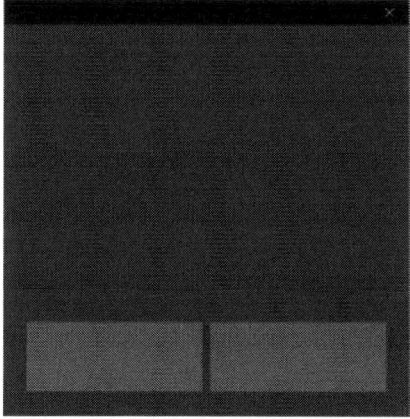

Figure 3.15

Chapter 3 – Configuring and Customizing Windows

Taskbar Corner Overflow
Windows will only place so many items in the Taskbar corner to avoid it getting too cluttered and taking up too much real estate on your taskbar. Any extra items will be hidden unless you click on the up arrow icon to the left of the displayed items.

Figure 3.16

The items you have here will vary depending on what programs you have running and what notifications your computer is configured to display. Common items you will find here are Windows Update notifications, antivirus software status and OneDrive access.

You can configure which items you wish to have displayed on the Taskbar and which items you wish to keep in the overflow section.

Taskbar Behavior
This section can come in handy if you really wish to customize how your Taskbar functions and looks.

- **Taskbar alignment** – If you wish to have your taskbar left justified as it was in Windows 10 then you can change that from here.

Chapter 3 – Configuring and Customizing Windows

- **Automatically hide the taskbar** – This option will hide the taskbar until you hover your mouse over where the taskbar normally is located.

- **Show badges** – Many Windows apps will have notification options like your smartphone apps do similar to the number 1 on my email app showing I have one new email and you can turn them on or off from here.

Figure 3.17

- **Show my taskbar on all displays** – If you have more than one monitor attached to your computer then you can choose if the taskbar is shown on only one monitor or both.

- **When using multiple displays, show my taskbar apps on** – Here you can decide if you would like all of your apps shown on only one taskbar or both when using dual monitors.

- **Select the far corner of the taskbar to show the desktop** – One of the most commonly used features of Windows that many people don't even know about is the show desktop button that is hidden away at the far right of the taskbar. In older versions of Windows, we had an actual show desktop icon but with newer versions, we can click this far right corner to have all of our open programs minimized at once so we can see the desktop.

Changing the Date and Time

One other thing I wanted to mention regarding the Taskbar since it's *on* the Taskbar, is how to adjust the date and time settings if needed. Sometimes when you get a new computer or have a new installation of Windows, your date and time settings may be incorrect. This may be because of the incorrect time zone being set, or if your computer's internal clock is off in the BIOS\UEFI on the motherboard and needs to be adjusted. If it's a case of an adjustment needed in the BIOS\UEFI, then you may have to go in there and fix it, because every time you reboot your computer it might revert back to that incorrect time. The BIOS (basic input-output system) and UEFI (Unified Extensible Firmware Interface) are beyond the scope of this book, but it's not too difficult to get in there to check.

Chapter 3 – Configuring and Customizing Windows

The method to do so varies depending on the motherboard manufacturer, but if you ever see a prompt at startup before Windows loads to press F2 or Del etc. to enter setup, then that's what you are looking for. You will usually have a menu driven system where you use the arrow keys and enter key to navigate around.

If it's just a case of setting the correct time zone or the Windows time itself is off, then all you need to do to fix it is to right click on the clock on the lower right-hand corner of the taskbar and choose *Adjust date/time*. In figure 3.18 you can see that there is a drop-down menu for the time zone as well as some other options. If the *Change* button next to *Set the date and time manually* is greyed out, that is because the *set time automatically* option is turned on, so if you want to manually assign the date and time, simply turn off this option. Then you will be able to click on the *Change* button. As you can see, there is also a setting for automatic daylight settings adjustments that you can turn on or off as needed.

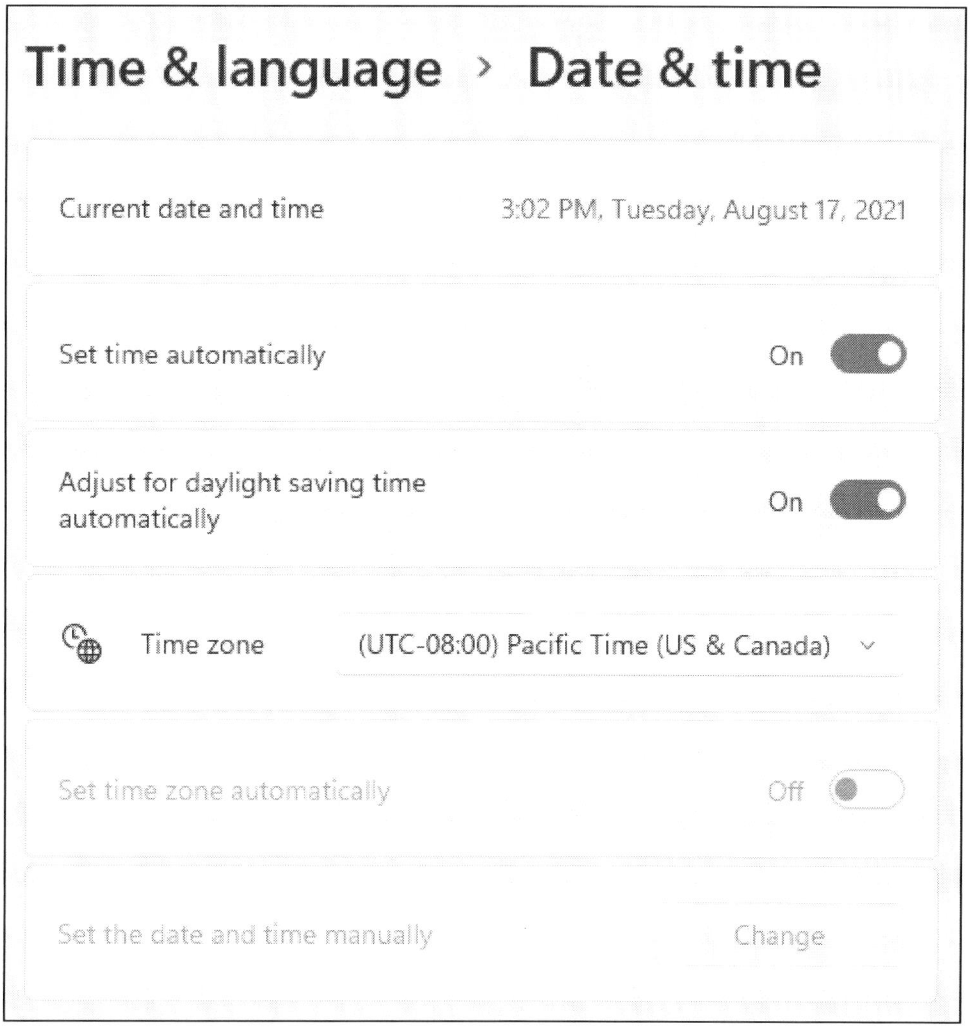

Chapter 3 – Configuring and Customizing Windows

Time & language › Date & time

Current date and time — 3:02 PM, Tuesday, August 17, 2021

Set time automatically — On

Adjust for daylight saving time automatically — On

Time zone — (UTC-08:00) Pacific Time (US & Canada)

Set time zone automatically — Off

Set the date and time manually — Change

Figure 3.18

Cortana

With Windows 10, Microsoft introduced its new virtual assistant named Cortana. Cortana is their version of Siri for Apple devices. You can use Cortana for a variety of things, such as setting reminders, making lists, tracking your tasks, and searching your computer, the web, and apps. When you configure Windows the first time it will ask you if you want to use Cortana or not, but even if you say no, you will still have the option to do so.

You can have the Cortana icon pinned to your Start menu or Taskbar if you plan on using it a lot the same way you would pin any other app.

Chapter 3 – Configuring and Customizing Windows

You might have noticed I have been using the words apps and programs to describe software on a computer. Windows uses both and apps are more of simple\single purpose software (such as solitaire or the weather) while programs are more complex and can do more (such as Photoshop or Word).

The first time you open Cortana it will want you to sign in with your Microsoft account. You can use the same account that you used to sign into Windows. Then you might be asked if you would like to allow your installed apps the ability to use voice activation so you can use your microphone to speak commands.

Chapter 3 – Configuring and Customizing Windows

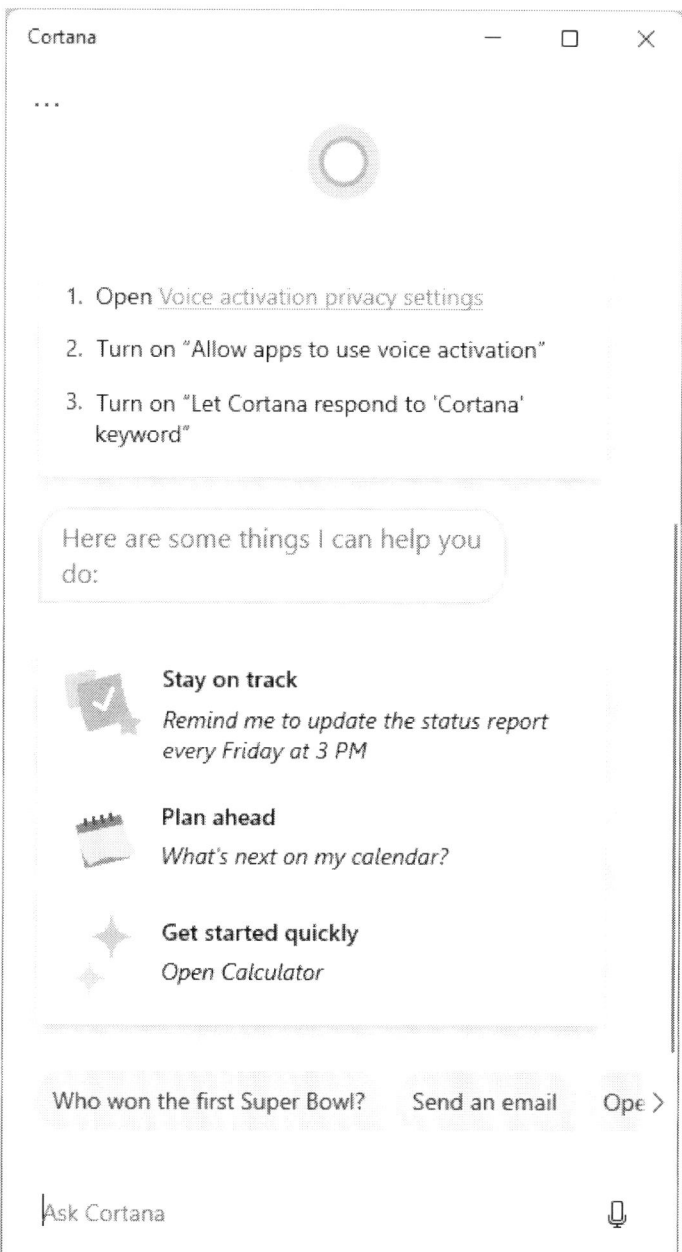

Figure 3.19

Once you are up and running you can ask Cortana to do things such as open an app or tell you the weather.

Chapter 3 – Configuring and Customizing Windows

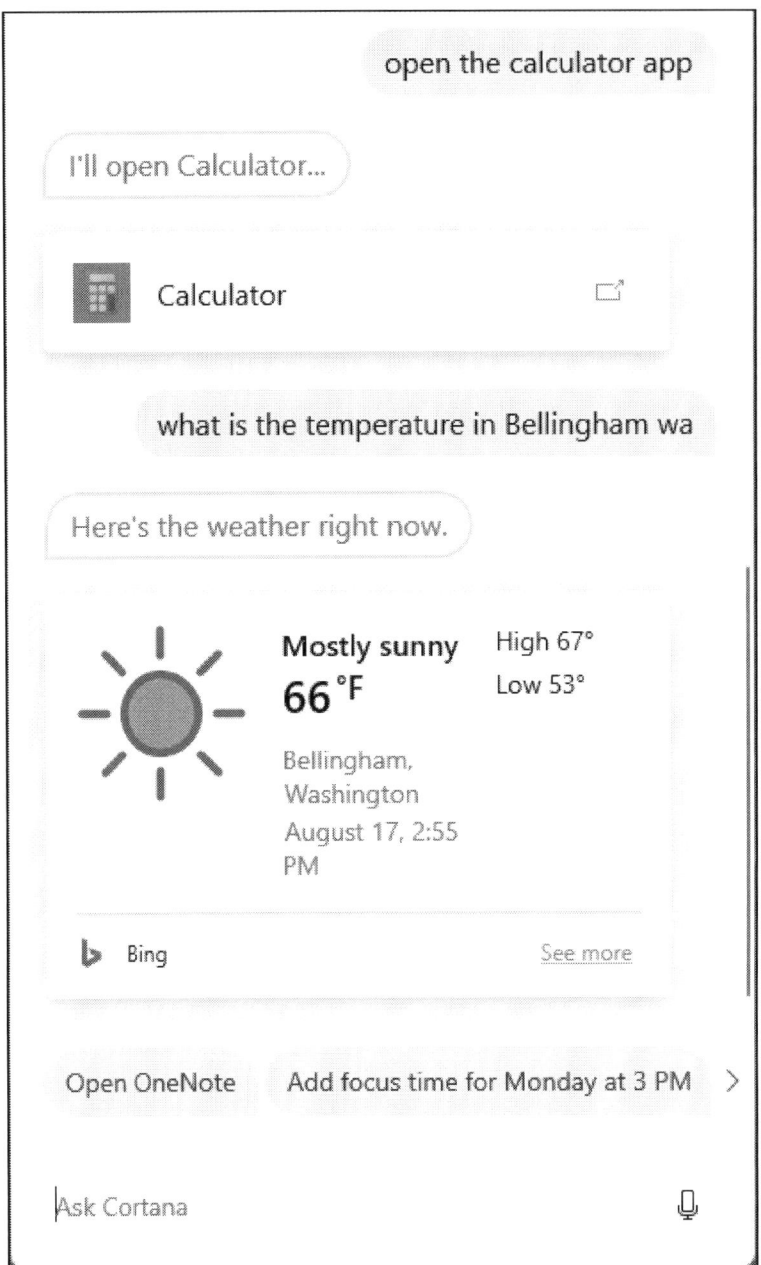

Figure 3.20

Windows Desktop
Another common item that people like to customize on their computer is the Windows desktop. Let's begin our discussion with what we call the "desktop". The word desktop is kind of a vague term that people use in different ways, but essentially the desktop when it comes to Windows is the main screen where you

Chapter 3 – Configuring and Customizing Windows

will have icons for programs and other items like folders and files that you regularly use. Think of it as the top of your desk that your monitor sits on top of. It's where you have an overview of everything and the place where you find the things you need to do your work. Here is what a typical Windows 11 desktop looks like. Notice the icons for programs and the other files and folders as well as the desktop background image?

Figure 3.21

The desktop is very customizable, and you can add whatever shortcuts to programs that you like, as well as create files and folders of any type on it. There are several ways to do this as well. For example, if you right click on a blank part of the desktop and then click on *New*, you will have several options for the types of items you can add to the desktop (figure 3.22). The important thing to keep in mind here is that the choices you will have after clicking New will vary on what programs you have installed on your computer, so your choices will most likely look different than the image below. My image shows the basics because it's a new installation of Windows and I don't have much else on this computer.

Chapter 3 – Configuring and Customizing Windows

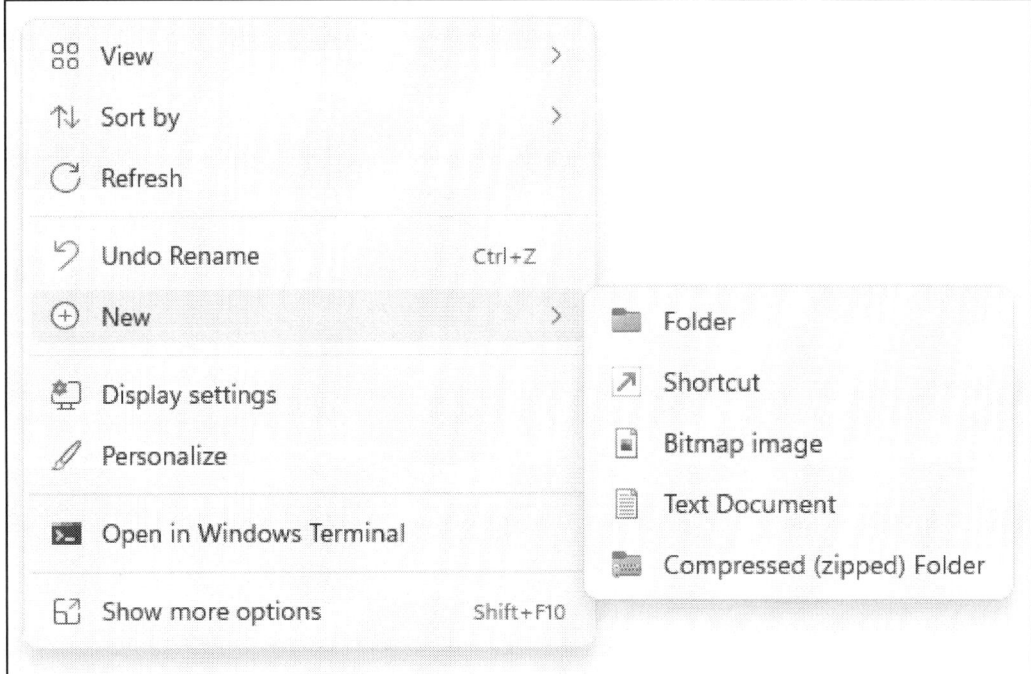

Figure 3.23

As you can see, you can create things like a new folder, shortcut, text document, and so on. It is also possible to customize what items are available from the New menu, but that's a much more advanced topic. So let's say we chose to make a new text document. After you clicked on *Text Document*, it would create the file on the desktop and allow you to name it whatever you like. Then when you open the text document it will be blank because it's a new file. You can get the same result by clicking on the *Notepad* app from your Start menu programs, creating a new document, and saving it on the desktop. As you will notice, there are several ways to do the same thing within Windows, and this really comes in handy when it comes to being efficient.

If you want to copy a file or folder from a different location to the desktop, it's as simple as finding the file or folder, right clicking it, choosing *Copy*, and then right clicking on the desktop and choosing *Paste*. I will discuss copying vs. cutting in Chapter 6, as well as deleting and renaming files and folders. You can also drag and drop files and folders from one location, such as a different folder on your hard drive, or even from a CD\DVD or external flash or hard drive to copy them to your desktop.

On a more advanced note, there are other ways to get to the files on your desktop. If you open File Explorer, you will see a shortcut icon for *Desktop* on the upper

Chapter 3 – Configuring and Customizing Windows

left-hand side of the folder tree. You will notice how the items in the Desktop folder match the items that are actually on the desktop except for the Recycle Bin.

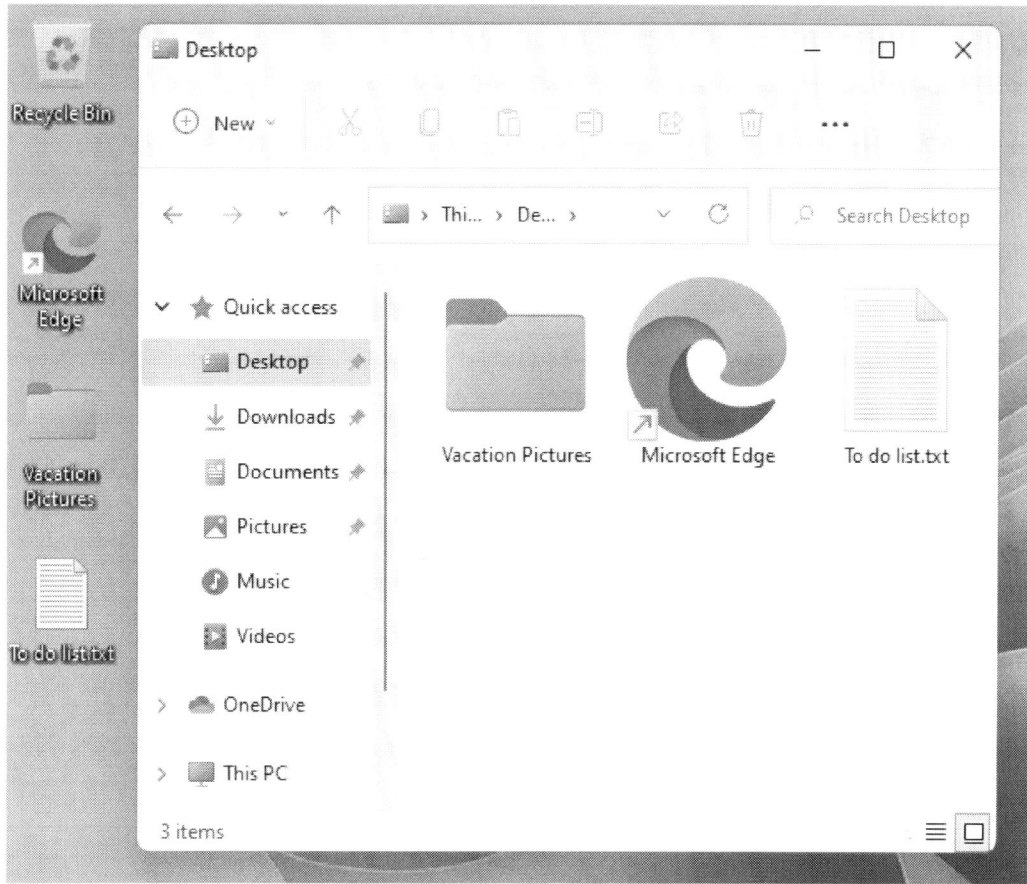
Figure 3.24

Another useful way to get to the Desktop folder is to find it under the *Users* folder on the system drive (usually the C drive) of your computer. Simply navigate to **C:\Users\username\Desktop**, where *username* is the user's account name that they log into the computer with. If you have other user accounts on your computer, you can get to their desktops as well, assuming you have permission to do so. (And by permission, I mean permissions configured on the computer, not from the person themselves!).

Changing Your Desktop Background
One of the most common ways people customize their desktop is to change the background picture of the desktop itself. Windows comes with some high quality

Chapter 3 – Configuring and Customizing Windows

pictures that you can choose from, or you can use your own pictures or even one you saved from a website.

To change your desktop background simply right click on a blank area of the desktop and choose *Personalize*. Here is an example of how you can do the same thing in Windows multiple ways because you can get to the same Personalization options by clicking on the Windows Settings gear icon and then going to Personalization.

Once you are in the Personalization settings go to the *Background* section (figure 3.25). Here you will have the option to have your background be either one of the included pictures, your own personal photo, a solid color or even a photo slideshow. The slideshow option will change the background image using pictures in a folder that you specify at an interval of your choosing. If you click the *Browse Photos* button, you can browse to a folder stored in a folder on your hard drive to use as a background image. The *Choose a fit for your desktop photo* setting will determine how the picture is displayed on your desktop. You can choose settings such as fill, fit, stretch, center tile, and so on.

Chapter 3 – Configuring and Customizing Windows

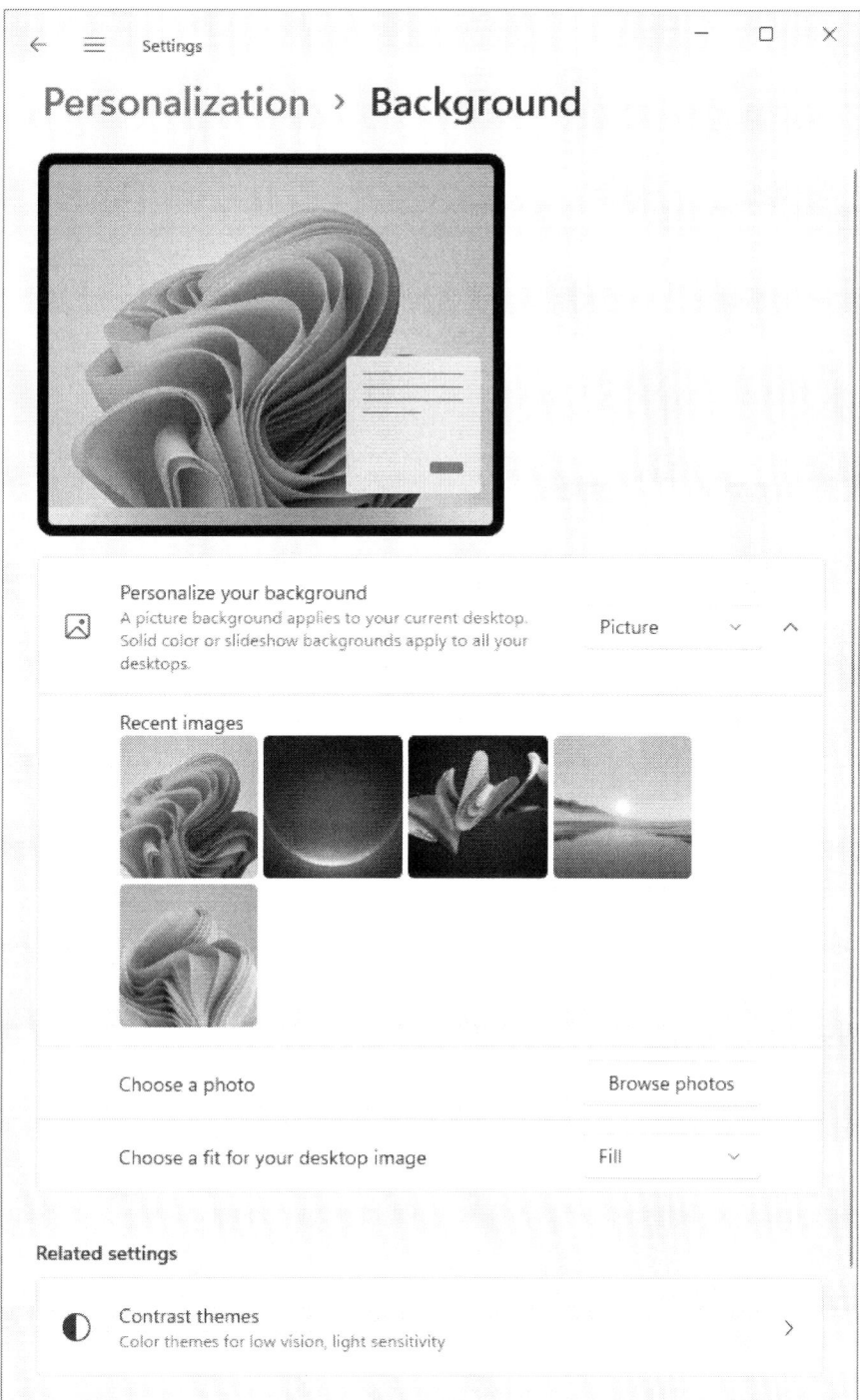

Figure 3.25

To use the slideshow option, you will need to click on Slideshow from the dropdown menu and browse to a folder on your computer that contains the photos you wish to use for your slideshow.

Chapter 3 – Configuring and Customizing Windows

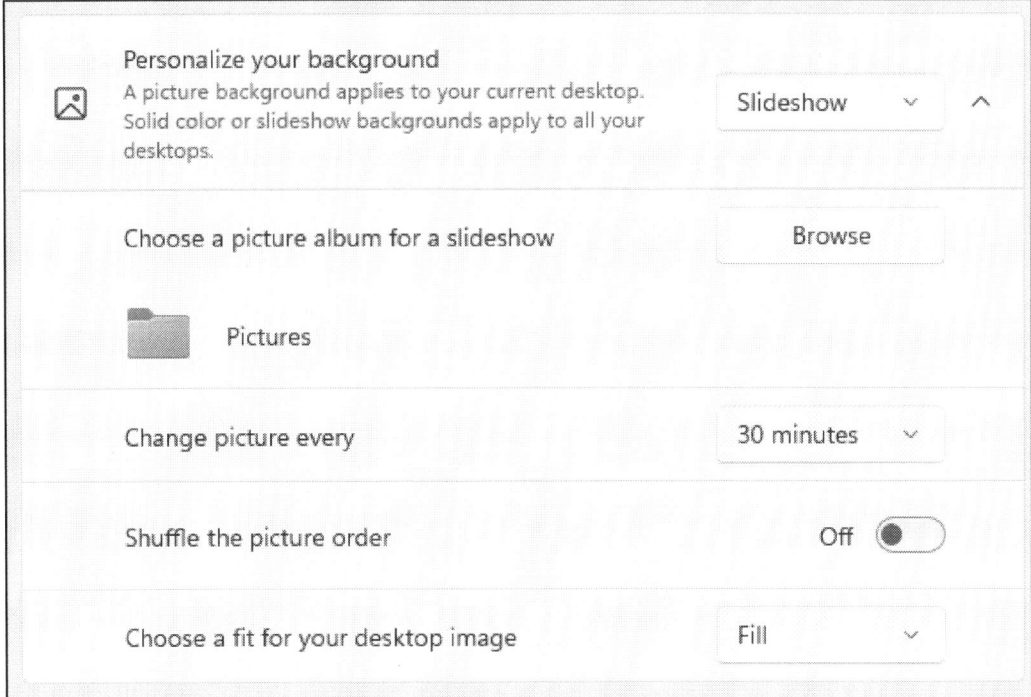

Figure 3.26

 If you are going to use your own picture for your desktop background, try and use a higher resolution image such as 300 dpi so it will look nice and clear when it's expanded to fill your desktop, especially if you have a larger monitor.

Changing Your Display Settings
Another thing I want to mention that is related to your desktop is the display settings. You can access these settings by right clicking on a blank area of the desktop and choosing *Display settings*, or from the Windows settings under the *Display* section. The Display settings allow you to change the resolution of your computer's display, so you get the best quality image for your monitor size. Windows will normally recommend a setting for you, but you don't have to use it. You can try out different resolutions and Windows will show you how it will look, and you can revert it back to the previous setting if you don't like the preview.

Chapter 3 – Configuring and Customizing Windows

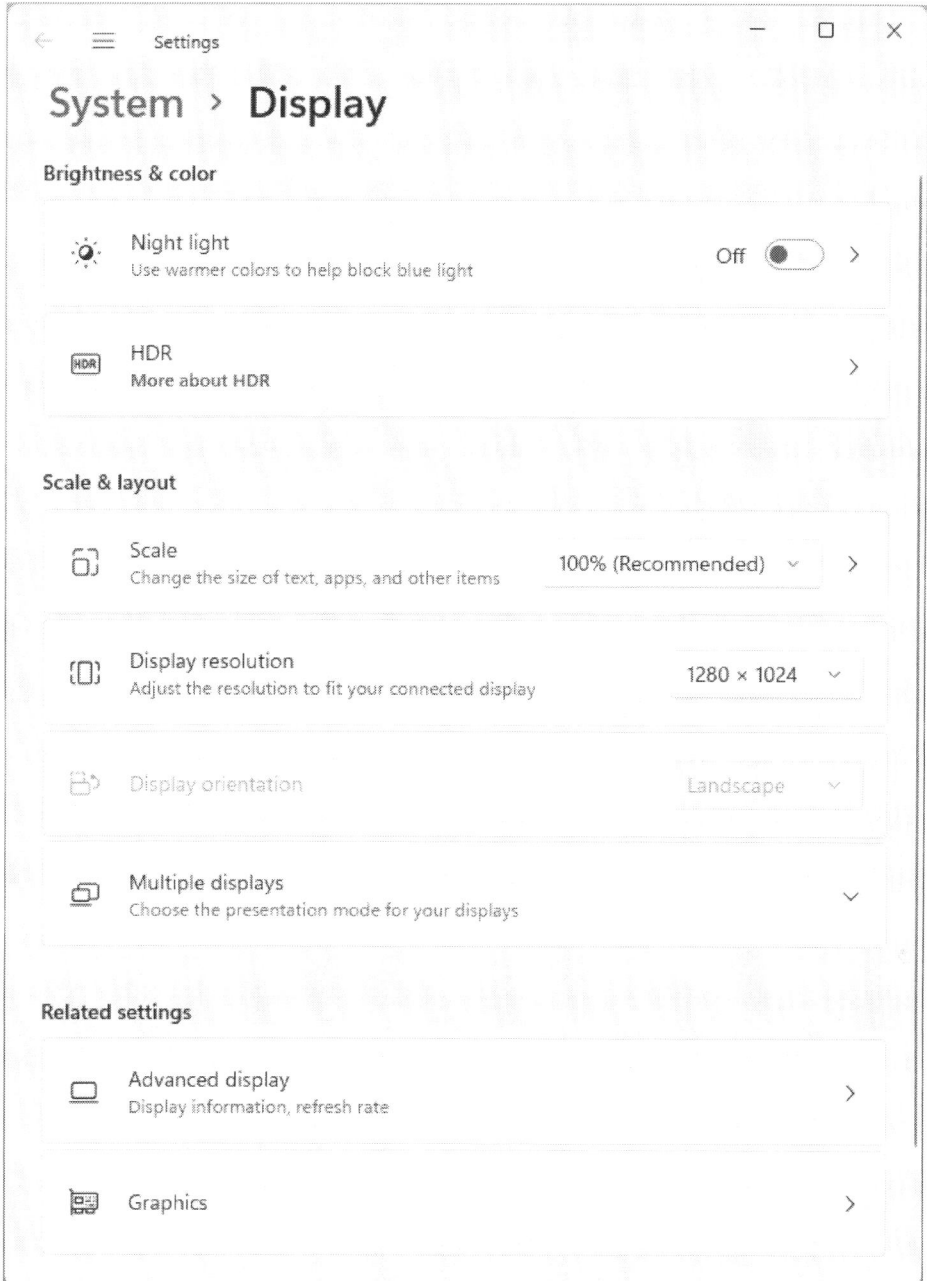

Figure 3.27

There are other options here for things like changing the size of text and apps if you need to enlarge them to make things easier to see. If you have a monitor that can rotate between landscape and portrait modes, then you can change the settings under the *Display orientation* section. And if you are the type that likes to have more than one monitor attached to your computer, then you can set up multiple displays from here as well.

Chapter 3 – Configuring and Customizing Windows

Changing Themes, Colors, and Sounds

Other popular items to customize in Windows include changing the Windows theme as well as the system colors and sounds. A theme is a grouping of settings including the background image, system colors, system sounds, and mouse cursor options. Windows 11 comes with some built in themes that you can choose from, or you can create your own and even download additional themes from the Microsoft Store (discussed in Chapter 5). You can even save a custom theme that you have created so you can go back to it later if you decide to change the settings of your current theme. Themes can be found under *Personalization* and then *Themes*.

I always like to play around with the themes and customize them so I can have my computer look exactly the way I like because it gives you a more pleasant experience when using your computer.

Chapter 3 – Configuring and Customizing Windows

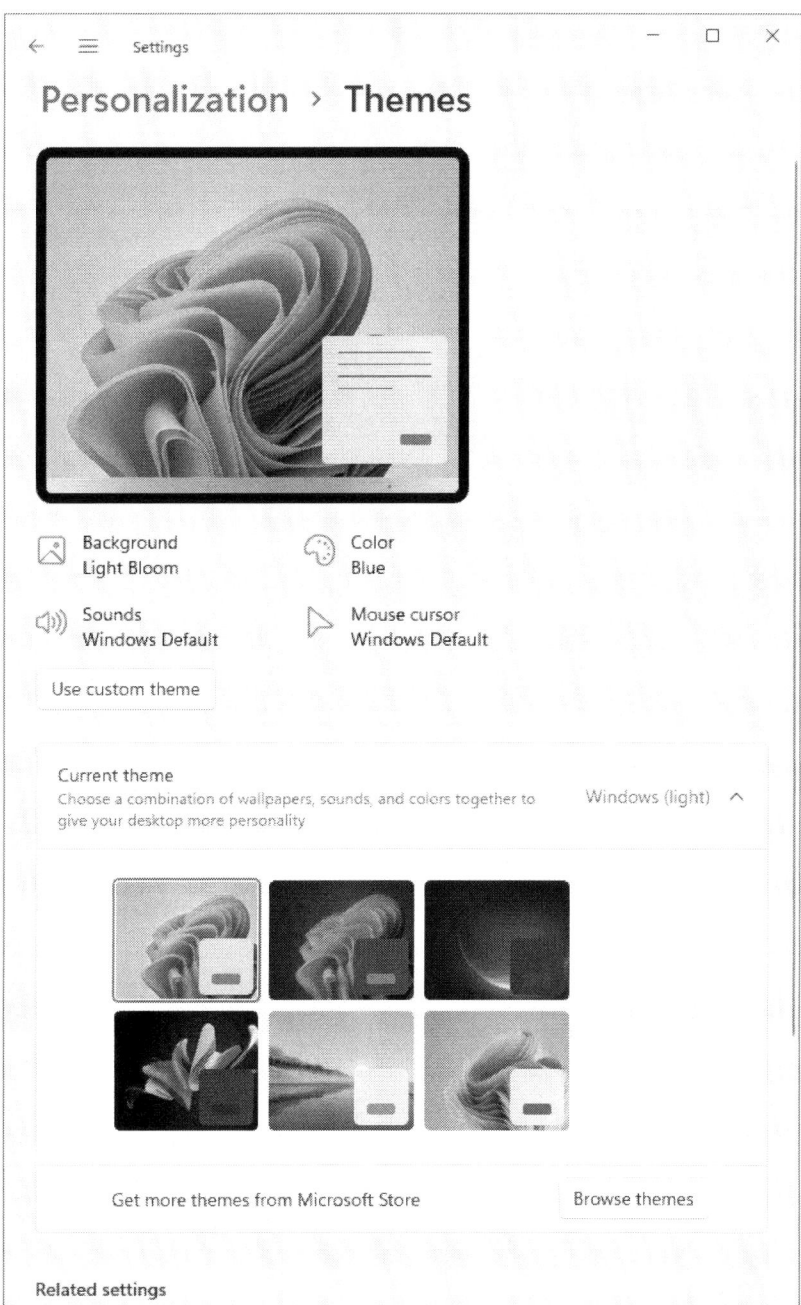

Figure 3.28

If you want to only change the colors or sounds Windows uses, you can do that from the Personalization settings as well. Clicking on *Sounds* will open the older Control Panel interface (discussed later in this chapter), so you can access the sound settings from there as well. Once you open the sound options, you will see that it's set to use the Windows Default sound scheme.

Chapter 3 – Configuring and Customizing Windows

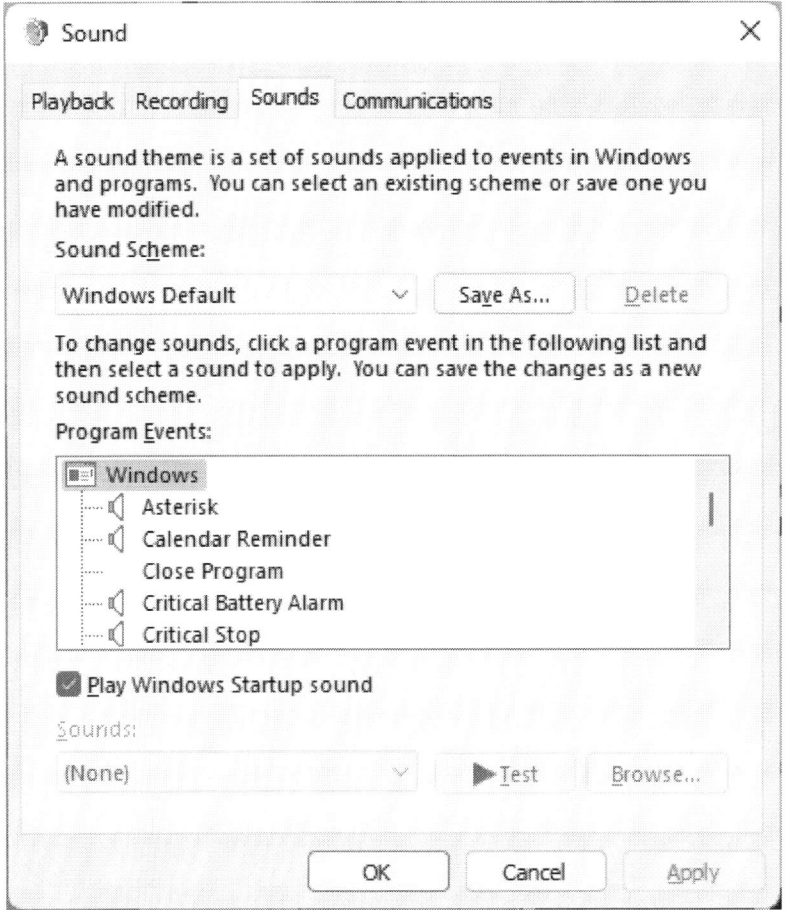

Figure 3.29

Under the section that says *Program Events,* you can change the sound for various events, such as when Windows starts up, when you connect a USB device, or when there is a system error. You can use the built in Windows sounds, which are WAV files, or you can even use your own WAV files if you have some. If you don't want to have a sound associated with an action, you can remove the sound from that action. I always like to set the sound scheme to *no sounds* because I like the peace and quiet!

Screen Savers
I'm not sure how many people really use screen savers anymore, but there is still an option to add one in Windows 11. And the interface you use to do so is the same one that has been around for many generations of Windows (figure 3.30). Maybe someday they will update the interface work like the background and colors sections.

Chapter 3 – Configuring and Customizing Windows

Figure 3.30

You can get to the screen saver settings from the *Lock screen* section in the Personalization settings. Once you have it open, you can choose which screen saver you want to use and how long before it kicks in. Depending on what screen saver you choose, the Settings button will allow you to customize it to suit your needs. If you want your computer to lock itself after you move the mouse to turn off the screen saver, then click the checkbox next to *On resume, display logon screen*.

Windows Power Settings
One thing people overlook when configuring their computer is the power settings. The power settings are where you can tell the computer to do things such as go to

sleep or hibernate after a certain period of time or turn off the monitor or hard drive after a period of non-use.

Sleep mode saves your open files and settings in memory (RAM) and then puts the computer in a low power mode. Hibernate mode saves your files to disk and then turns off the computer. Then when you move the mouse or press a key on the keyboard the computer will wake up and things will be the way that you left them. I never like to use sleep or hibernate mode because it takes longer to get back to your work when you move the mouse to have the computer "wake up", and sometimes you will find that it doesn't wake up at all and you have to reboot it.

I do like to use the turn off display option so when you walk away from your computer the monitor will power off after a set amount of time that you determine. Then when you move the mouse, it will come back on. There are other power settings you can configure as well, such as turning off the hard disk after a period of time to save power. Today's computers are pretty energy efficient, so you can get away with keeping things running and be ok. On the other hand, if you are using a laptop running on battery power, you might want to use some of these power saving features.

In the Windows settings under System, there is a *Power* section where you can configure the options for turning off your monitor and putting the computer to sleep.

Chapter 3 – Configuring and Customizing Windows

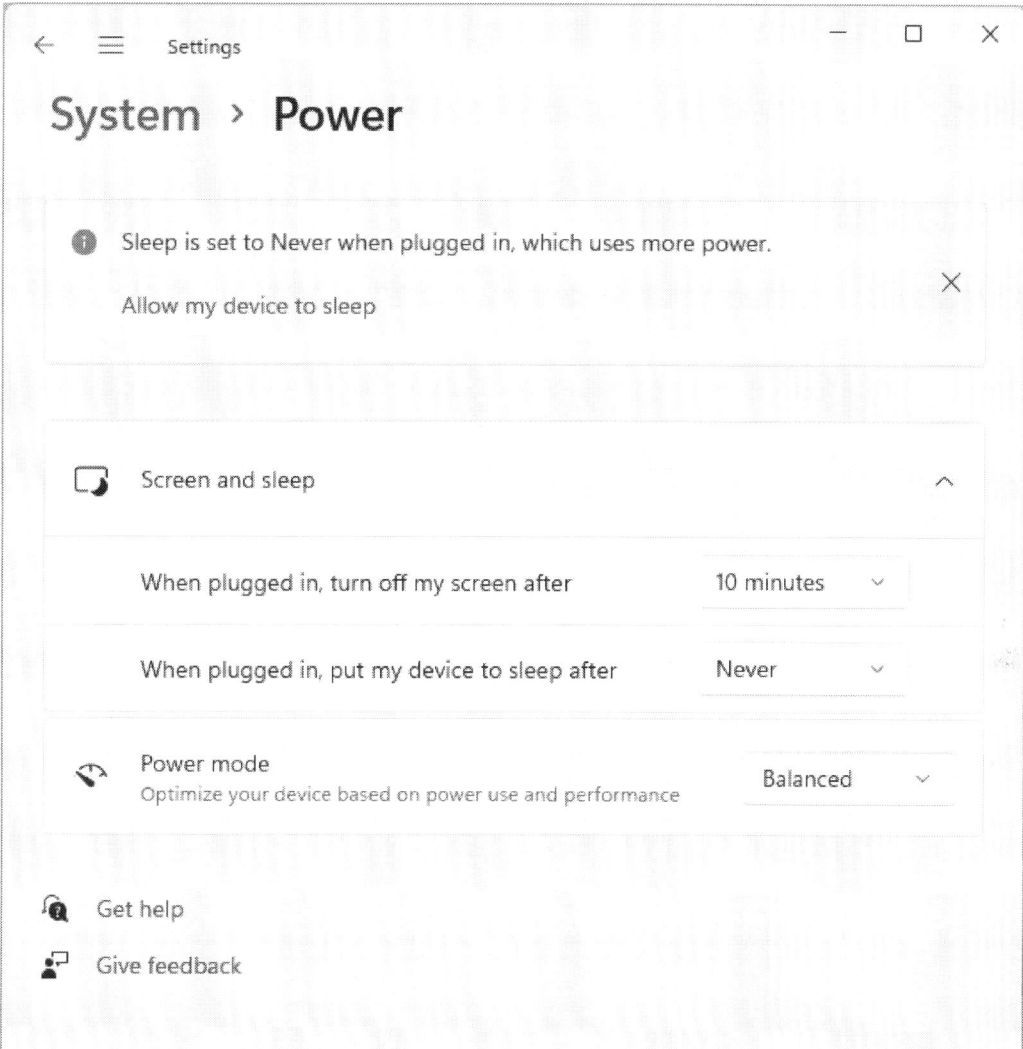

Figure 3.31

If you want to change the more advanced options, you will need to go to the *Power Options* utility in Control Panel as seen in figure 3.32.

Chapter 3 – Configuring and Customizing Windows

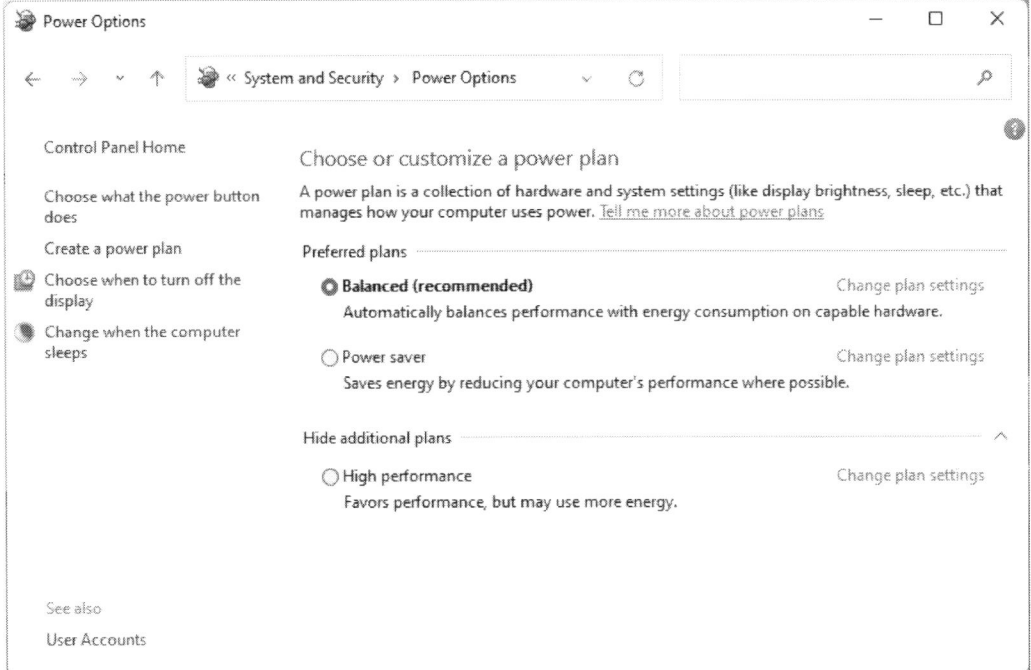

Figure 3.32

Here you can choose one of the preconfigured plans and then change the settings by clicking on the *Change plan settings* link. Once you do that, you can click on the *Change advanced power settings* link to get to the advanced options, as shown in figure 3.34.

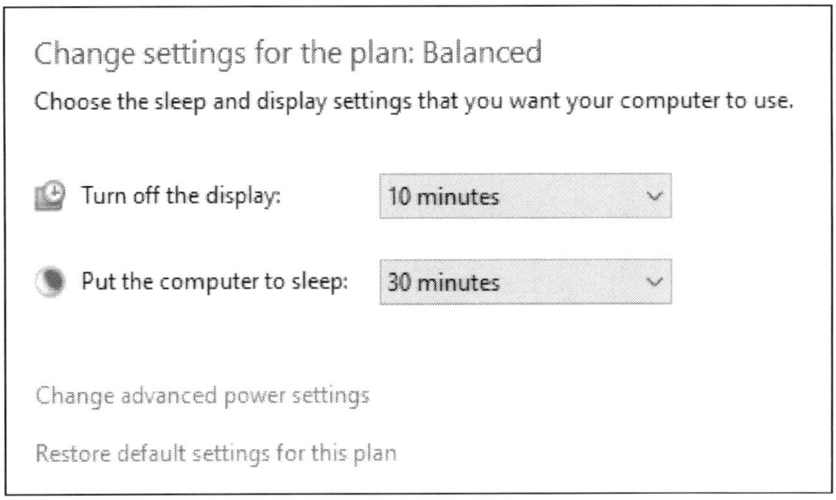

Figure 3.33

Chapter 3 – Configuring and Customizing Windows

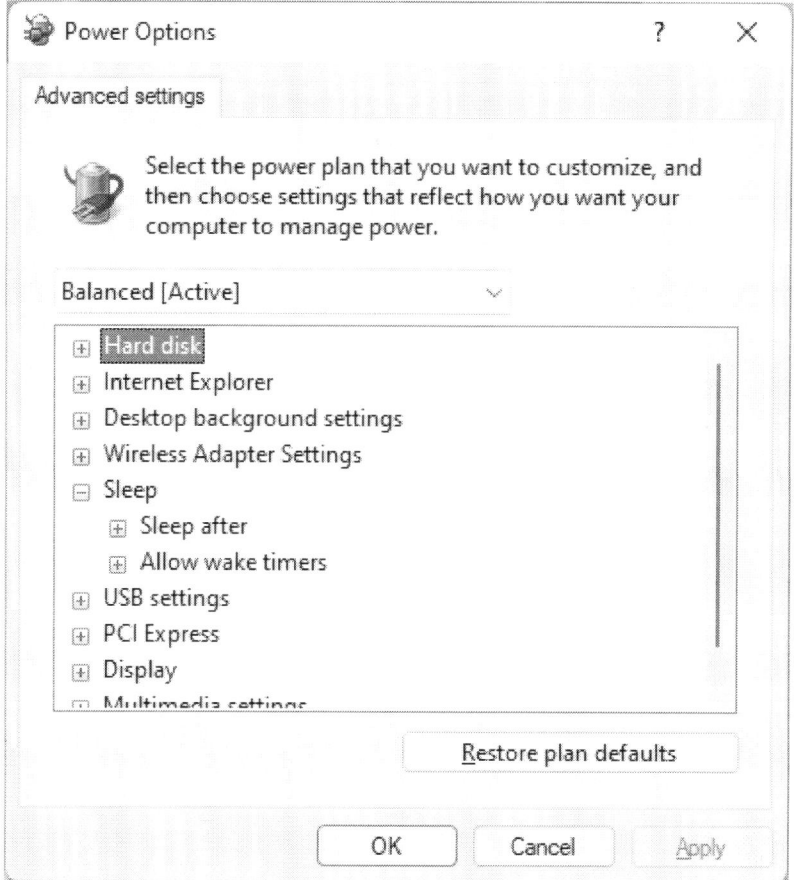

Figure 3.34

At the top of the window, there is a dropdown menu where you can choose the power plan, and then you can customize it with the options underneath. If you want to change things back to the default, then you can click on the *Restore plan defaults* button.

Windows Control Panel
If you plan on being a serious Windows user, or even if you just plan on tweaking your computer's settings, you will need to get yourself familiar with the Windows Control Panel. This is where you can go to get to many of the Windows configuration settings and options to change the way Windows operates, or to fix problems you may run into. Many of these settings can be done via the Windows 11 Settings (discussed in Chapter 9) but for some things you will need to use Control Panel and for other things the Control Panel method is just easier!

Chapter 3 – Configuring and Customizing Windows

The easiest way to get to the Control Panel is to just type in **control panel** from the search box from the Start menu or from Cortana. If it's the first time you have opened Control Panel, then it will most likely be in the category display view, but if you click the down arrow next to *View by*, then you can change it to large icons or small icons and see everything in one place (figure 3.36).

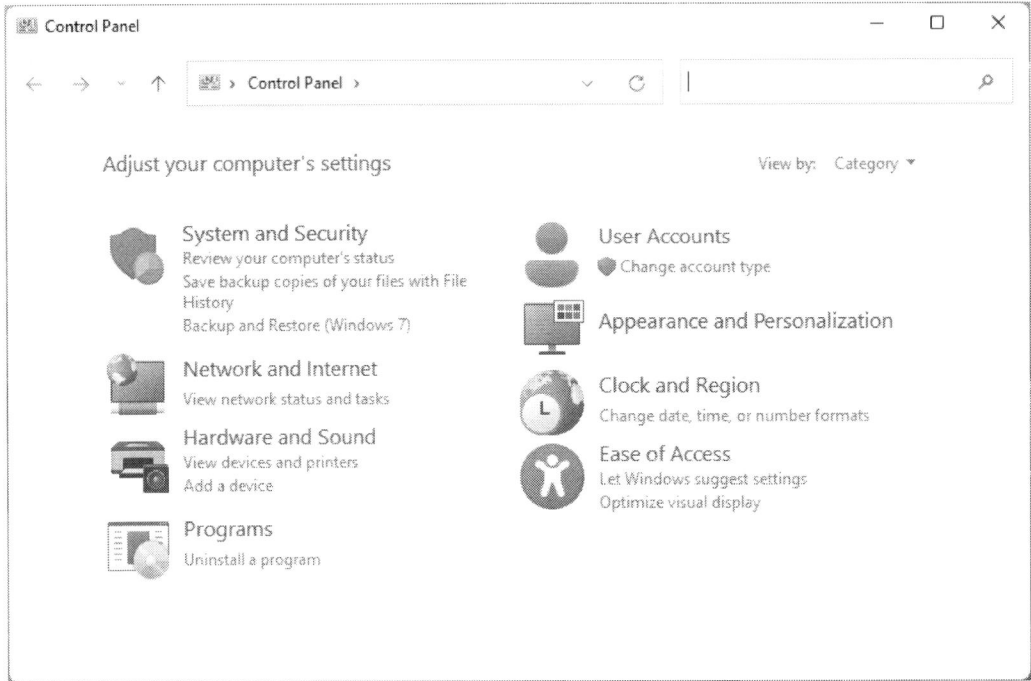

Figure 3.35

Chapter 3 – Configuring and Customizing Windows

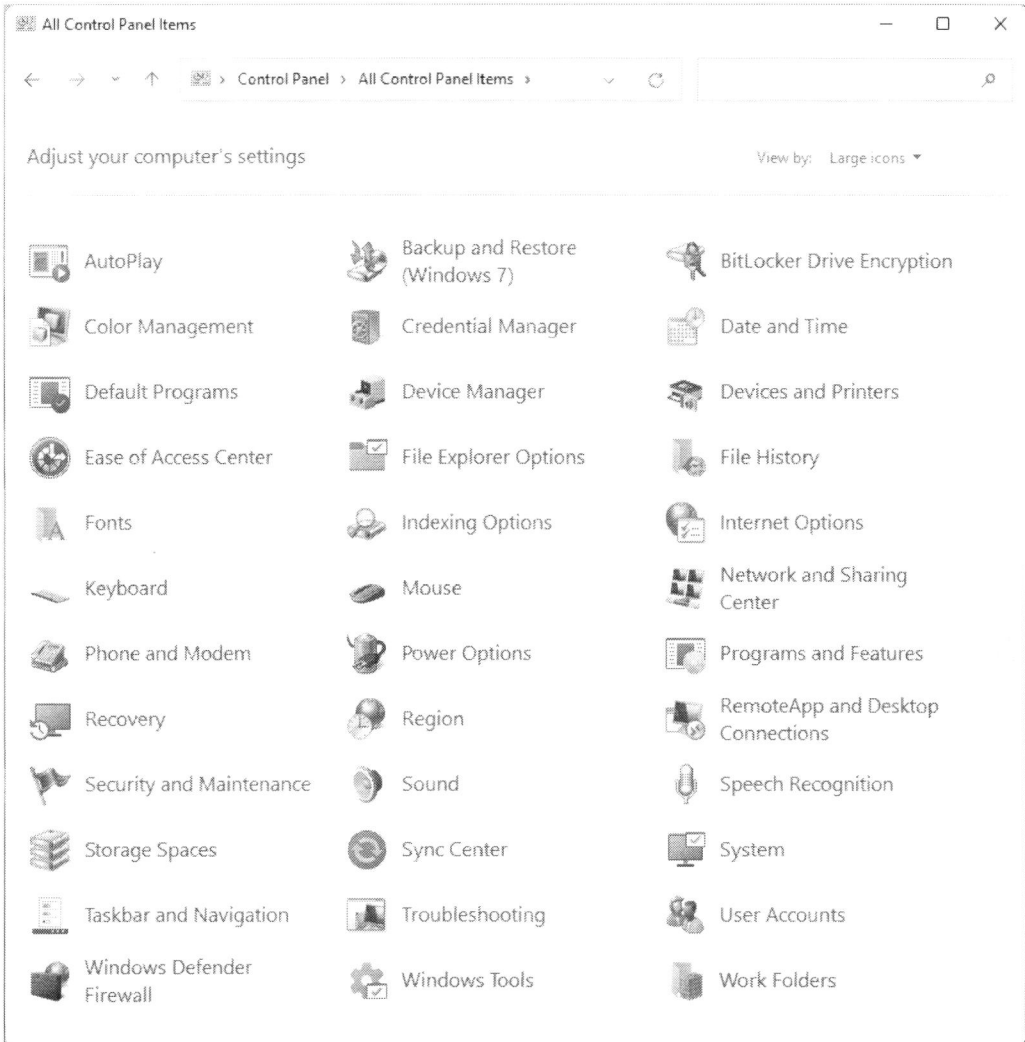

Figure 3.36

As you can see, there are many settings to choose from, but keep in mind yours may vary a little depending on your computer's configuration. Rather than going over each utility, I will discuss some of the more commonly used ones. (You can experiment with the others on your own, though some of these you will never have a reason to use at all). Some of the Control Panel settings will actually open the Windows 11 newer style settings interface.

- **Default Programs** – Used to tell Windows what program to use as the default for types of files.

- **Ease of Access Center** – Allows you to set options that make the computer easier to use.

Chapter 3 – Configuring and Customizing Windows

- **Fonts** – This is where you can see installed fonts and also add and remove them.

- **Devices and Printers** – Here you can manage your printers as well as install new printers and other devices.

- **Network and Sharing Center** – Allows for the configuration of network settings and connections.

- **Sound** – Used to configure Windows sounds as well as recording and playback options for your sound hardware.

- **System** – This is where you can find information about your computer, as well as get to other settings such as your network, privacy or Windows Update settings.

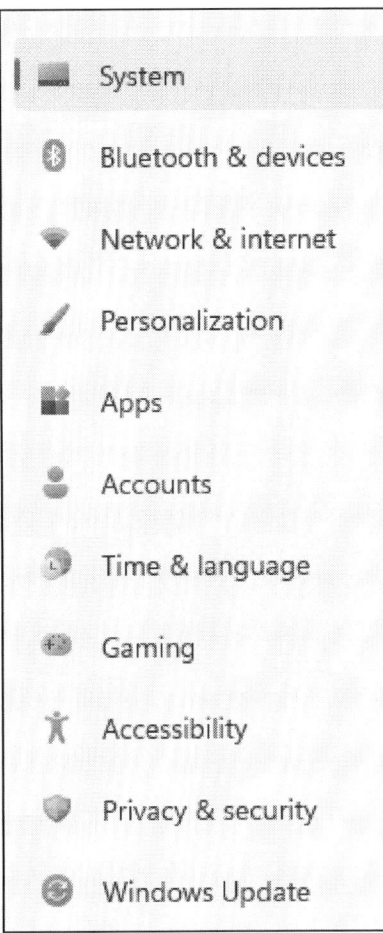

Figure 3.37

Chapter 3 – Configuring and Customizing Windows

- **Power Options** – Controls how Windows manages power for your hardware (previously discussed).

- **User Accounts** – This is where you manage your local users for the computer (discussed in Chapter 7).

Chapter 4 – Installing Devices

At some point in time, you are going to want to add some kind of new device to your computer to improve its functionality. It may be a new printer, webcam, flash drive or a variety of different things. Regardless of what you are trying to attach to your computer, you will need to know how to configure it, otherwise you might not be able to use it until you do. Some devices will configure themselves while others require additional software that you will need to install.

Installing Printers\Scanners
Printers are one of the most common devices that people add to their computers. These days most printers are what they call all-in-one printers, where they can print, scan, copy, and fax. And with these printers costing so little, they are affordable to just about everyone.

Most printers will install the same way no matter if it's an all-in-one printer, photo printer, or laser printer. There are a few different ways to connect them to your computer though, so let's talk about that first.

It used to be that using the USB connection was the most common way to connect a printer to a computer. USB stands for Universal Serial Bus and has been around since 1996. It has had several versions, including 1.1, 2.0, 3.0, and 3.1, with each version becoming considerably faster than the previous version. Computers will typically have around 2-6 USB ports in the rear, and usually a couple in the front of the computer for easy access. It involves connecting a USB cable from your computer to the printer and is as easy as that.

Until USB 3 becomes the standard implementation of USB, you might notice that your computer has USB ports that are a different color, such as red rather than just black. This usually indicates that they are USB 3 ports. They may also have SS written next to the port for Super Speed.

Another connection method that is becoming one of the most common ways to connect printers is to use a wireless connection. This method will probably be the standard way to connect soon, at least for home users. When you use a wireless connection, you can have multiple computers connect to one printer rather than

Chapter 4 – Installing Devices

being stuck with only one computer using the printer because there is only one USB port on the back of the printer. This method is a little more complicated to set up because you will need to connect your printer to your Wi-Fi router\modem first and then have your computer search for an available wireless printer to connect to.

The last connection method I will mention is using a network connection. Many printers have network ports on the back that allow you to connect them to your home or office network and share them that way. This method also requires a bit more work to configure since you will need to know how your network is configured to be able to set up the printer properly. When it's ready to go, then you can print to the networked printer from multiple computers, just like with the wireless setup.

If you would like to learn more about networking concepts and how they allow our devices to communicate, then check out my book titled **Networking Made Easy**. https://www.amazon.com/dp/1720034109

Once you get the connection method figured out, you will need to install some software called a *driver* on your computer. Drivers allow the operating system (Windows) to communicate with the hardware device, in our case, the printer. Sometimes you will get lucky and Windows will already have a driver for your printer built in and configure it for you. If not, then you will either have to use the software CD that came with the printer or download a driver from the manufacturer's website.

There is more than one way to install your printer software. If you install the software from the supplied CD, then it usually comes with the driver plus additional software for things like scanning and faxing. It's up to you which components you want to install, but you do definitely need the driver. To install the driver and additional software from the CD, simply put it in the drive and it should automatically run. If not, then you need to use File Explorer to browse to the CD itself and find the setup file and run it from there.

Chapter 4 – Installing Devices

Another way to install a printer is from the *Bluetooth & devices* section in the Windows 11 settings. Once you are there, you will click on *Printers & scanners*. Then you can click on the *Add device* button to add a printer or scanner.

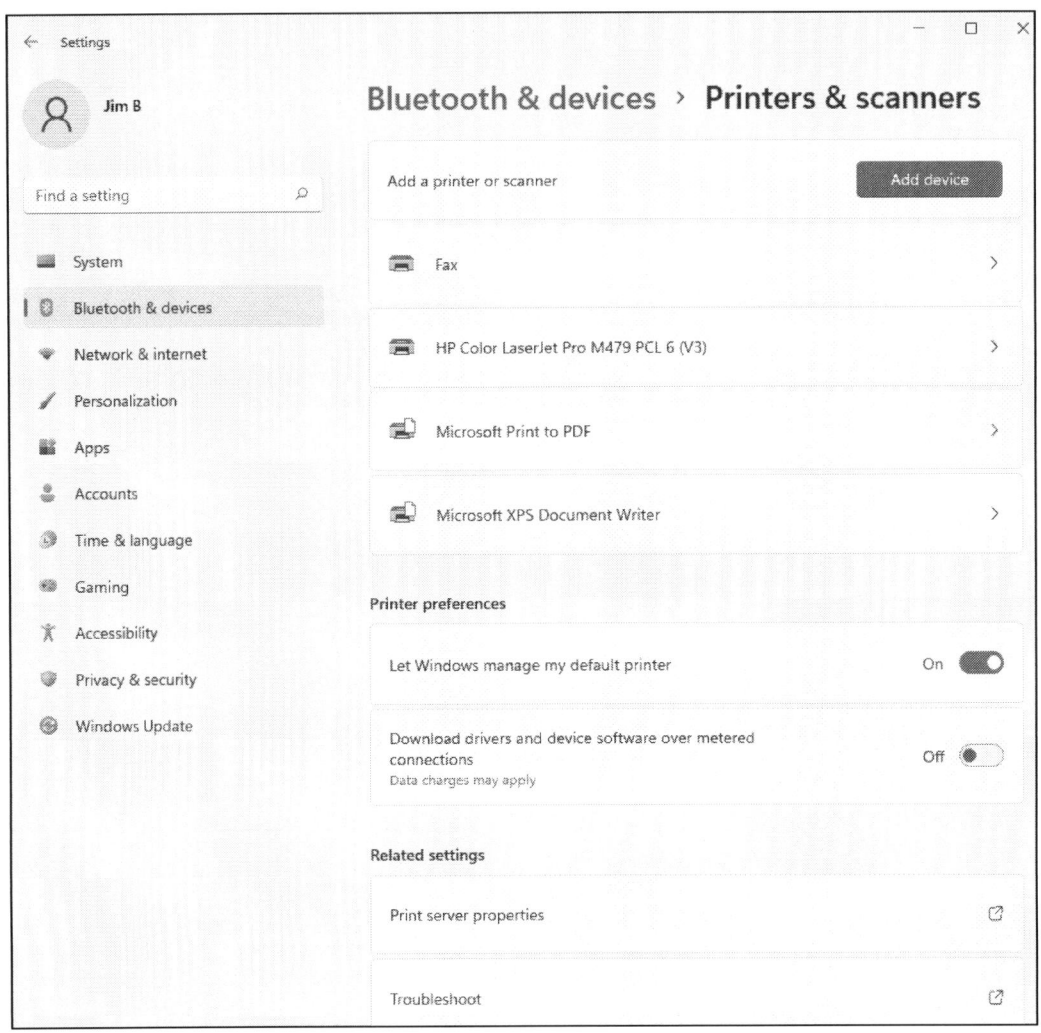

Figure 4.1

Windows will then search for any new printers that are connected to your device. Once it finds your printer, it will prompt you for the location of the software drivers and then proceed to install the printer.

Once you have a printer or printers installed, you can then click on them to do things such as see what is in the print queue, print a test page, troubleshoot printing problems and see the various properties of that particular printer.

Chapter 4 – Installing Devices

> **HP Color LaserJet Pro M479 PCL 6 (V3)**

HP Color LaserJet Pro M479 PCL 6 (V3)
Printer status: Idle

[Remove]

Printer settings

Open print queue

Print test page

Run the troubleshooter

Printer properties

Printing preferences
Orientation, page order, pages per sheet, borders, paper source

Hardware properties

Figure 4.2

Another place you can manage your printers from is called *Devices and printers* in Control Panel. It's the place you used to go for printer-related tasks in older versions of Windows, but is still included in Windows 11, and some people like it better than the method I just covered.

Chapter 4 – Installing Devices

Connecting a Smartphone to Your Computer
Many people like to connect their smartphones to their computers via a USB cable to transfer pictures and movies off of their phones and onto their computers. You can also charge your phone while it's connected to your computer through the USB cable, but it typically won't charge as fast as if you used your wall charger.

There are different makes and models of smartphones, but as of now it's basically a choice of using an Apple iPhone or a Google Android based smartphone. There are many manufacturers who make Android based phones, and they often customize the interface the way they like, so one manufacturer's phone most likely will look and behave a little differently than another's. iPhones typically stay the same, but Apple adds more features as the newer models come out.

Depending on what model of phone you have, when you connect your smartphone to your computer a few different things might happen. If it's the first time you have connected it to your computer, it may take Windows a while to recognize your phone for the first time. Then you may or may not get a window that pops up showing the folders contained on your phone's internal storage. Some Android phones, for example, make you pull down from the notification area a menu that has connectivity options such as *transfer files* or *charge the phone only*. iPhones will typically pop up a message asking if you want to trust this computer, and you have to confirm before it will let you access the phone's storage from your computer. Once you get into the phone's storage, you will typically want to look for a folder that is called *DCIM*, which will have your pictures and video files stored in it. Once you open this folder, you can drag and drop the files onto the desktop of your computer or into another folder of your liking. From there you can print them out, email them, upload them for professional printing, or copy them to a flash drive or external drive to access from a different computer.

If you want to learn more about Android smartphones and how to get the most out of these devices, then check out my book titled **Android Smartphones Made Easy**.
https://www.amazon.com/dp/1086026837

Mouse Settings

You might think that a mouse is just a mouse and they are all pretty much the same. For the most part, all mice pretty much do the same thing, but there is actually some customization you can do with your mouse to make it work the way you want it to work.

Some mice will have additional buttons besides the two default buttons that are programmable to allow you to assign certain functions to them, but it might require you to install additional software to do so. That doesn't mean that you can't configure mouse options on a standard mouse without software installed. Windows gives you many options to configure your mouse when it comes to mouse buttons, pointers, and so on. There are some mouse options you can play within the Windows 11 Settings under *Bluetooth & devices*, and you can get additional configuration options from the Mouse utility in Control Panel (figure 4.4).

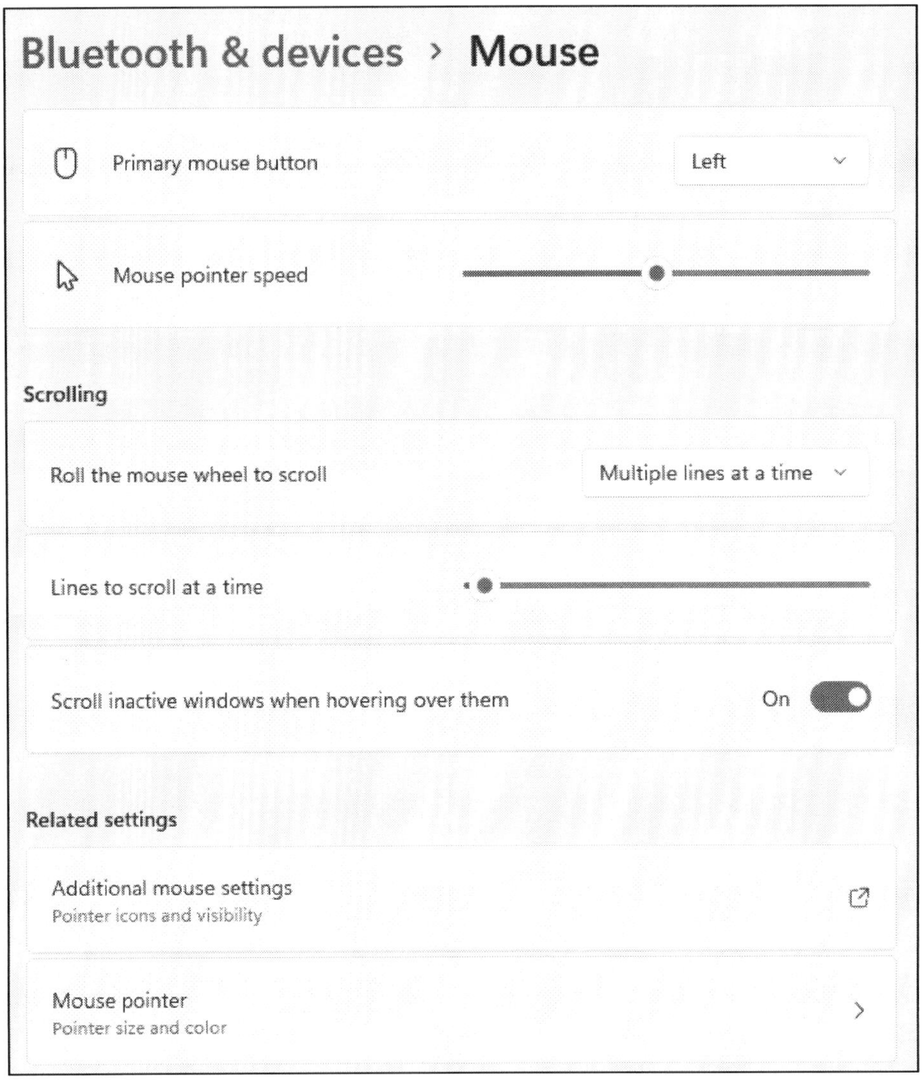

Chapter 4 – Installing Devices

Bluetooth & devices > Mouse

Primary mouse button — Left

Mouse pointer speed

Scrolling

Roll the mouse wheel to scroll — Multiple lines at a time

Lines to scroll at a time

Scroll inactive windows when hovering over them — On

Related settings

Additional mouse settings
Pointer icons and visibility

Mouse pointer
Pointer size and color

Figure 4.3

Chapter 4 – Installing Devices

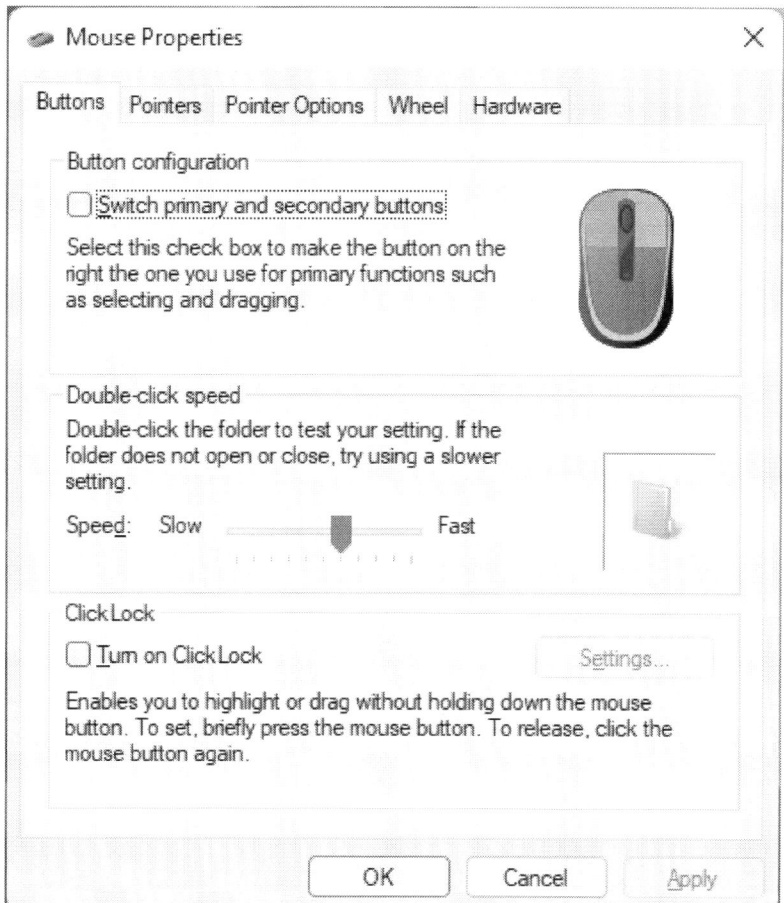

Figure 4.4

From here you can do things like assign functions to mouse buttons and change the mouse pointer to a different style. On the *Pointer Options* tab, you can choose how fast the mouse moves across the screen, which is a nice thing to configure because the default speed doesn't always work best for everyone. Most mice have a center wheel that you can use to scroll up and down pages and this is configurable as well from the Wheel tab.

 One important thing to remember when it comes to using a mouse in Windows is that the right click button is used for many different things, so be sure to play around by right clicking on items within your software.

Chapter 4 – Installing Devices

Installing USB Devices
Most of the devices that you will attach to your computer will connect via a USB port, and since all computers have multiple USB ports in the front and rear of the computer, you will usually have a port that is free to use. USB devices tend to be plug and play, which means you simply connect them to a USB port, they configure themselves, and you are good to go. You may run into a situation where a USB device requires some sort of driver or software like a printer does in order to get it up and running.

External USB hard drives and flash drives will usually work without any additional configuration. Once you plug them in, Windows will assign them a drive letter, and then you will be able to copy files to and from the drive. These external drives work just like an internal hard drive except that you can disconnect them from your computer and then connect them to a different computer and use them the exact same way.

Other examples of common USB devices include game controllers for those who like to play video games on their computers, and also webcams that can be used to make video calls with software such as Skype or Zoom. You can even have a USB headset and microphone to use with your video calls or online games. And if you run out of USB ports, then you can get a USB hub, which will take one USB port and expand it to 4 or more ports.

Dual Monitor Setup
Many people who like to have a lot of windows open at one time will install a secondary monitor so they can have more screen "real estate" and be able to see more of what they are working on all at once. To use dual monitors with Windows 11, you need to have a video card that supports this and has two video output connections on the back of it.

If you look at figure 4.5, you will see there is a section to configure multiple displays under the *System > Display* section Windows will even allow you to connect to a wireless monitor, which is becoming more common now. If you click on the *Detect* button, Windows will try and configure your other monitor. After it finds it, you will have options to tell Windows which is the primary monitor, and which is the secondary monitor. You can then decide if you want to extend the displays (which will make both monitors act like one giant monitor) or duplicate the displays so you have the same thing on both monitors.

Chapter 4 – Installing Devices

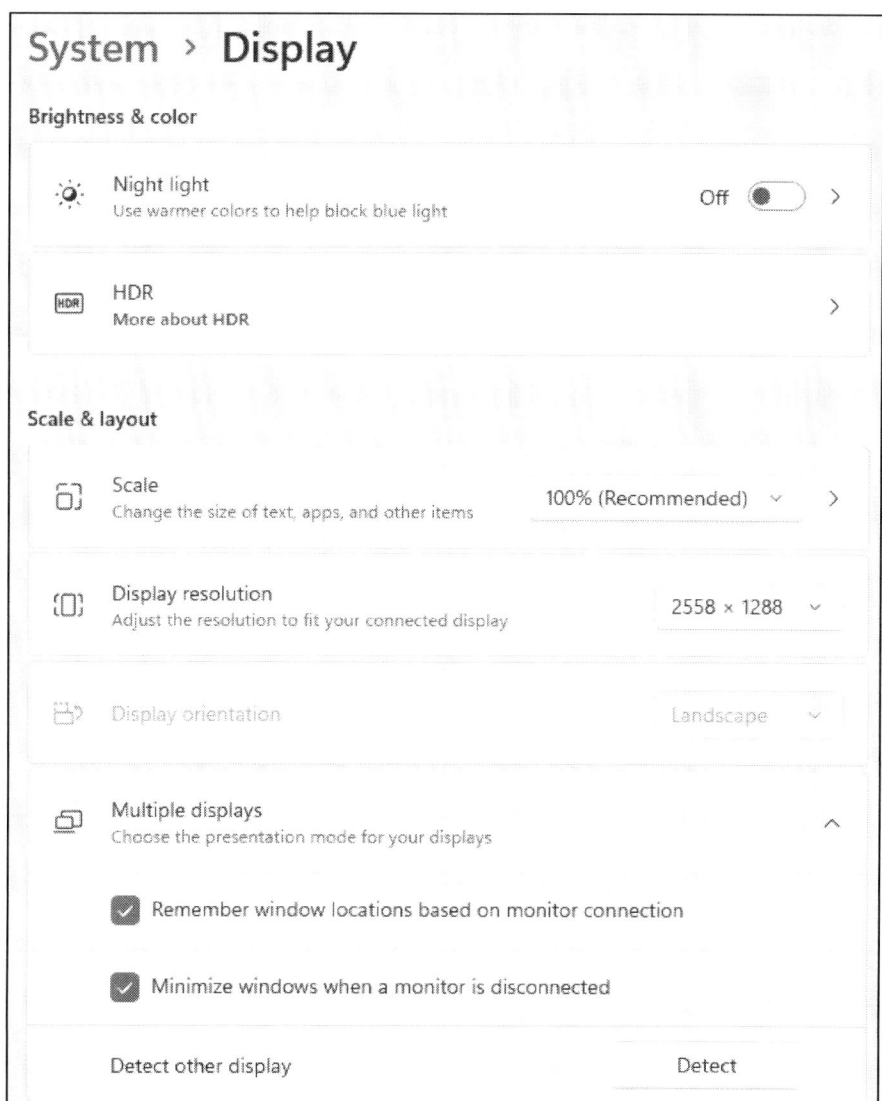

Figure 4.5

Chapter 5 – Windows Apps

Starting with Windows 8, Microsoft decided that it wanted to have a common interface for the version of Windows running on tablets and the version running on desktop PCs. Unfortunately for them, this idea didn't work out too well. Windows 8 was kind of a flop and didn't last too long. Even though Windows 10 and 11 are a huge improvement over Windows 8, Microsoft still has some of that tablet interface aspect built into Windows both of them, but this time it works, for the most part.

Apps vs. Programs
Even though most of us are used to running programs like Microsoft Word or Adobe Photoshop, that doesn't mean that they are the only types of software we can run. Windows 11 comes with apps that are preinstalled on your computer and also allows you to install more apps for things like games, photo editing programs, and so on. There *is* a difference between a program and an app, even though they may function in a similar way.

A Program (also called Desktop App) is a traditional Windows software package that you install on your computer, and it can be from any number of software manufacturers. Programs will have a specific type of interface designed to be used with a mouse and keyboard and will only run on PCs, not smartphones or tablets. Windows Apps on the other hand look and feel more like an app you would use on your smartphone or tablet and run on all types of devices. Figure 5.1 shows the program called Microsoft Excel, which is a desktop app, and figure 5.2 shows the built in Windows weather app.

Chapter 5 – Windows Apps

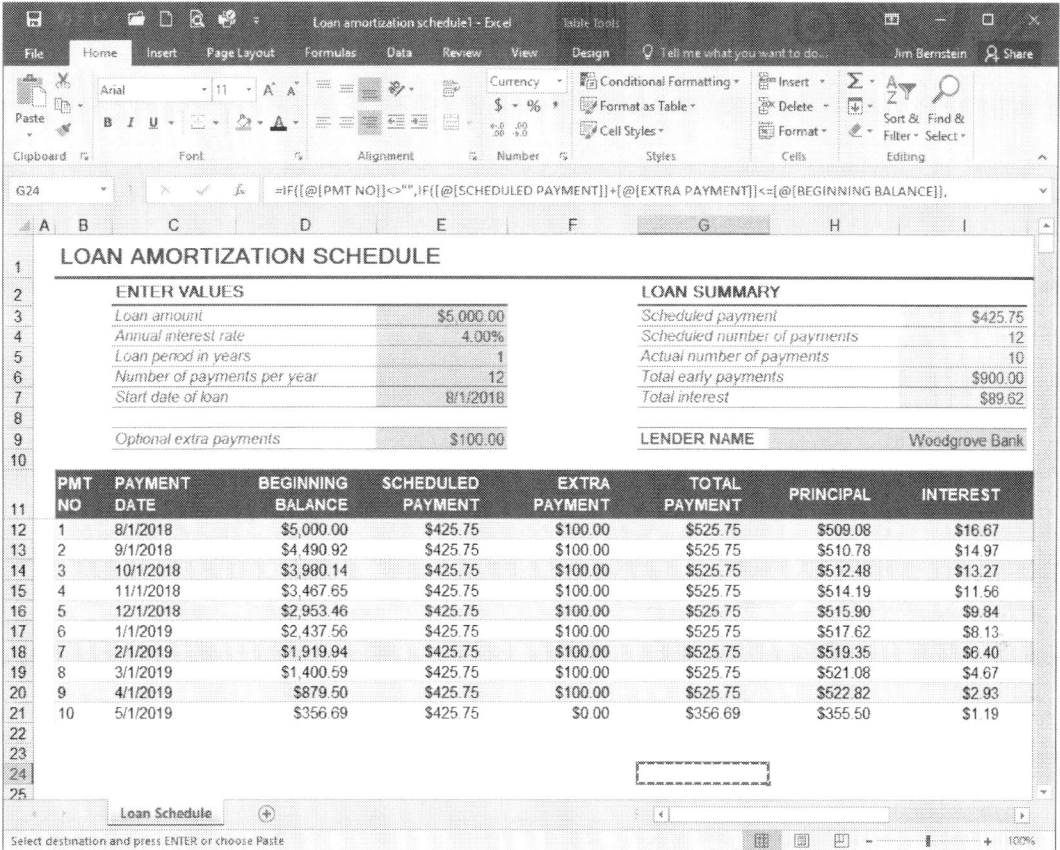

Figure 5.1

Chapter 5 – Windows Apps

Figure 5.2

Windows 11 comes with a bunch of apps preinstalled, and you can find these apps on the Start menu. They will be listed alongside your desktop apps. Some examples of common default Windows 11 apps include Groove Music, Microsoft News, OneDrive, Sticky Notes, Snip & Sketch, and Xbox Game Center.

Microsoft Store Apps
If you have a smartphone, you have most likely used the App Store (Apple) or Google Play (Android) to get more apps for your phone or tablet. Windows 11 comes with the Microsoft Store that lets you search and download new apps that can be used on your computer. There are many free applications to choose from

Chapter 5 – Windows Apps

as well as more advanced apps that you can purchase. You can even rent movies and listen to music.

To get to the Microsoft Store simply find it on your Start Menu or search for it using the search feature. After you find and open the app, you will see a window similar to figure 5.3. As you can see, the Microsoft Store is categorized by types of apps such as games and productivity on the top and then has a search function over to the right.

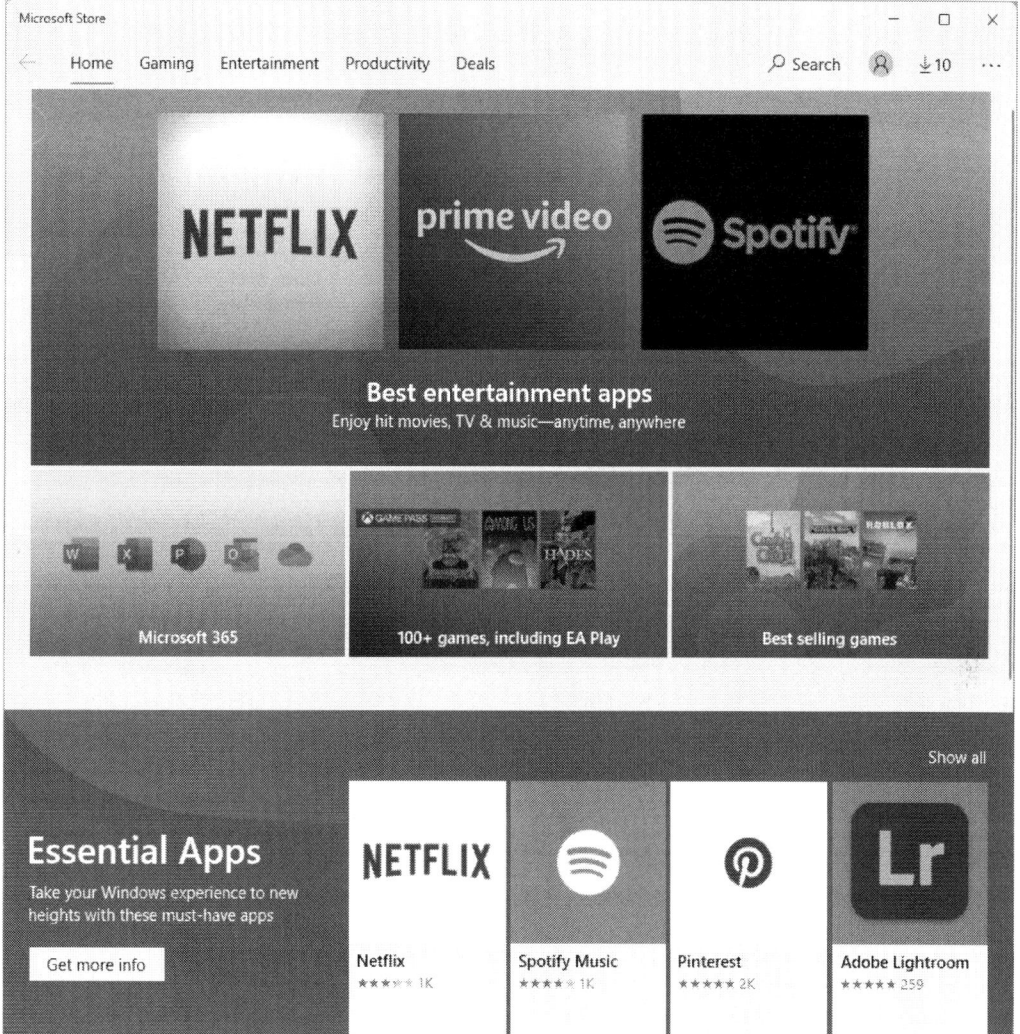

Figure 5.3

Once you find an app you want to try out, simply click on the *Get* button or free apps or the *Buy* button for pay for apps to have Windows download and install the app for you. If you scroll down past the Get or Buy button you will see the system

Chapter 5 – Windows Apps

requirements for the app as well as additional information such as the developer's name, release date, and size of the app itself. Just like with your smartphone, there are many apps that you can download and try out for free and many that you can purchase, but just remember that when you install these apps on your computer, they will take up disk space, just like regular programs will.

Uninstalling Apps

If you are the type that likes to try new things, then there is a chance you might go overboard at the Microsoft Store and download one too many apps while checking things out. If this is the case, there is no need to worry because it's easy to uninstall these apps once you have installed them.

The process is very similar to uninstalling regular programs, so if you have ever used the *Programs and Features* utility in Control Panel to uninstall software, then removing apps should be a no brainer. As you can see in figure 5.4, the listing of programs looks similar to the ones in the *Apps & features* section of the Windows 11 settings (figure 5.5). The main difference is that the Apps & features section will show **both** the Windows Apps and the regular Windows programs (Desktop Apps), so technically you can just use Apps & features to uninstall any software you need to remove. And if you want to remove an app, you will have to do it from the Apps & features section exclusively.

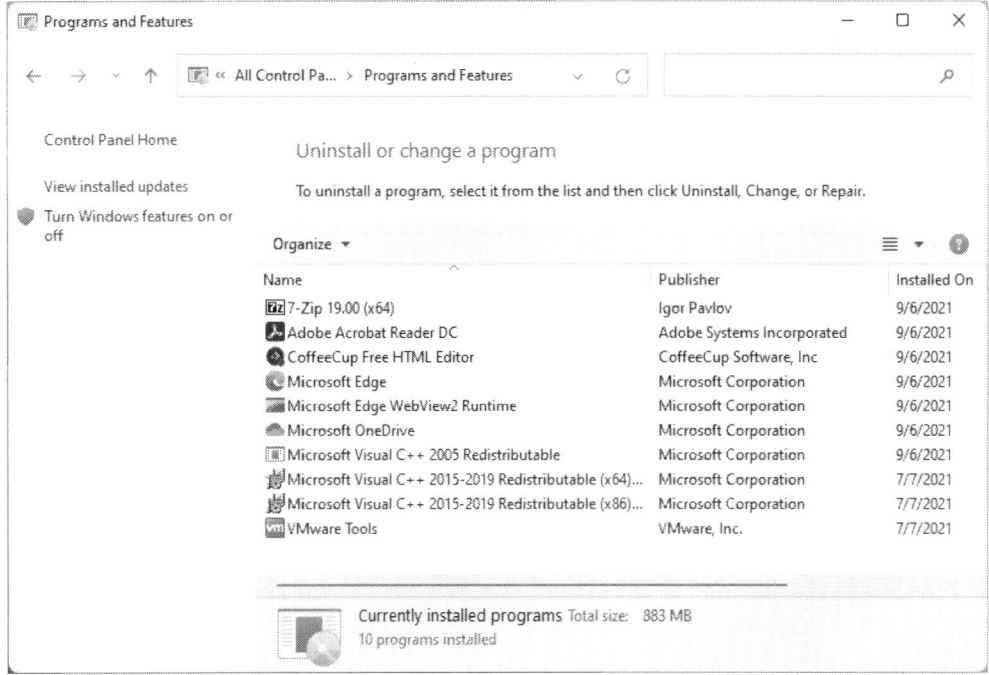

Figure 5.4

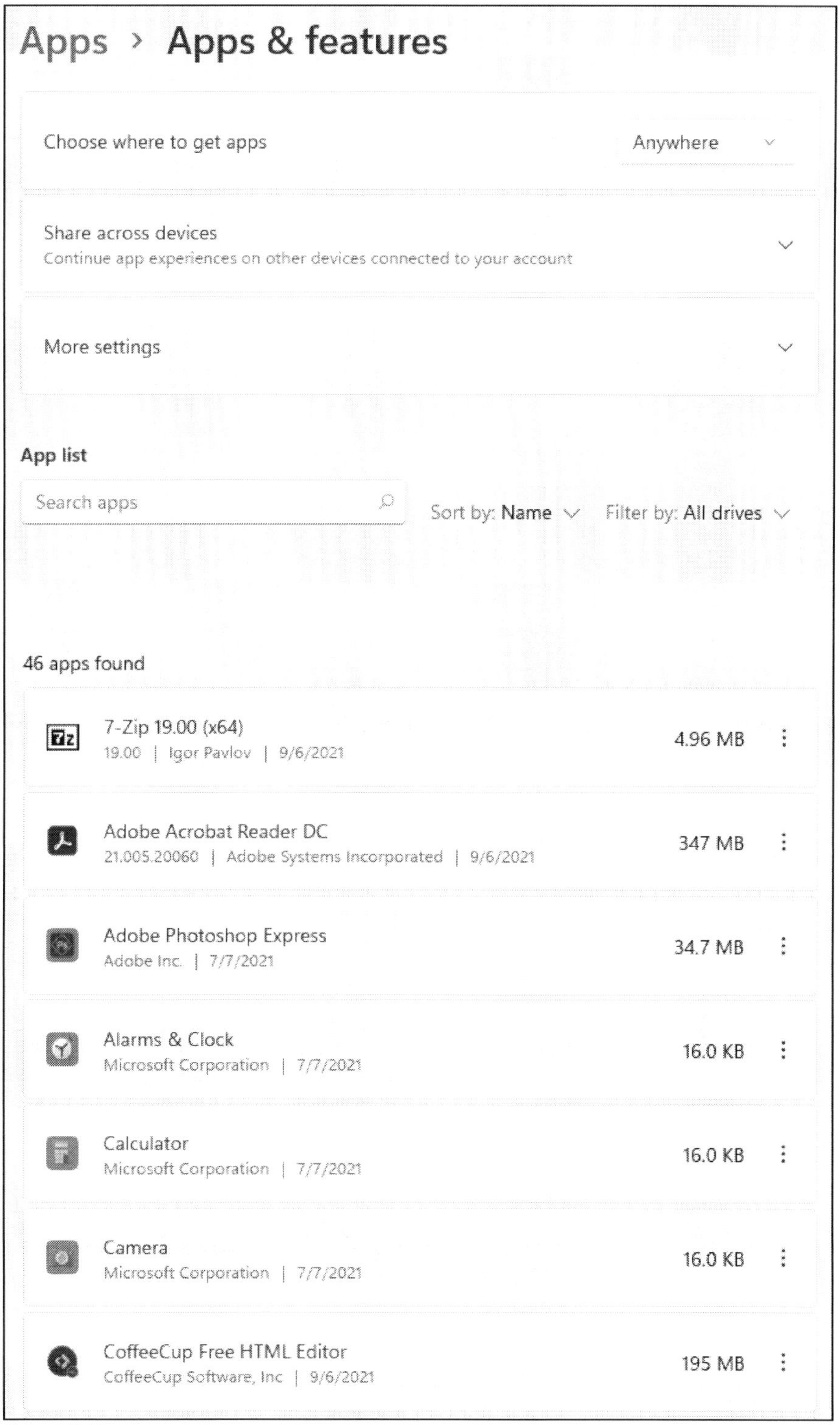

Chapter 5 – Windows Apps

Apps > Apps & features

Choose where to get apps — Anywhere

Share across devices
Continue app experiences on other devices connected to your account

More settings

App list

Search apps   Sort by: Name   Filter by: All drives

46 apps found

7-Zip 19.00 (x64) 19.00	Igor Pavlov	9/6/2021	4.96 MB	⋮
Adobe Acrobat Reader DC 21.005.20060	Adobe Systems Incorporated	9/6/2021	347 MB	⋮
Adobe Photoshop Express Adobe Inc.	7/7/2021	34.7 MB	⋮
Alarms & Clock Microsoft Corporation	7/7/2021	16.0 KB	⋮
Calculator Microsoft Corporation	7/7/2021	16.0 KB	⋮
Camera Microsoft Corporation	7/7/2021	16.0 KB	⋮
CoffeeCup Free HTML Editor CoffeeCup Software, Inc	9/6/2021	195 MB	⋮

Figure 5.5

Chapter 5 – Windows Apps

To uninstall a Windows App or Desktop App simply click on the 3 vertical dots next to the app or program name and you will have an option to uninstall the app or program. As you can see in figure 5.6 there is also a *Modify* button that is used to run things like the program's repair or customize feature if it has one. If the button is greyed out, then the program or app doesn't support any additional functionality.

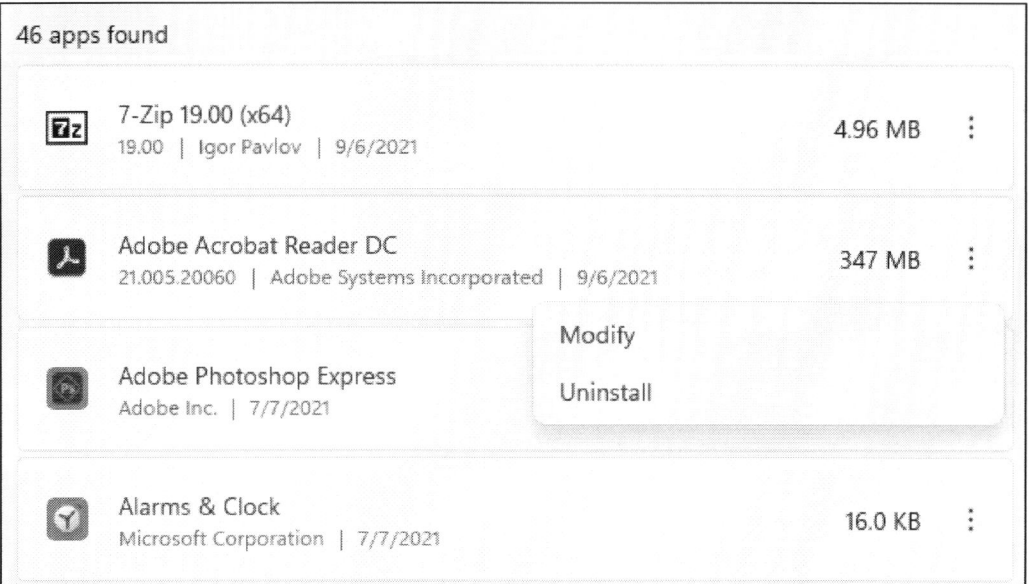

Figure 5.6

Many Windows apps will have a choice called *Advanced options* that will let you modify specific settings for that app. Then for apps that you have installed from the Microsoft Store, you will have a *Move* option that will let you move the location of the app on your hard drive to a different drive altogether.

Chapter 6 – File and Folder Management

I mentioned earlier how knowing how to manage your files and folders is one of the key things you need to know in order to be a successful Windows user, and now I am going to go over some things you should know to help get you on your way. Most of this information will apply to other versions of Windows as well.

Windows File Structure
Windows uses a tree structure for its folders with files and\or subfolders within folders. As you can see, there is a folder tree in the left pane with the contents of the Users folder displayed underneath it, and as well as in the right pane.

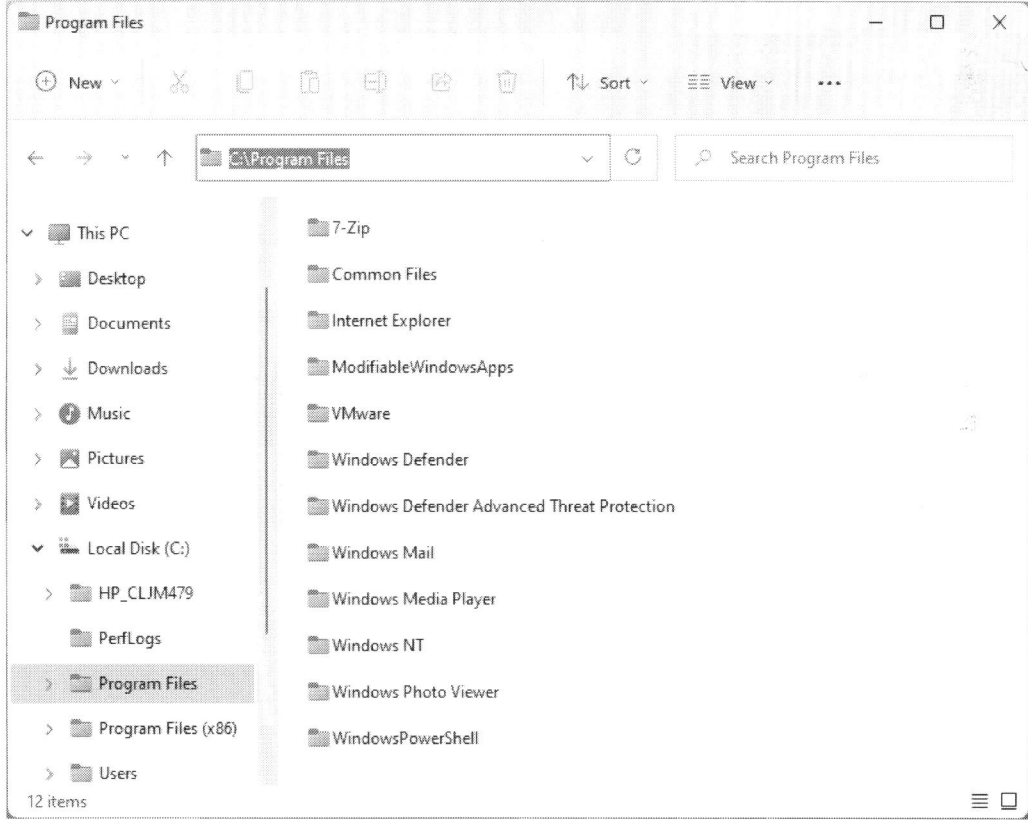

Figure 6.1

To access your files and folders you can use File Explorer (Previously known as Windows Explorer). The easiest way to open this app is to right click on the Start button and choose *File Explorer* and you will see a window similar to figure 6.1.

Chapter 6 – File and Folder Management

Within this window there is the left pane, which will show all your installed drives such as your hard drive(s), DVD drive, and any USB connected flash drives or hard drives. Each drive is assigned a letter, with the Windows\system drive assigned the letter C by default. The name of your C drive will vary depending on what the drive label was named during its initial configuration. As you add drives to your computer, Windows will assign the next available drive letter to that drive. It is possible to customize these drive letters, but that is a more advanced topic. When you click on a folder in the left pane, the contents of that folder will be displayed in the right pane. You can drill down into these folders and subfolders to see their contents. On the top address bar you will see the path to the current folder that is highlighted. In figure 6.1 the path is **C:\Program Files**. If you were to drill down to the 7-Zip folder, the path would then be **C:\Program Files\7-Zip** and so on.

Changing File and Folder Views

If you don't find the files and folders easy to work with, then you can change their view to another format, such as details, list, tiles, large icons, small icons, and so on. To do so, go to the *View* menu and choose the view that best suits your needs (figure 6.2). You can try out different views until you find the one you like best. If you use the details view, then you can sort the files or folders by name, date, size, type, and add other attributes by right clicking a blank spot on the title bar while in detail view mode. The *Show* option will allow you to change how your File Explorer interface looks as well as giving you the option to show file extensions which comes in very handy. Figure 6.2 shows the same folder with the *Large icons* view selected.

Chapter 6 – File and Folder Management

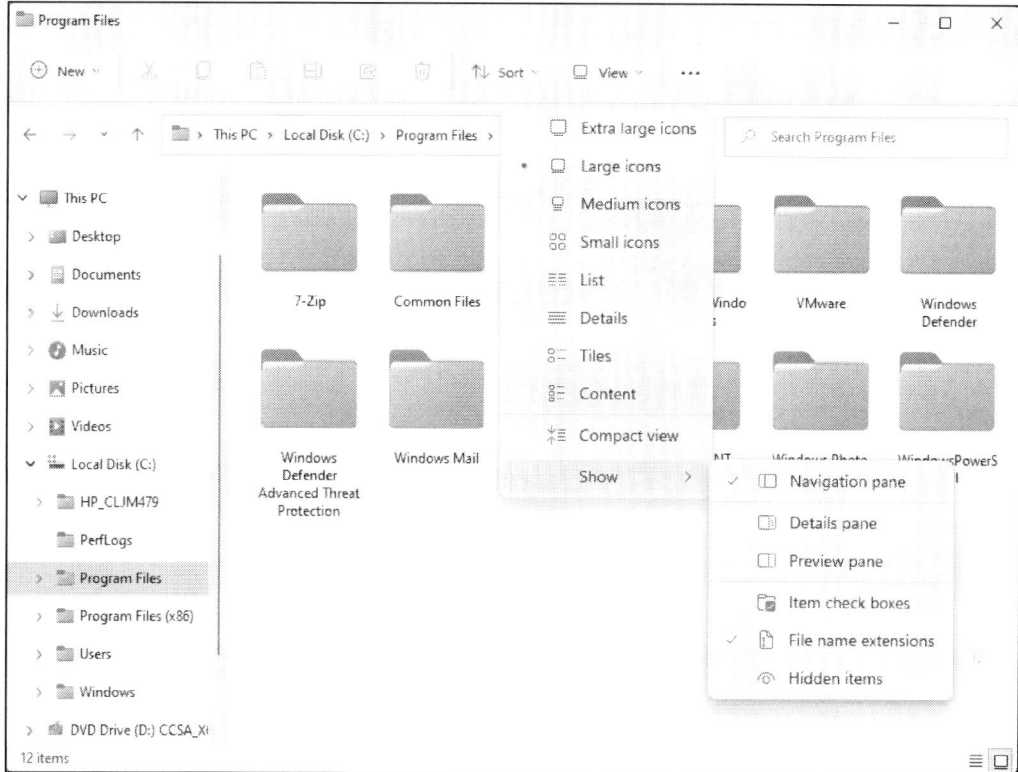

Figure 6.2

Keep in mind that this view will only apply to the folder you are currently in. To make it apply to all of your folders, you will need to choose a folder and change the view to the setting you like. Then you will need to go to the Windows Folder Options which you can get to by clicking the ellipsis on the toolbar and then on *Options*. From there you will click on the *View* tab and click the button that says *Apply to Folders*.

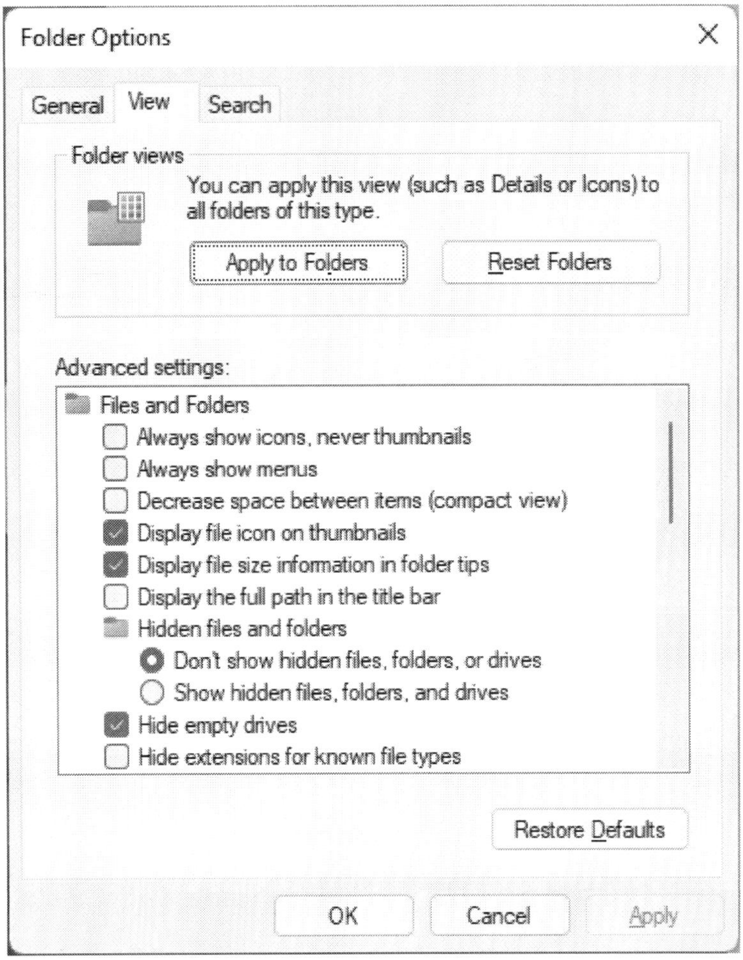

Chapter 6 – File and Folder Management

Figure 6.3

There are other options you can apply here before clicking on Apply to Folders, such as having Windows show hidden files or have Windows show file extensions (discussed next). If you make a mess of things and want to go back to the way things were at the beginning, then you can click the *Reset Folders* or *Restore Defaults* button and then OK.

File Extensions

File extensions are used to tell Windows what program to open a certain type of file with. If they weren't used, then every time you double clicked a file you would be asked what program you wanted to open it with, and if you didn't know what type of file it was, then that would make things very difficult. File extensions are hidden by default in Windows (with a few exceptions). A file extension consists of a period followed by three or more letters (or sometimes numbers) afterward denoting what program the file is to be associated with. For example, with a file called **resume.docx,** the file name is **resume** and the extension is **.docx,** and **.docx** is the file extension associated with Microsoft Word. So, when you double-click the resume.docx file, Windows knows to open it with Microsoft Word. However, if you don't have Microsoft Word installed, it won't know what to open it with because Word will register that extension with Windows only after you install it on the computer. If you want to have Windows show all file extensions (which is usually a good idea) then uncheck the box that says *Hide extensions for known file types* in figure 6.3.

If you have a need to, you can try to open one type of file with another program other than the one the file extension is associated with by right clicking on the file and choosing *Open With*.

Moving, Copying, Renaming and Deleting Files
One thing you will be doing a lot of once you are more comfortable with your file management skills will be copying, moving, renaming, and deleting files as needed. But before we begin our discussion, we must say BE CAREFUL when doing so to files, because you can cause your programs or even cause Windows to stop working if you play around with the wrong files. And, of course, you can also misplace or delete your own personal files, which is never a good thing.

Manipulating file locations is very common because you have so many options as to what you can do with your files and where you can store them. This all applies to folders as well, by the way, so keep that in mind. If you are working on a document, for example, and want to save it, then you can pretty much save it wherever you want on your hard drive, even someplace you shouldn't like the Windows folder. So, what do you do if you need to relocate a file that you saved someplace you didn't want to save it at? The answer is easy. You move it! I will now go over how you can move a file from one folder to another.

The first thing you need to do is to locate the file you want to move, and that can be done with File Explorer. Once you've found the file, simply click on it once to highlight it. Then you can find the scissors icon on the toolbar (figure 6.4), which is used to "cut" the file.

Chapter 6 – File and Folder Management

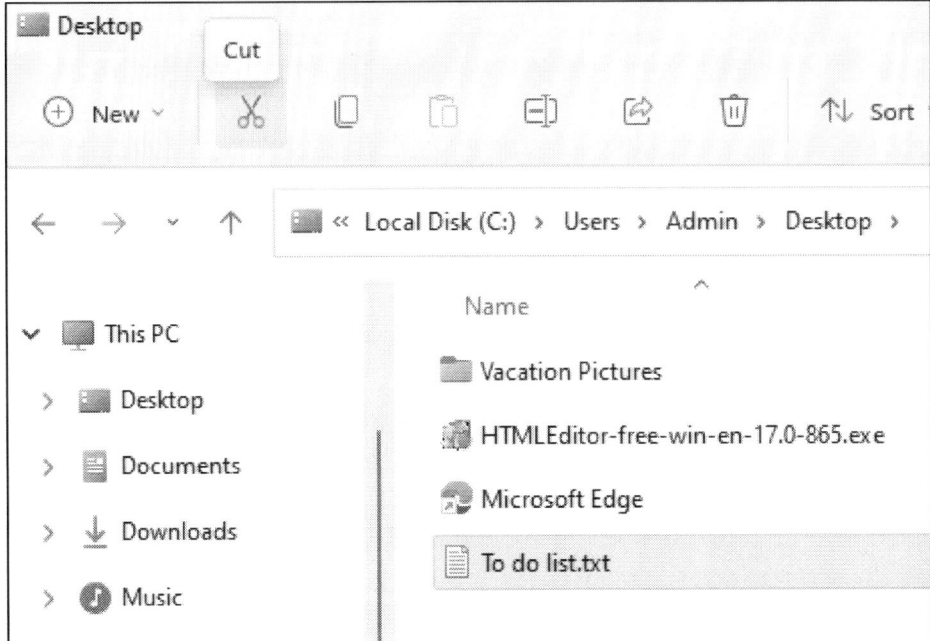

Figure 6.4

You can also right click the file or folder and click the scissors icon as well as use the keyboard shortcut *Ctrl-x*. Each one of these methods will achieve the same result. You will also notice that the file icon and text fades\greys out a bit indicated that it has been cut. If you decide you don't want to move\cut the file or folder you can simply do nothing or press the Esc key on your keyboard to cancel the process.

Now that the file is cut, you can browse to the folder you want to move it to, right click on a blank area, and choose *Paste*. Just be careful not to choose *Paste shortcut*, because that is not the same thing, and we will be discussing what that is later in the chapter. You can also use the *Ctrl-v* keyboard shortcut or the Paste icon on the File Explorer toolbar. If you change your mind or picked the wrong folder, simply use the keyboard *Ctrl-z* shortcut to undo the last move you made.

If you have both the source and destination folders open in two File Explorer windows or can see both of them in one File Explorer window, then you can simply drag the file from the source folder to the destination folder to move it. This will only work if the source and destination folders are on the same physical hard drive, otherwise it will copy the file instead.

You can do the exact same thing to copy a file from one folder to another, except you will use the *Copy* icon on the toolbar or right click the file and choose the *Copy*

Chapter 6 – File and Folder Management

icon rather than *Cut*. You can also use the *Ctrl-c* rather than the *Ctrl-x* keyboard shortcut to copy, and then use the same *Ctrl-v* keyboard shortcut to paste the file into the destination folder. The drag and drop method will not work for copying files unless it's from two separate drives because it will move them rather than copy them, but you can use the right mouse button to drag the file over and then let go and choose *Copy here*.

Deleting files is pretty straightforward, and all you have to do is highlight the file and click the trash can icon from the File Explorer toolbar. Or you can right click a file and choose the same trash can icon or press the *Delete* key on your keyboard. By default, Windows will send the file to the Recycle Bin rather than delete them permanently. If you made a mistake and want the file back, you can use *Ctrl-z* to undo the action and have the file undeleted from the Recycle Bin and returned to its original location. Keep in mind that Ctrl-z only works for the last operation performed, so if you've deleted another file since the one you wanted to be recovered, it won't work, and you will have to go into the Recycle Bin to get it back.

If you want to see all the files you have deleted, you can open the Recycle Bin from the desktop, or, if for some reason you don't have an icon for it, you can get to it by typing **C:\$Recycle.Bin** in the File Explorer address bar, but you will need to have the *hide protected operating system files* option unchecked from the Windows Folder Options settings previously discussed.

Once you are in the Recycle Bin you can sort the deleted files and folder by things such as name, size, original location, date deleted, and so on. If you want to recover a deleted file or folder, then simply right click on it and choose "Restore". You can also do this for multiple files and folders at a time. This will move the file back to its original location. You can also right click the file, choose *Cut*, and then paste it wherever you like or simply drag it out of the Recycle Bin to a different location.

If you right click the Recycle Bin and choose *Properties*, or click the Properties icon in the toolbar, you will see its location and how much hard drive space is allocated to hold recycled files.

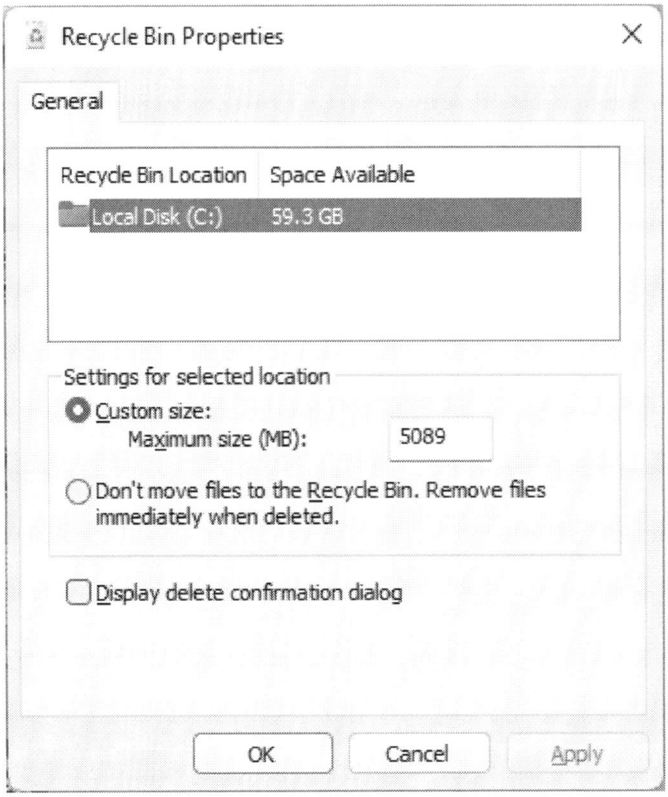

Figure 6.5

These settings can be modified to give you more space for recycled files and folders if needed. You can also see that there is an option to bypass the Recycle Bin and delete the files off the computer instead. This can also be accomplished manually by holding down the *Shift* key while deleting files or folders. Just know that if you do this, the files are gone for good (unless you use some type of file recovery software to get them back). Plus, there is never a guarantee that the recovery will work, and the longer you wait to recover them, the more likely the sectors the file occupies on the hard drive will get overwritten with new data.

Another common thing you will most likely do with your files and folders is rename them. Once again, be careful when doing this, and don't try to rename any Windows system files or files belonging to other software because you are only asking for trouble. Try and stick with only renaming personal files such as documents, pictures, music, etc. Also, be sure not to alter file extensions such as changing resume.**docx** to resume.**me** because Windows won't know what program to open the file with if you do so.

The procedure for renaming files is similar to copying or moving files. Once you highlight the file or folder you want to rename, you can click on the *Rename* button in the File Explorer toolbar or you can right click the file and choose the same button. You can also press the F2 key on your keyboard. Then simply type in the new name, press Enter, and you are all set. If you want to rename a bunch of files, you can highlight them all and right click on the first one, choose the rename button, type in a new name, and press Enter. It will name all the files the same but will add numbers after them such as Resume (1).docx, Resume (2).docx, and so on. In Windows, you can't have two files with the same name in the same folder or two subfolders with the same name within the same parent folder.

Now, if you want to perform any of these file and folder operations to multiple files or folders, you can simply select the ones you want and then take action on them after they are selected. For example, you might want to delete a bunch of files, but don't want to have to delete them one at a time. There are two ways to select multiple files depending on whether you want to select a concurrent list of files or just certain ones.

To select an entire row of files simply click on the first file in the group, hold down the *Shift* key, and then click on the last file in the group. This will highlight all the files in that particular grouping of files or folders (figure 6.6). To select a non-contiguous listing of files you can click on one file, hold down the *Ctrl* key, and then click on whichever files you want to highlight, and it won't highlight the entire group of files (figure 6.7).

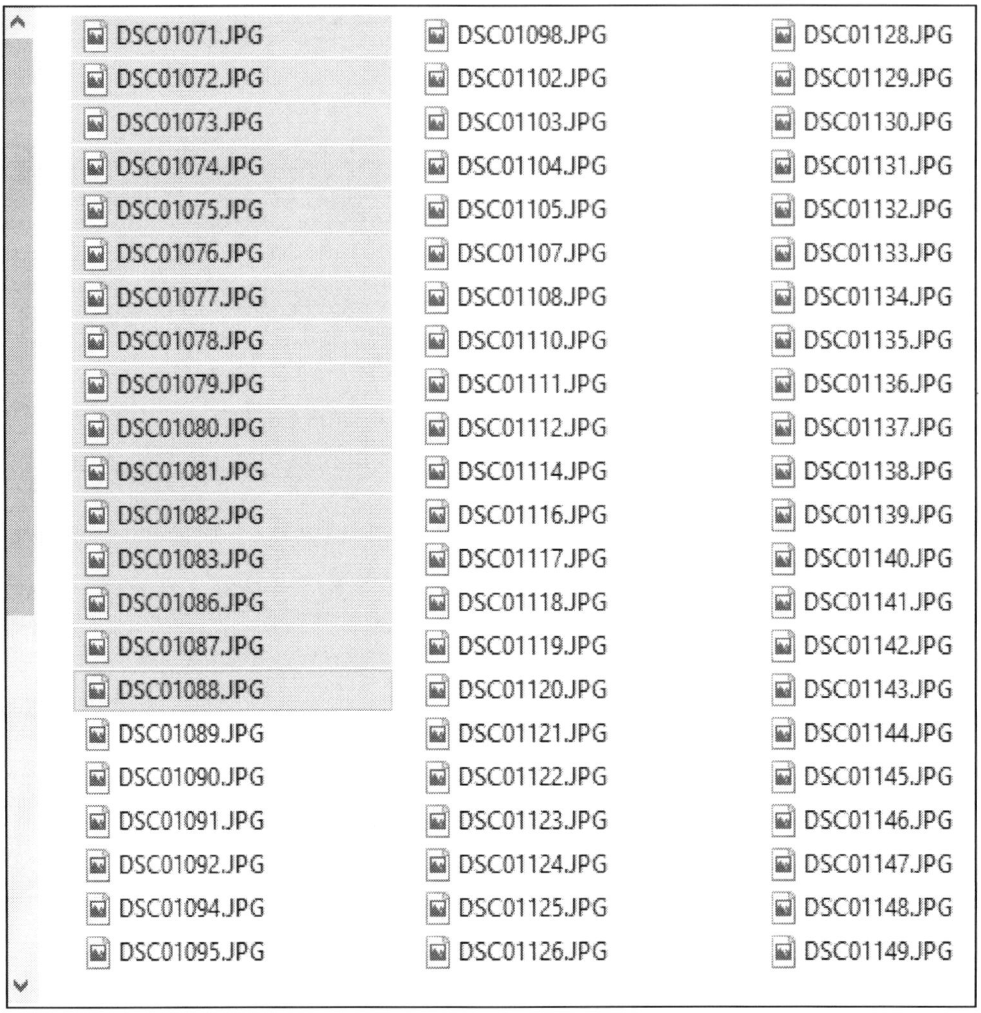

Chapter 6 – File and Folder Management

DSC01071.JPG	DSC01098.JPG	DSC01128.JPG
DSC01072.JPG	DSC01102.JPG	DSC01129.JPG
DSC01073.JPG	DSC01103.JPG	DSC01130.JPG
DSC01074.JPG	DSC01104.JPG	DSC01131.JPG
DSC01075.JPG	DSC01105.JPG	DSC01132.JPG
DSC01076.JPG	DSC01107.JPG	DSC01133.JPG
DSC01077.JPG	DSC01108.JPG	DSC01134.JPG
DSC01078.JPG	DSC01110.JPG	DSC01135.JPG
DSC01079.JPG	DSC01111.JPG	DSC01136.JPG
DSC01080.JPG	DSC01112.JPG	DSC01137.JPG
DSC01081.JPG	DSC01114.JPG	DSC01138.JPG
DSC01082.JPG	DSC01116.JPG	DSC01139.JPG
DSC01083.JPG	DSC01117.JPG	DSC01140.JPG
DSC01086.JPG	DSC01118.JPG	DSC01141.JPG
DSC01087.JPG	DSC01119.JPG	DSC01142.JPG
DSC01088.JPG	DSC01120.JPG	DSC01143.JPG
DSC01089.JPG	DSC01121.JPG	DSC01144.JPG
DSC01090.JPG	DSC01122.JPG	DSC01145.JPG
DSC01091.JPG	DSC01123.JPG	DSC01146.JPG
DSC01092.JPG	DSC01124.JPG	DSC01147.JPG
DSC01094.JPG	DSC01125.JPG	DSC01148.JPG
DSC01095.JPG	DSC01126.JPG	DSC01149.JPG

Figure 6.6

Chapter 6 – File and Folder Management

DSC01071.JPG	DSC01098.JPG	DSC01128.JPG
DSC01072.JPG	DSC01102.JPG	DSC01129.JPG
DSC01073.JPG	DSC01103.JPG	DSC01130.JPG
DSC01074.JPG	DSC01104.JPG	DSC01131.JPG
DSC01075.JPG	DSC01105.JPG	DSC01132.JPG
DSC01076.JPG	DSC01107.JPG	DSC01133.JPG
DSC01077.JPG	DSC01108.JPG	DSC01134.JPG
DSC01078.JPG	DSC01110.JPG	DSC01135.JPG
DSC01079.JPG	DSC01111.JPG	DSC01136.JPG
DSC01080.JPG	DSC01112.JPG	DSC01137.JPG
DSC01081.JPG	DSC01114.JPG	DSC01138.JPG
DSC01082.JPG	DSC01116.JPG	DSC01139.JPG
DSC01083.JPG	DSC01117.JPG	DSC01140.JPG
DSC01086.JPG	DSC01118.JPG	DSC01141.JPG
DSC01087.JPG	DSC01119.JPG	DSC01142.JPG
DSC01088.JPG	DSC01120.JPG	DSC01143.JPG
DSC01089.JPG	DSC01121.JPG	DSC01144.JPG
DSC01090.JPG	DSC01122.JPG	DSC01145.JPG
DSC01091.JPG	DSC01123.JPG	DSC01146.JPG
DSC01092.JPG	DSC01124.JPG	DSC01147.JPG
DSC01094.JPG	DSC01125.JPG	DSC01148.JPG
DSC01095.JPG	DSC01126.JPG	DSC01149.JPG

Figure 6.7

To select all the files in a folder or all of the subfolders within a folder, you can click on *Select all* from the ellipsis menu, or you can use the *Ctrl-a* keyboard shortcut. When copying, moving, renaming, and deleting files, just remember that *Ctrl-z* (undo) is your friend, and if you mess something up and want to go back a step, you can use that to make your life easier.

Creating a New Folder or File
As you save files on your computer you will need a place to store them, and that place is called a folder. There are default folders within Windows (discussed next) used to store documents and pictures etc., but sometimes you will want to create your own folder for a specific purpose. This process is easy to do, and here is how you do it. Once again, open File Explorer and decide where you want your new folder to go. Next, you will find a blank spot within that folder, right click there,

Chapter 6 – File and Folder Management

choose *New* on the drop-down menu, and then *Folder*. Then type a name for the new folder and press Enter. Another method is to go to the New menu in the toolbar and click on the *New folder* button. As for the permissions on the new folder you create, they will be inherited from the parent folder (unless you have *disable inheritance* turned on). Any files you put in this new folder will inherit the permissions as well.

The process for creating new files works a little differently. Normally you create new files when you save your work in one of your programs. For example, if you are working on a new document in Microsoft Word and decide to save it to your desktop, a file will be created on your desktop and named whatever you called it when you saved it. If you want to create a new blank Word document on your desktop, simply right click an empty spot on your desktop, choose *New*, then *Microsoft Word Document*, type in a name, and press Enter. The file type choices you will have will vary depending on what software you have on your computer and if that software puts an entry under the New right click menu. There is a way to customize what items are under the New menu, so if you are feeling up to the challenge, you can do a little research and figure out how to customize the menu.

Default Windows Folders
Windows comes with many default folders that can be used to store a variety of files to help keep things organized. You may have noticed some folders named Desktop, Documents, Downloads, Music, Pictures, and Videos. These folders are created when Windows is installed and are meant to be used as a place to hold certain types of files. That doesn't mean you have to use them, but many programs will default to these folders when you click on *save* within that program. Of course, these options can usually be changed, just like everything else.

Let's focus on the *Downloads* folder for a minute since the rest of them are pretty self-explanatory. When you are using a web browser and download a file or program from a website, most of the time these files will go into your Downloads folder. Some web browsers use this by default, and others don't. Microsoft's web browsers (Edge) will use the Downloads folder unless you configure it otherwise. If you download something from a website and don't recall where you saved it to or just clicked on save without looking when it asked where you want to save it to, then it's most likely in the Downloads folder, so you can go there and browse for it. If you are using the *Details* view, then you can sort by date and have the newest files be at the top of the list to help you find your most recently downloaded file.

Chapter 6 – File and Folder Management

Searching for Files and Folders

Another important file management task that you will need to learn to do is to search for files and folders because you will not always remember where certain files and folders are located, and maybe not even remember what they are named! Searching for files and folders is pretty easy, and you can fine tune your searches to really narrow things down. The easiest way to search is to open File Explorer and navigate to the folder you want to search. If you don't know what folder the file might be in, then you can search the entire PC by clicking on *This PC*. The search box is located at the upper right-hand side of the window, and you can then type in the word or phrase you are looking for.

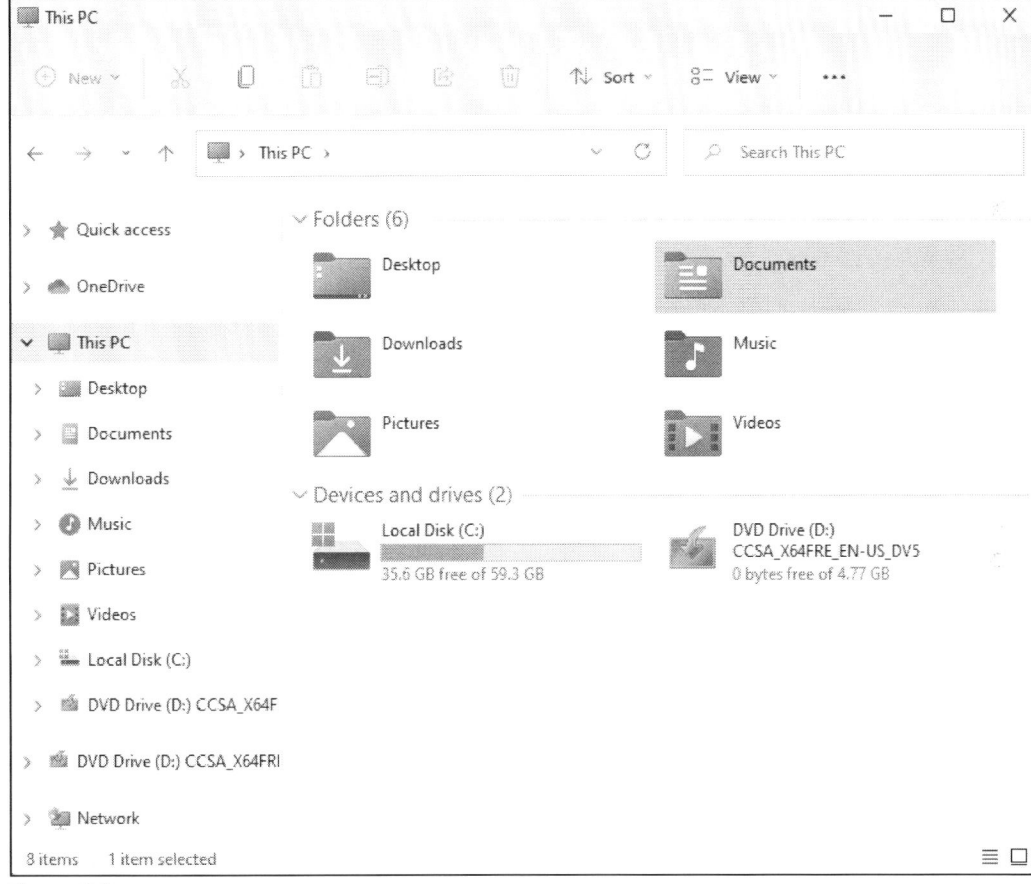

Figure 6.8

To do a simple search, type in the file or folder name you want to search for. Windows will begin searching automatically and show you the results as it finds them. You can use the options from the *Search options* button that appears during a search (figure 6.9) to fine tune your searches, such as specifying the type of file or the size of the file and so on. You can also search by date modified and have it

Chapter 6 – File and Folder Management

search within files using the *File contents* option. If you only want to search the current folder, then click on the *Current folder* button, otherwise use the *All subfolders* option to search all the subfolders of the folder you are currently in.

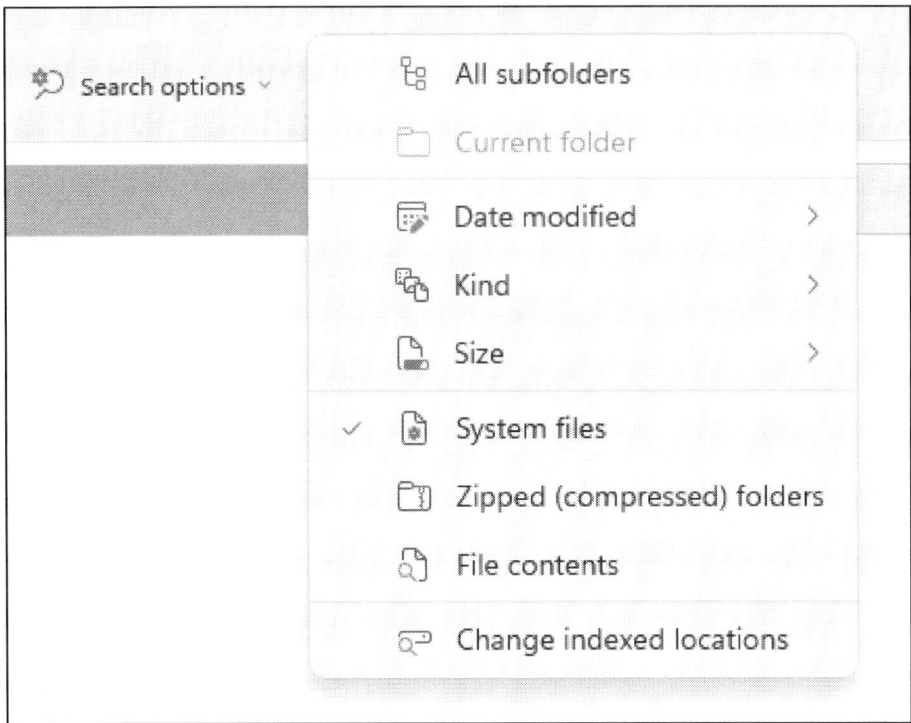

Figure 6.9

One effective way to search for files is to use wildcards. These come in handy when you know part of the name, or at least know what type of file it is that you are looking for. For example, if you know you have a file that might have been called **Birthday2022,** or maybe **Bday2022,** but aren't sure, you can use the wildcard symbol, which is an asterisk (*), and search for ***2022** to bring up any file that has some characters and then 2022 afterward. Or, if you want to search for all the jpeg images on your computer, you can search for ***.jpg**, which will search for any file with .jpg on the end (which is the file extension for jpeg images).

Shortcuts vs. Actual Files
I have been discussing files for some time now, so you should be pretty familiar with what they are and how to manipulate them. But let's say you have a shared file that multiple people need access to, and you want to be able to quickly open the file from your desktop, but don't want to give other users access to your desktop itself and its other files. This is where a shortcut comes into play. A

Chapter 6 – File and Folder Management

shortcut is simply a pointer to a file, which means it's an icon for that particular file that points to the actual location of that file. So, if you have a file called **Sales.xlsx** in a folder on your C drive under **c:\finances\business\Sales.xlsx** and want to open that file from your desktop, rather than having to navigate to c:\finances\business\Sales.xlsx each time, you would simply create a shortcut file on your desktop that points to the actual file.

There are a few different ways to create a shortcut file, but the easiest method is to locate the actual file, right click on it, and choose *Copy*. Then go to the location on your computer where you want the shortcut to that file to be (such as your desktop), then right click and choose *Paste **shortcut*** rather than choosing Paste itself as I discussed in the section on how to copy and move files. In figure 6.9, the file on the left is the original Sales.xlsx file, and the file on the right is what you will see after you paste a shortcut. Notice how it keeps the same name and just adds - **Shortcut** after it. The icon also has a blue arrow indicating that it's a shortcut and not the actual file. You can rename the file to take off the shortcut label and the blue arrow will stay so you will still be able to tell it's a shortcut and not the actual file itself.

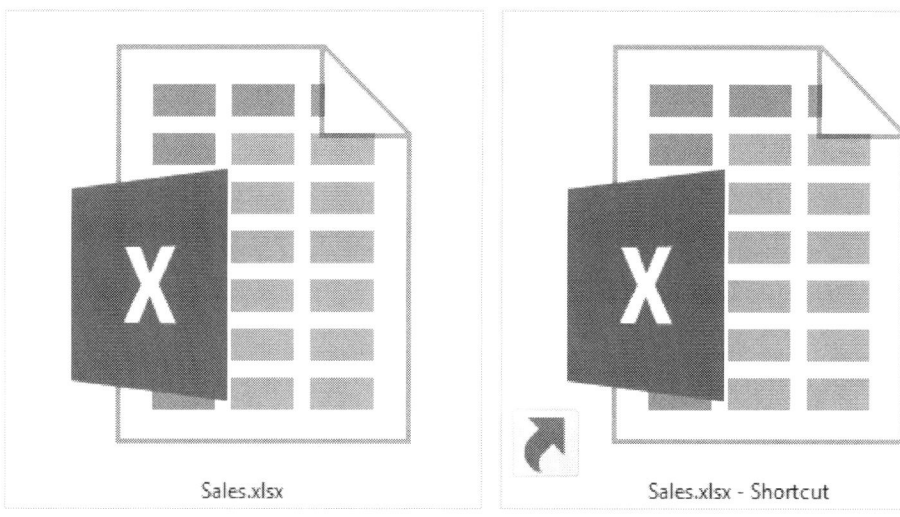

Figure 6.9

Other users on the computer can do the same thing, and you can have as many shortcuts to the same file as you like. Creating shortcuts to files is very common when the files are stored on file servers on a network where you might not know how to find the real file, or don't want to have to navigate to a networked server every time you want to open your files. Right clicking on a shortcut file and choosing *Properties* will tell you the path (or target) to the actual file if you want to know what your shortcut is pointing to. If you decide you don't want a shortcut to a file anymore, you can simply delete the shortcut and the actual file will not be affected. (Just be careful that you are deleting the shortcut and not the file itself!).

Chapter 7 – User Accounts

One thing you will definitely need to have to use a Windows computer is a user account. User accounts are required to make sure people are allowed to access the computer only if the owner wants them to. In order to use a Windows computer, you will need a user account that has been configured for you by an administrator or when you first set up your new computer. There are many reasons why Windows has user accounts, including the following:

- Having a way to protect their personal files from being accessed by others (unless they want them to be accessed).

- Providing a way to assign permissions to shared files and folders on the local computer or network.

- Determining what type of functions that person is allowed to perform on the computer itself.

- Tracking things such as login times, failed login attempts, and file access using event logging.

- Setting allowed times for users to be able to log onto a computer or network.

- Saving the personal settings of your computer, such as your desktop background and installed printers etc.

- Assigning levels of access for software usage.

Keep in mind as a home user you won't have to worry about most of these because your user account will mainly be used to save personalization settings that you customized for your user account and to keep your documents from being accessed by other users. As usual, Microsoft has given us a couple of ways to work with user accounts, and each way works a little differently, but we will get to that later on in this chapter.

User Account Types
There is more than one type of account for a Windows user, and this makes sense because different people need different levels of access and permissions. The two

main types of user accounts that you will be dealing with are the standard user and the administrator.

Standard user accounts are for people who need to do everyday tasks on the computer such as run programs, go online, print, and so on. Standard users can also install and uninstall certain software as well. It's usually a good idea to make everyone on your computer a standard user, and then if they need something done that requires higher privileges, they can have an administrator do it. And by administrator, I mean you!

Administrator user accounts have full control over the computer and can do things such as install or uninstall any software, add or remove user accounts, add or remove hardware, and make changes that affect Windows itself. If you are logged in as a standard user and need to do something that requires administrator access, many times you will get prompted to enter the username and password of an administrator so you don't need to actually log out and then back in as an administrator to get the job done.

Creating User Accounts
With social media being all the rage and everyone and everything connected to each other, Microsoft decided that it wanted to use what they call a *Microsoft account* to log into your computer with. This way whenever you log into another device with the same account, it will use many of the same settings for a universal experience each time. A Microsoft account uses an email address to log in rather than a standard username.

But if you are the type that likes to keep things old school (and simple), then you can still use a standard user type to log in with. Even if your computer was initially configured with a Microsoft account, you can convert it to a standard account fairly easily. I find that local accounts are much easier to troubleshoot when it comes to login problems.

To view the user accounts on your computer, go to the *Windows 11 Settings* and click on *Accounts* and you will see the information for the user you are currently logged in as. Figure 7.1 shows that my account is configured as an administrator since it says Administrator under my name.

Chapter 7 – User Accounts

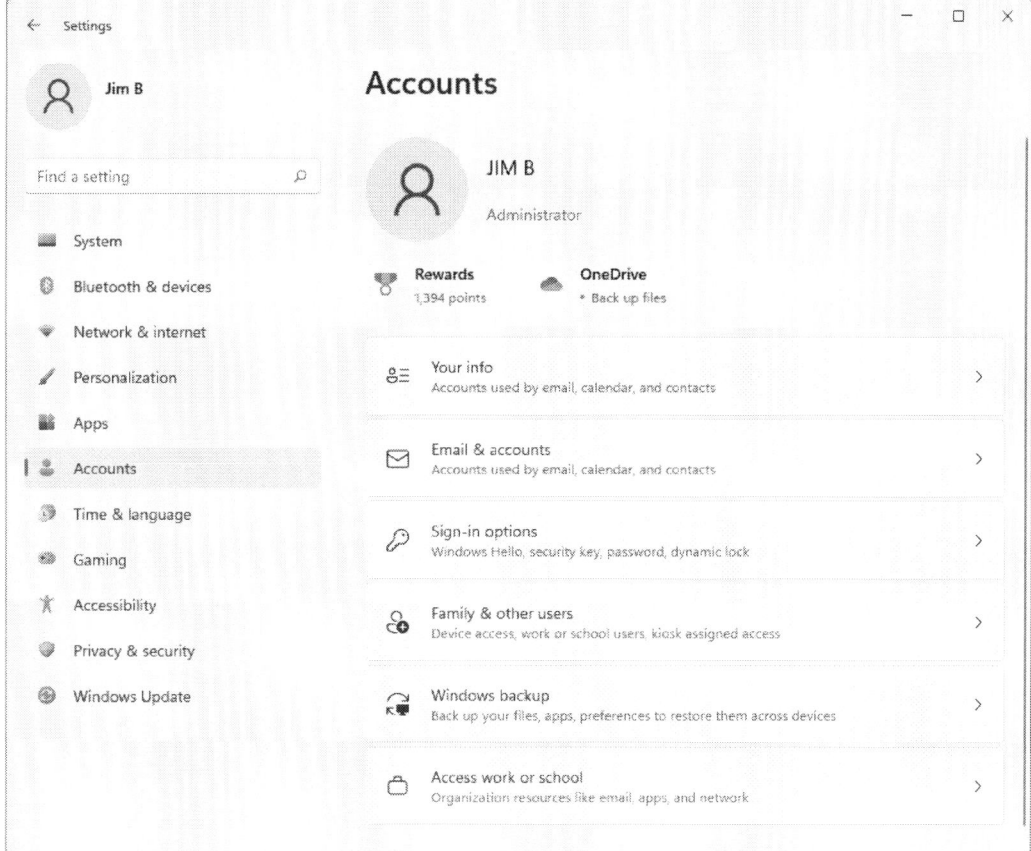

Figure 7.1

Clicking on *Email & accounts* will allow me to manage my account or create a new one. I can also delete an account from here if needed. There are two types of accounts you can create here. The first account type is one that can be used by your email, calendar and contacts while the second type is one that you can use for other types of apps.

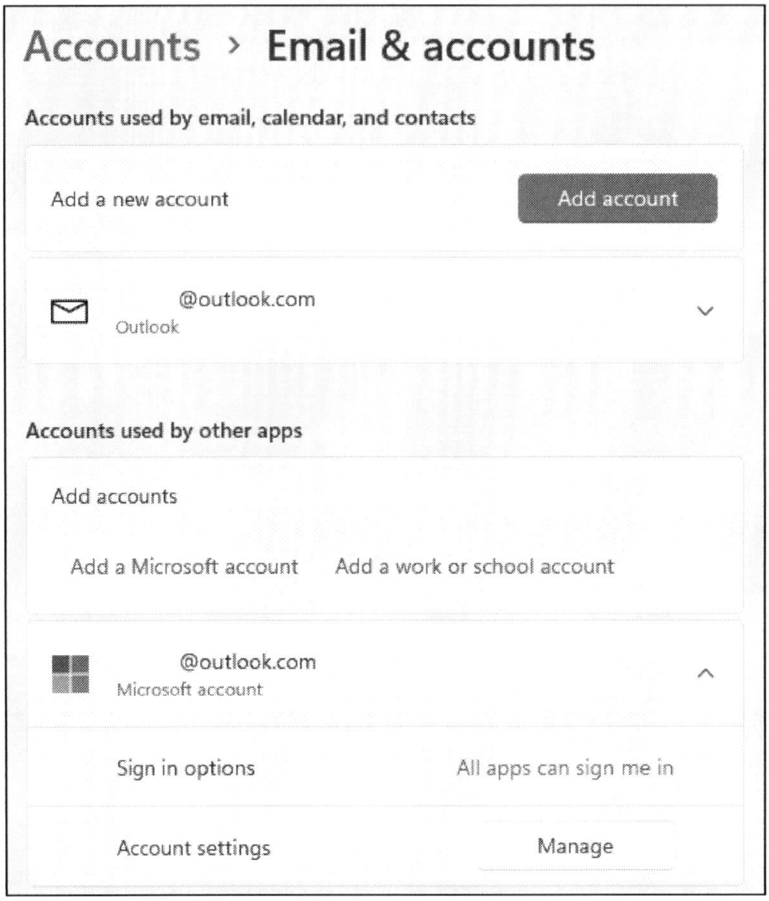

Chapter 7 – User Accounts

```
Accounts › Email & accounts

Accounts used by email, calendar, and contacts

    Add a new account                        Add account

    ✉  @outlook.com                                    ⌄
       Outlook

Accounts used by other apps

    Add accounts

        Add a Microsoft account    Add a work or school account

    ⊞  @outlook.com                                    ⌃
       Microsoft account

        Sign in options            All apps can sign me in

        Account settings                      Manage
```

Figure 7.2

To create a new account, I will need to click on the *Add account* button and then choose the type of account I want to add (figure 7.3). The process for creating an account will vary depending on which type you choose.

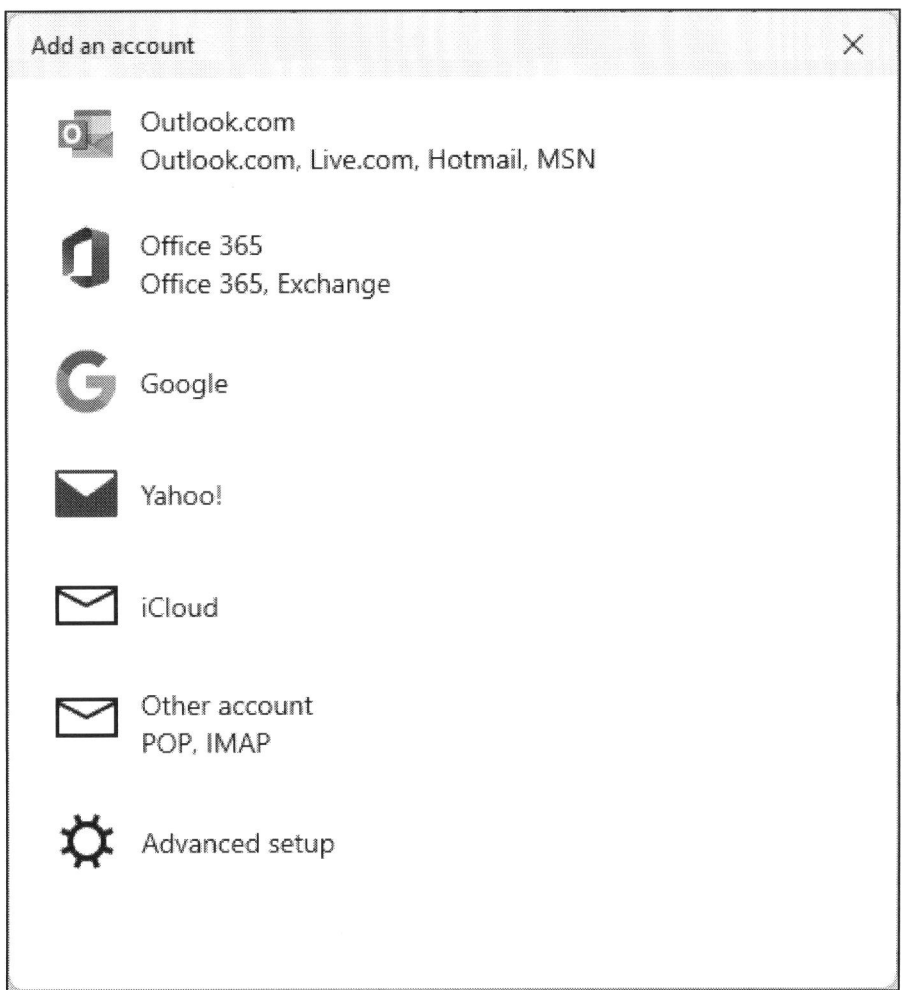

Figure 7.3

For example, if I wanted to add an Outlook.com account I would need to enter my Microsoft email and password or create a new one on the spot. Or if I wanted to use my Google account, I would need to enter my Gmail address and password and then Google would want to verify it was me by sending a notification to my smartphone.

I added my Google account to my computer so now it shows up along with my previous account.

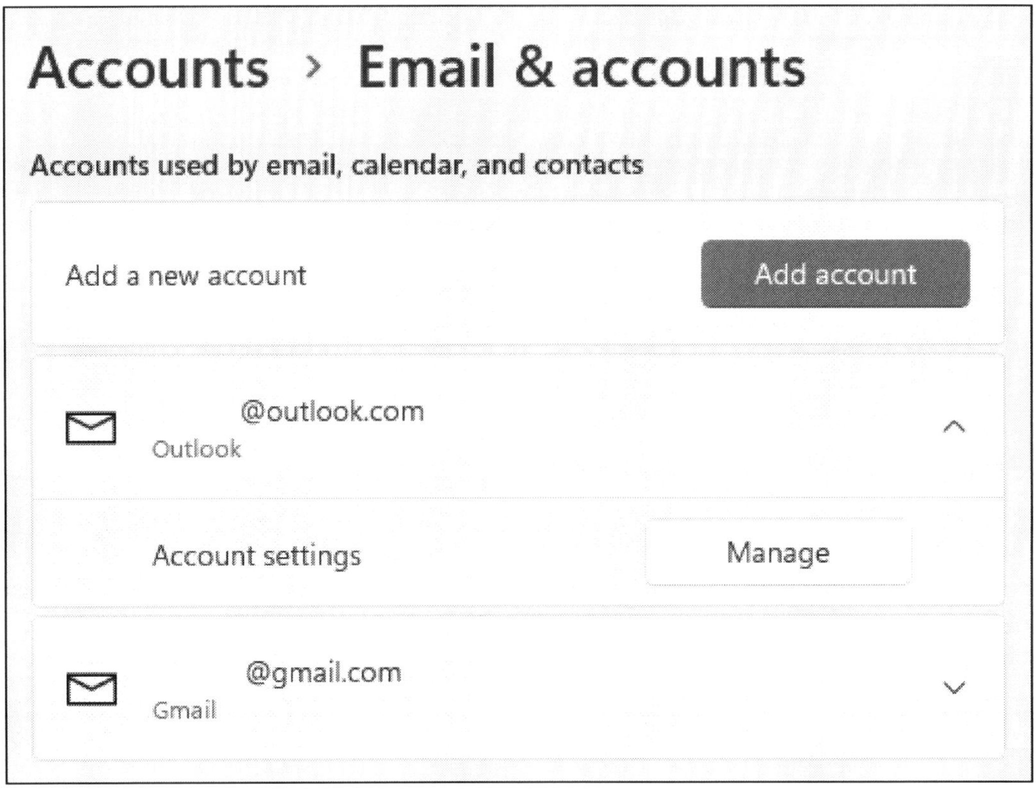

Chapter 7 – User Accounts

Accounts › Email & accounts

Accounts used by email, calendar, and contacts

Add a new account   Add account

✉ @outlook.com
   Outlook   ︿

       Account settings   Manage

✉ @gmail.com
   Gmail   ﹀

Figure 7.4

To add an account that can be used to log into my computer I will need to go back to the main Accounts screen and click on *Family & other users*. From there I can choose the *Add a family member* option or *Add other user* option. The family member option is used to add members of your family (like kids) where you want to restrict access to things like certain websites or games. The other user option is where you would go to add a new standard or administrator user. I will now add a new user using the *Other user's* choice.

Chapter 7 – User Accounts

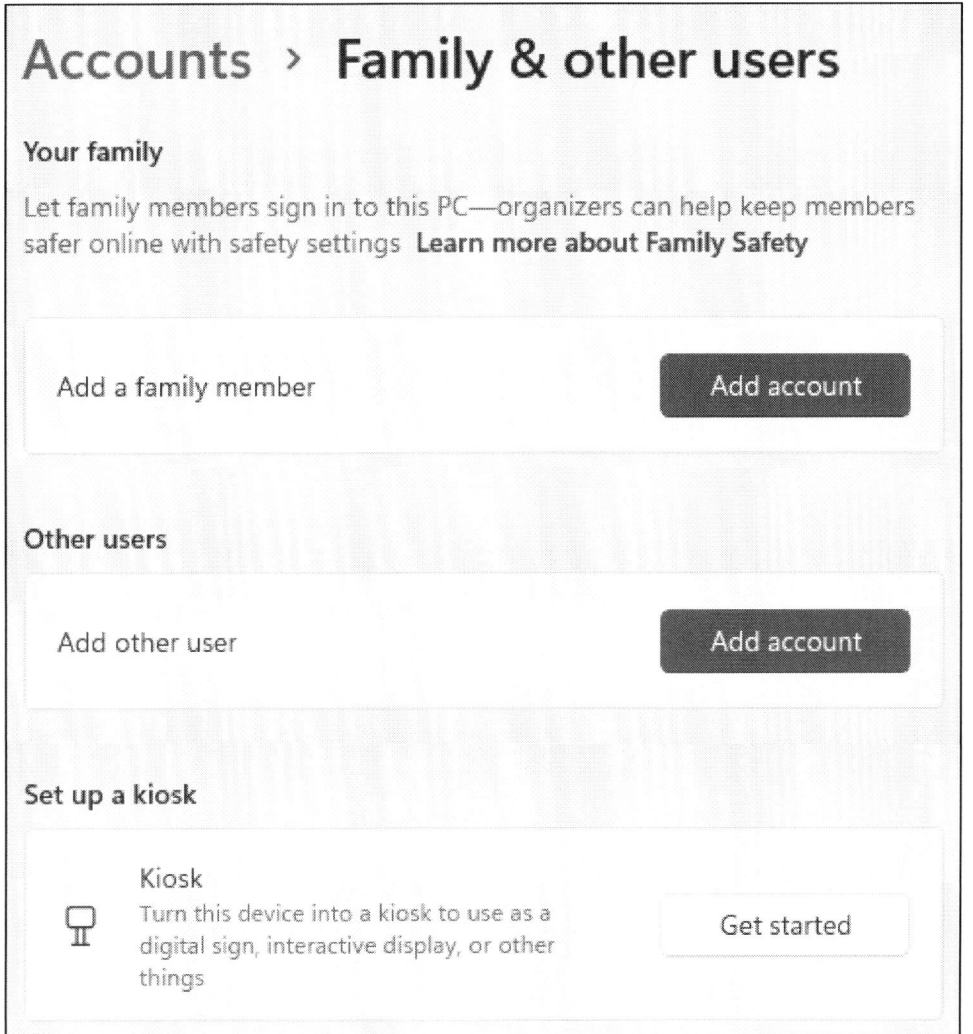

Figure 7.5

I will now create a local user account rather than a Microsoft account. To do so, you would need to click on *I don't have this person's sign-in information* at the bottom of the window.

Chapter 7 – User Accounts

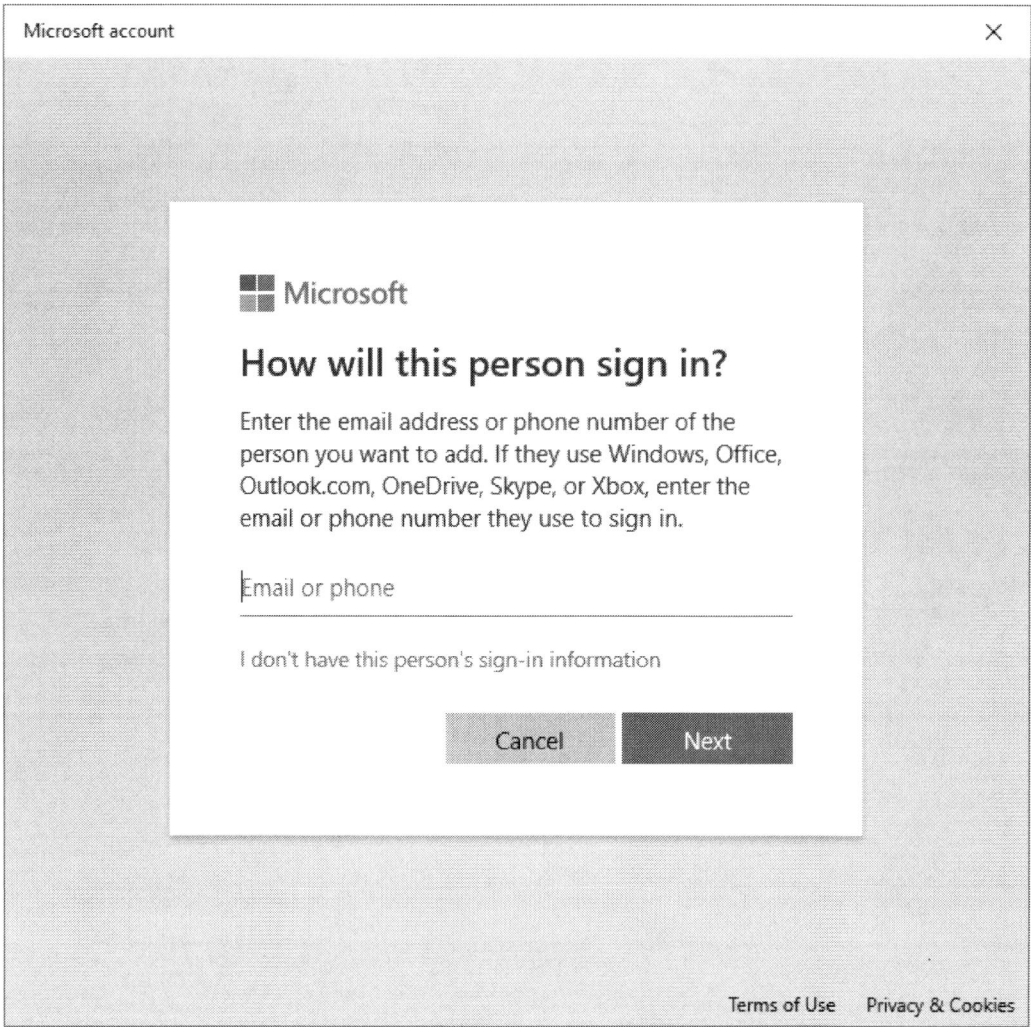

Figure 7.6

Then, on the next window where it asks for an email address again, click on the link that says *Add a user without a Microsoft account*.

Chapter 7 – User Accounts

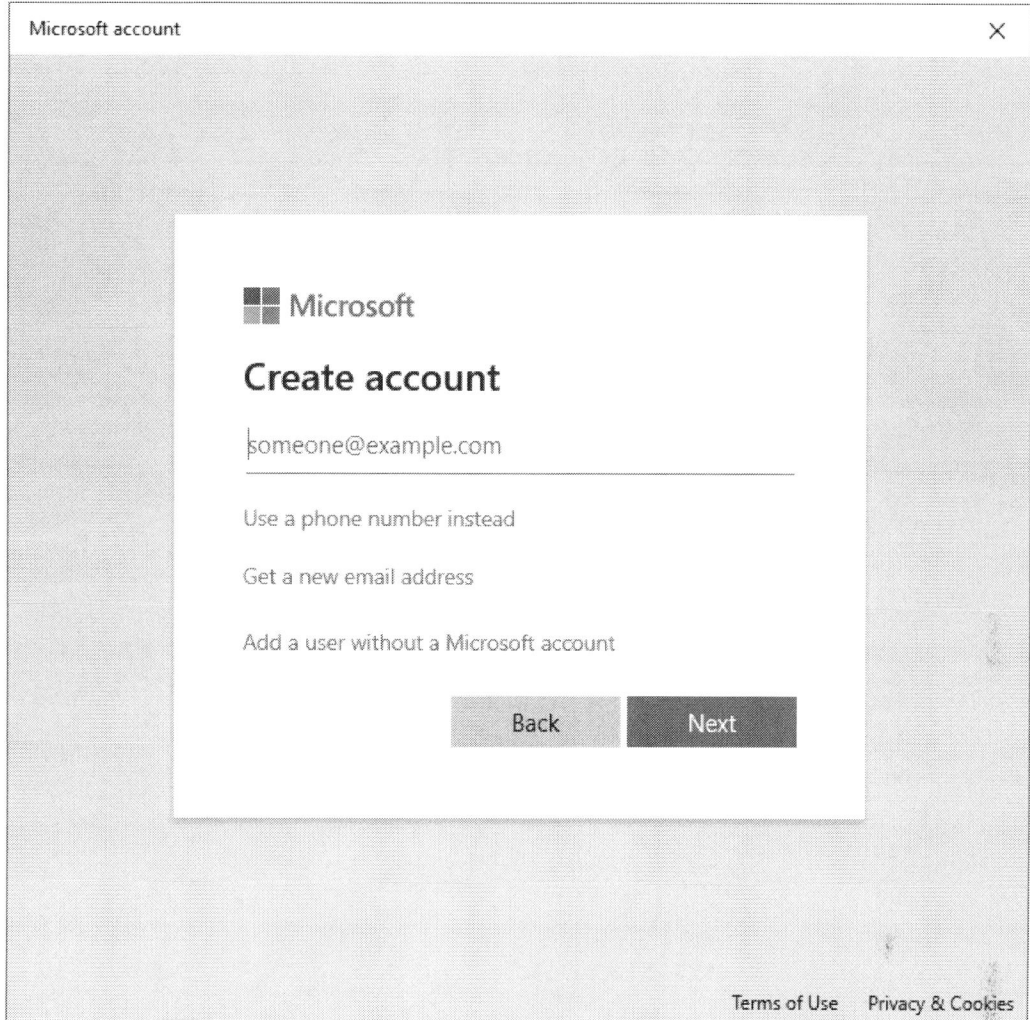

Figure 7.7

Next, you will be able to type in the username and password for your new local user. Windows will also want you to answer some security questions in case you forget your password and want to try and recover it.

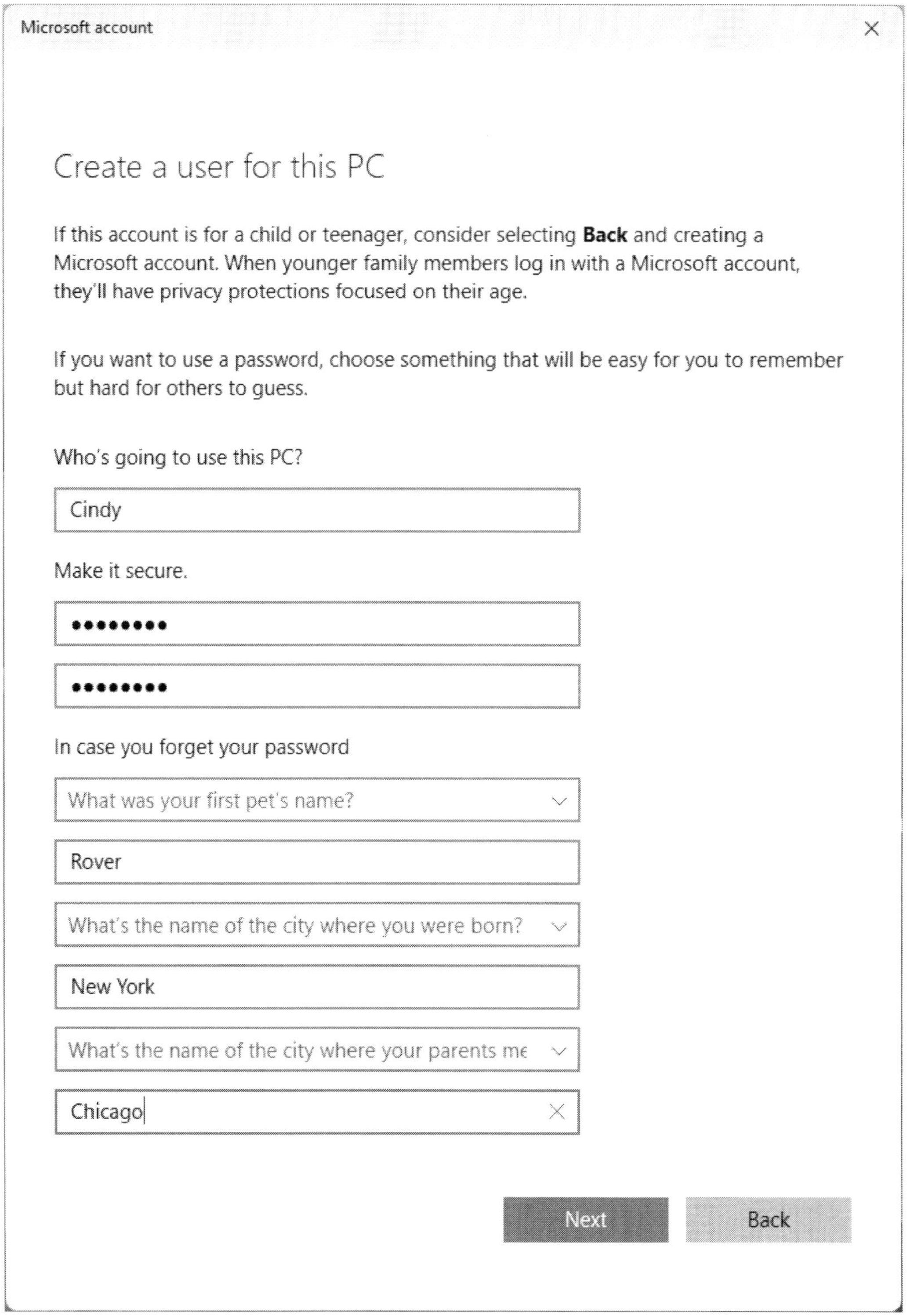

Chapter 7 – User Accounts

Create a user for this PC

If this account is for a child or teenager, consider selecting **Back** and creating a Microsoft account. When younger family members log in with a Microsoft account, they'll have privacy protections focused on their age.

If you want to use a password, choose something that will be easy for you to remember but hard for others to guess.

Who's going to use this PC?

    Cindy

Make it secure.

    ●●●●●●●●

    ●●●●●●●●

In case you forget your password

    What was your first pet's name?

    Rover

    What's the name of the city where you were born?

    New York

    What's the name of the city where your parents me

    Chicago

                                    Next   Back

Figure 7.8

Chapter 7 – User Accounts

Once you have the account created, you can go back to the *Other people* section where your user accounts are listed, click on the user account, and then click the *Change account type* button to make the user an administrator if needed.

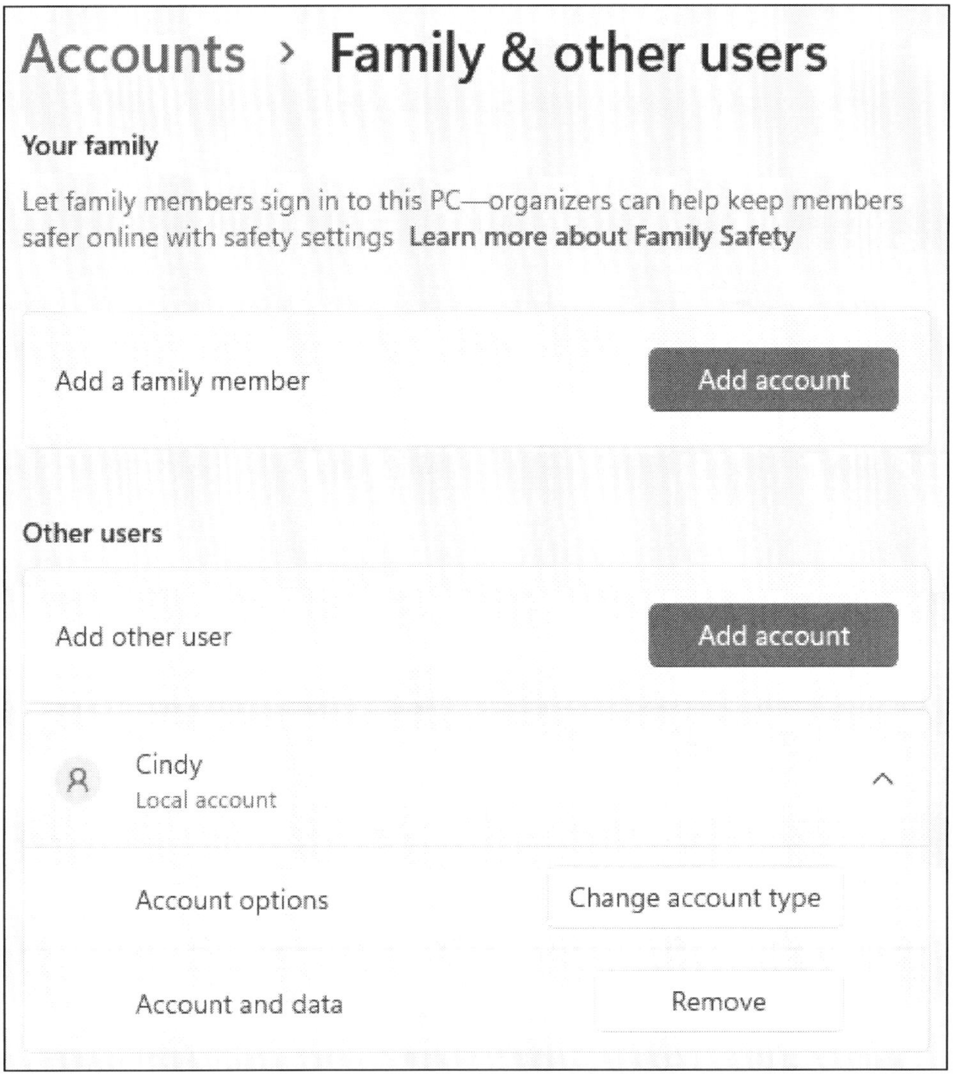

Accounts > Family & other users

Your family

Let family members sign in to this PC—organizers can help keep members safer online with safety settings **Learn more about Family Safety**

Add a family member — Add account

Other users

Add other user — Add account

Cindy
Local account

Account options — Change account type

Account and data — Remove

Figure 7.9

You can also remove user accounts from this section. One thing to keep in mind when removing a user account is that it will also delete their data, such as documents, downloads, photos, and so on, so it's a good idea to back up their files first.

Chapter 7 – User Accounts

Changing Passwords

There may come a time when you want to change your password for security reasons or change another user's password because they feel that they have been compromised, or you simply need to reset their password because they forgot it. Once again, there are several ways to do this, and I will go over some of the methods.

If you are signing in with a Microsoft account, then you will need to change your password from the Microsoft account settings portal online and the changes will then apply to your computer when you log in.

If you are using a local account like the one I made for Cindy, you can simply press *Ctrl+Alt+Del* on your keyboard and choose the *Change a password* option.

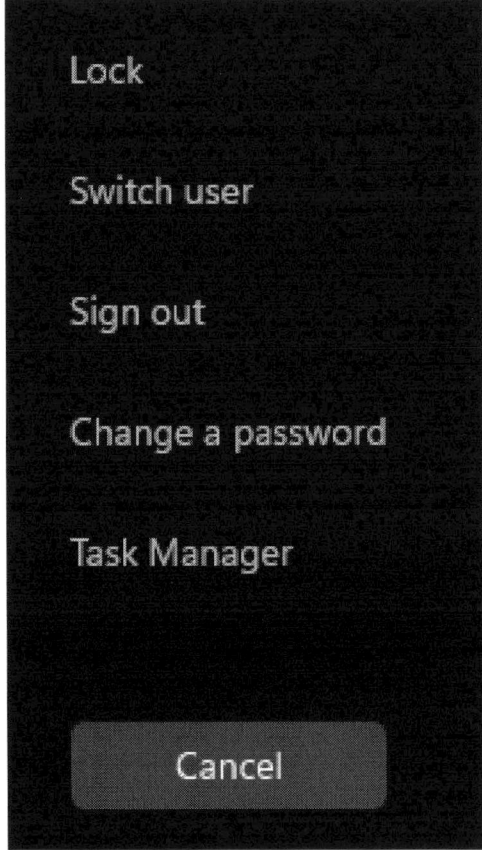

Figure 7.10

Chapter 7 – User Accounts

Figure 7.11

Then you will be prompted to enter your current password, as well as a new password, which you will have to type in again to confirm (figure 7.11). Notice at the bottom of figure 7.11 that there is a *Create password reset disk* option, which I will be discussing at the end of this chapter.

Chapter 7 – User Accounts

Another way to change your own password is back at the *Accounts* section of the Windows 11 Settings. Just go to the *Sign-in options* section and find the area that says *Password* and click on *Change*. You will be prompted to enter your current password and your new password twice, and then add a password hint to help you remember your password in case you forget it. Remember that to get to the Windows 11 Settings click on the Start button and then the gear icon.

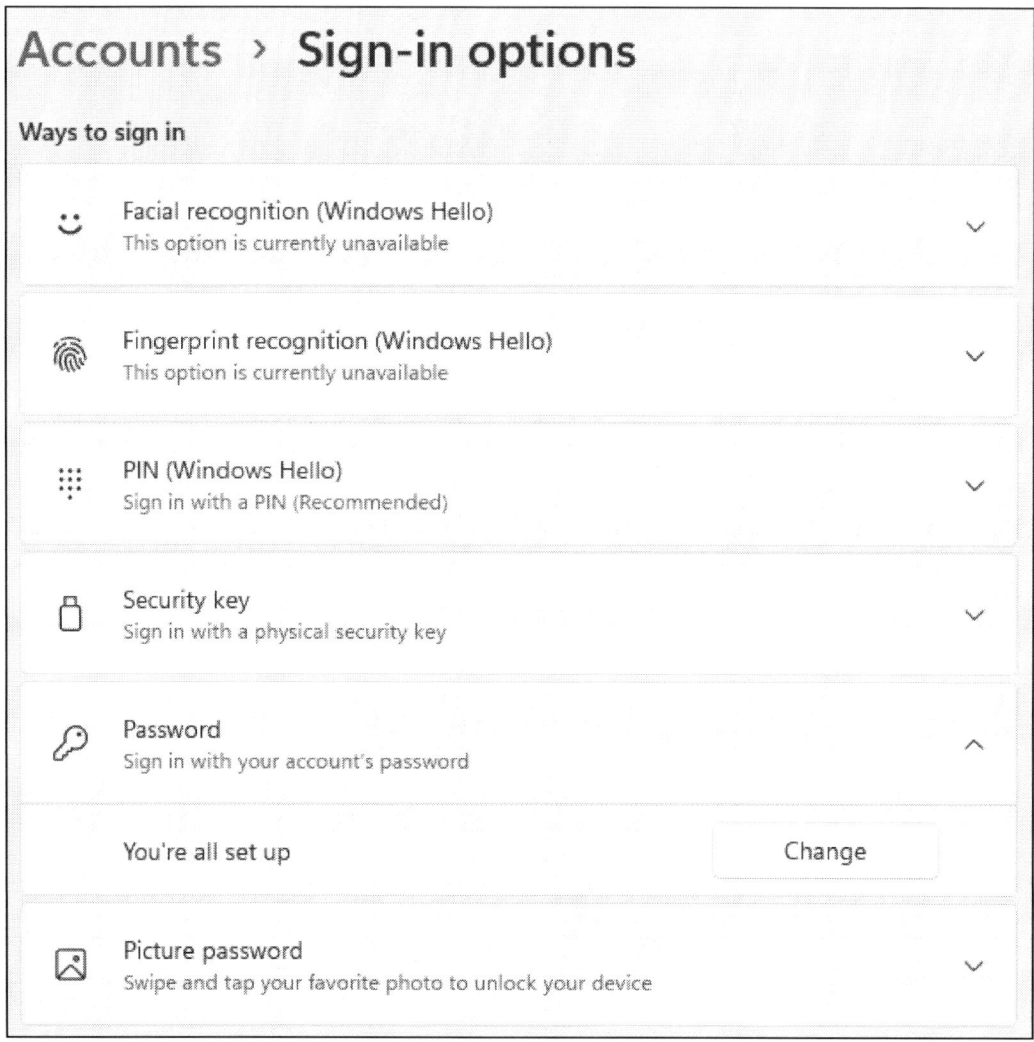

Figure 7.12

You might have noticed the *Windows Hello PIN* option above the password option. You can use this option to set a PIN number that you can use to log in rather than typing in a password.

To change another **local** user's password, you will need to go into Control Panel and then to the *User accounts* utility. From there you will click on the link that says *Manage another account*. Next click on the user account that you will want to manage and then click on the link that says *Change the password*. As you can see in figure 7.11, it's the same type of procedure as you would do from the Windows 11 Settings for your own account with the password confirmation you will also need to add a password hint to help that user remember their password if they forget. The main difference here is that you don't need to know their current password in order to change it, but you do need to be an administrator to change someone else's password.

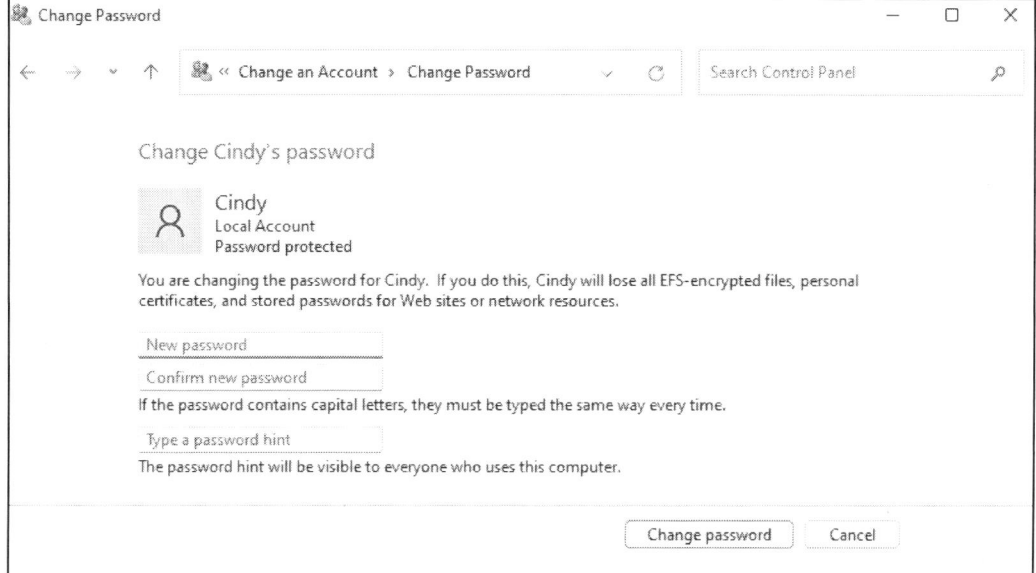

Figure 7.11

Switching Users

If you have more than one user account on your computer, then most likely you will run across a situation where one of the other users wants to use the computer while you are in the middle of something. This is where user switching comes in handy. Rather than having to save all of your work, close everything out, and log off, you can simply switch user accounts and let the other person log on and do what they need to do.

When you switch accounts, it leaves your current login state as is so you don't need to worry about losing any information. When the other user is done, they simply log off and you can connect back into your session and carry on with what

Chapter 7 – User Accounts

you were doing. Or you can switch back and forth between accounts as needed if both of you need to leave your login sessions open.

To switch user accounts simply click on Start and then click on the user icon and choose which account you want to switch over to. It will also show you if another user is currently logged into the computer like Cindy is in figure 7.12. Just keep in mind that if another user shuts down the computer then your open session will be closed and any unsaved documents you have opened will not be saved.

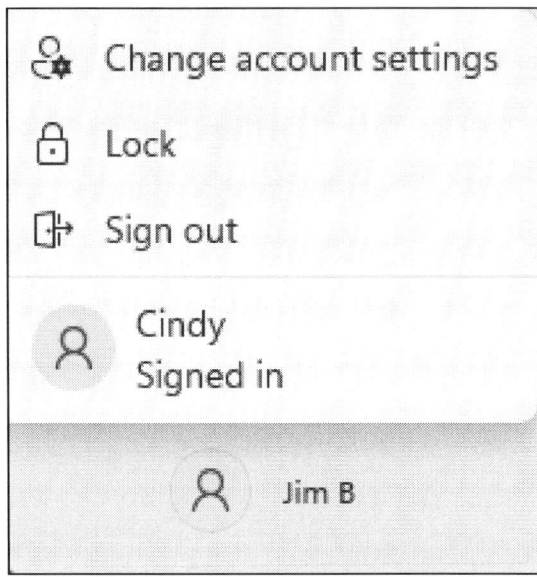

Figure 7.12

Creating a Password Reset Disk
There will come a time in your life where you will forget your password on at least one of your devices, if not many of them. When this happens, you will be locked out of your computer with no way back in. If you have another user on the computer with the appropriate rights to reset your password, then it's an easy fix (we discussed that a little bit ago). But what if you are the only user on the computer? If that's the case, then hopefully you made a password reset disk before forgetting your password. A password reset disk is used to reset your password in case of an emergency.

To make a password reset disk, type in *password reset* from the search box or Cortana and follow the prompts to make the password reset disk using a USB flash drive. (And no, we don't know why they call it a reset "disk"). All you need to do

Chapter 7 – User Accounts

is insert a USB flash drive, type in your current user password, let it do its thing, and then store the flash drive in a safe location.

Then, if you forget your password and enter it incorrectly, you will notice a link under the password box that says *Reset password* (figure 7.13). You will also be able to use your security questions to try and get back into your computer. If you don't know the answers to these then you can click on *Use password reset disk instead* as seen in figure 7.14. You will then be prompted to connect your password reset flash drive and have your password recovered.

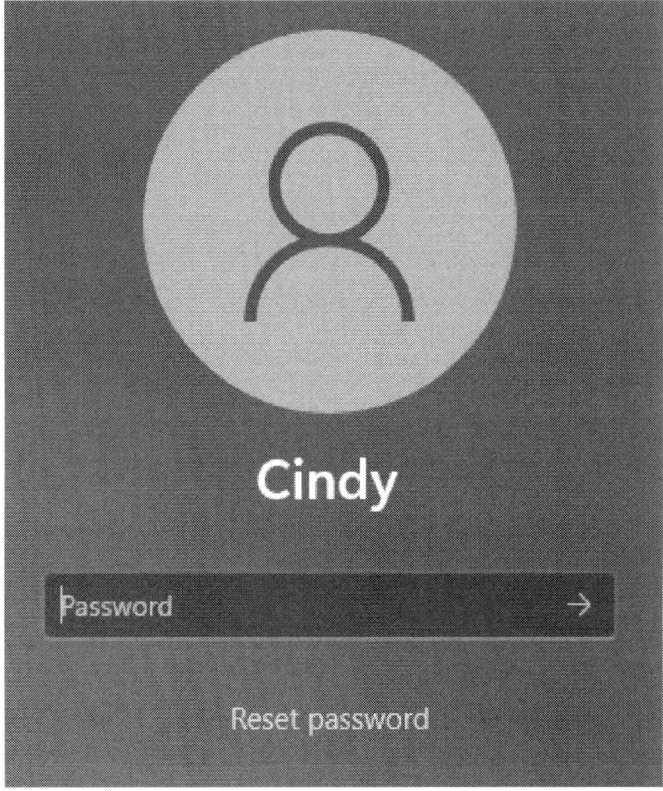

Figure 7.13

Chapter 7 – User Accounts

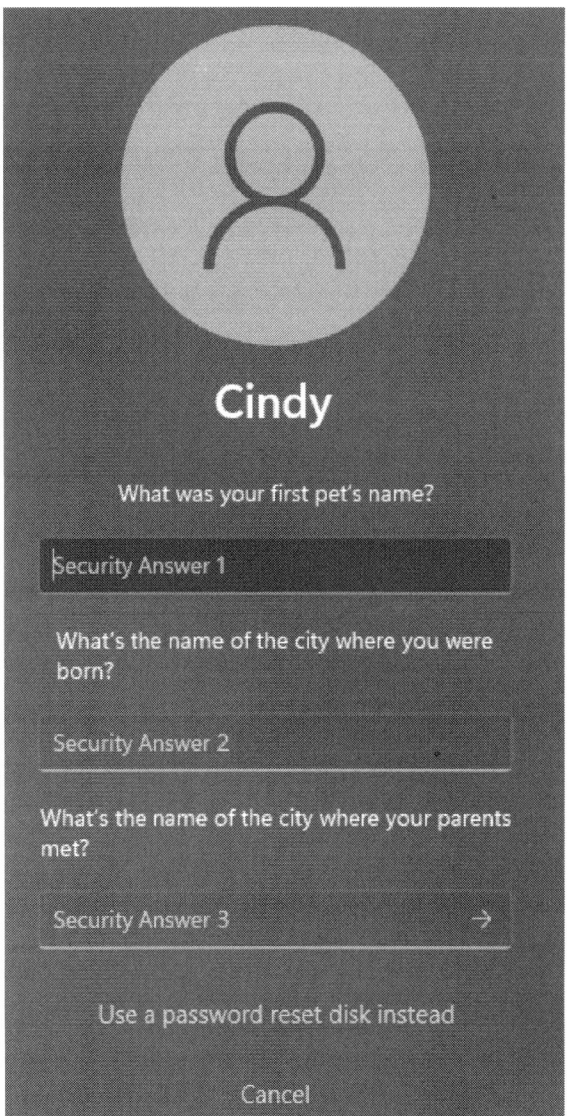

Figure 7.14

 When creating a password reset disk on a USB flash drive, make sure you don't need to keep any of the information on that drive because it will be wiped out in the process. So in other words, back it up first!

Chapter 8 – Microsoft Edge Web Browser

One of the most popular things that any computer user will do is browse the Internet. In fact, sometimes that's all certain people will use a computer for! Web browsers have been around as long as Windows has been around, and there are plenty to choose from such as Mozilla Firefox, Google Chrome, and Apple Safari.

Introducing Microsoft Edge
As you may or may not know, Internet Explorer has been the built in web browser for Windows since the beginning of web browsers. With Windows 10 they switched to their new browser called Microsoft Edge, and it's actually a Windows App rather than a Desktop App (or program). In Windows 10, Internet Explorer was still part of the operating system, even though Edge was the "official" browser of Windows. For Windows 11, Microsoft has completely removed Internet Explorer so you will have to use Edge or download another browser from the internet.

The way Edge works is similar to all the other web browsers, and you should definitely try it out and see if you like it. Microsoft claims it's faster than Chrome and Firefox, and also says it's a good browser to use if you are into staying safe on the Internet. And since you can run multiple browsers on your computer at the same time, it never hurts to have a couple that you like since some pages work better in different browsers.

As you can see in figure 8.1, Microsoft Edge looks like your typical web browser, with the address bar at the top, back and forward buttons, and the ability to open multiple tabs within one browser window. You can add a home button to Edge from the settings even though I think it should be there by default.

Chapter 8 – Microsoft Edge Web Browser

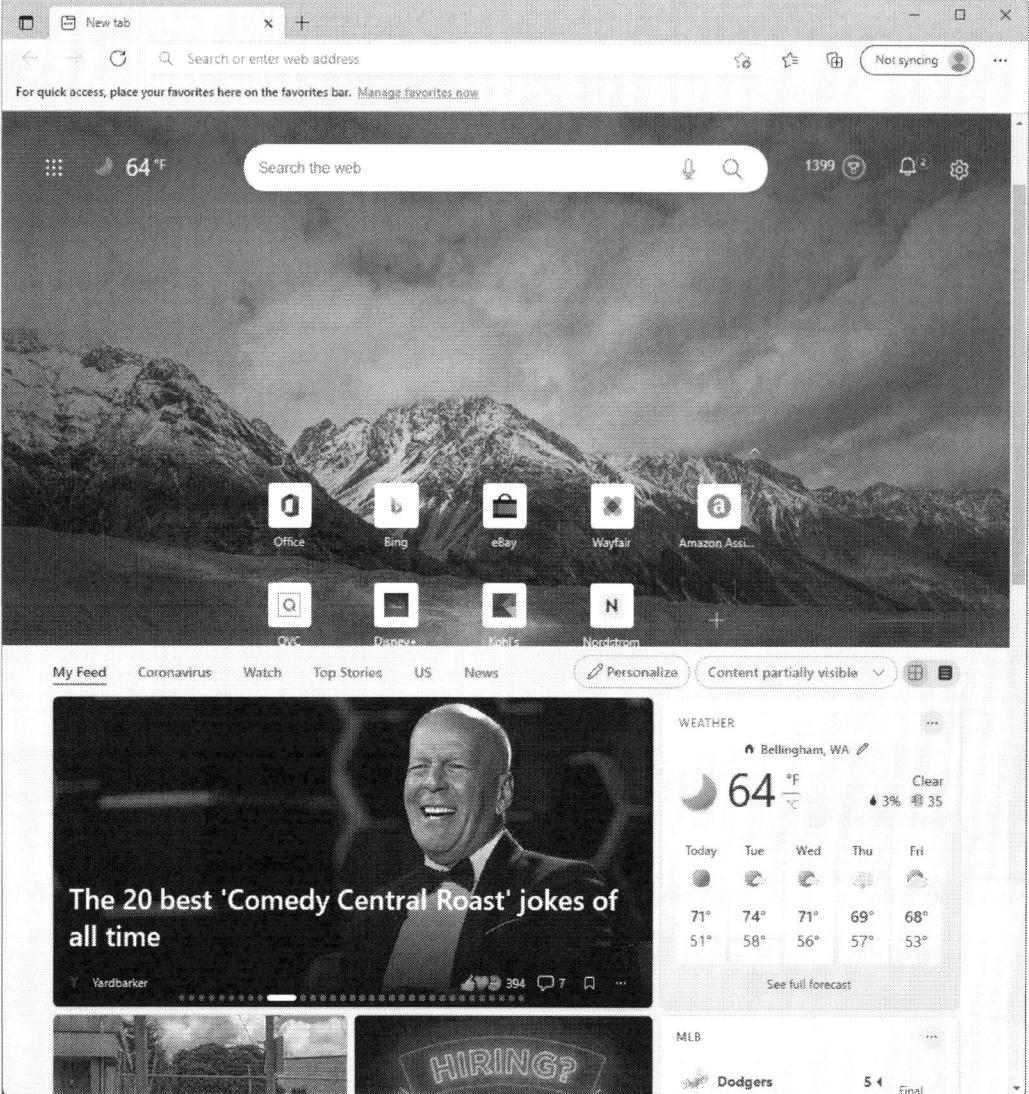

Figure 8.1

Since Microsoft Edge is an app rather than a typical program like Internet Explorer, you won't have the typical text based menus on the top like you are used to seeing in other browsers. That doesn't mean it's not easy to use, but rather just requires a little getting used to.

Using Microsoft Edge

If you have ever used a web browser such as the old Internet Explorer, Chrome, or Firefox, then you shouldn't have too much trouble using Microsoft Edge. It works the same way once you get your home page configured so it has a familiar

Chapter 8 – Microsoft Edge Web Browser

look when you start it up. There are only a few areas you really need to get familiar with before you will be up and running (figure 8.2).

Figure 8.2

- **Address Bar** – This is where you type the website addresses you want to go to if you prefer to do that rather than do a search for the site.

- **New Tab Button** – All modern browsers allow you to have multiple website pages open within one web browser session. Simply click the new tab button and it will open up another page that you can use to browse to another site while leaving your other pages open.

- **Add to Favorites Button** – Use this button to add websites that you are on to your favorites so you can easily find them later and go back to them.

- **View Favorites** – If you go here, you can view your favorites or bookmarked sites, as well as organize them into folders etc.

Chapter 8 – Microsoft Edge Web Browser

- **Home Button** – Clicking on this button will take you to your home page, which can be customized to whatever you want it to be. (I will show you how to do this later in the chapter.)

- **Refresh Button** – If you want to reload the web page you are on to check for updates or in case it doesn't seem to be responding, you can press this button. (F5 on the keyboard will do the same thing.)

- **Back & Forward Buttons** – You can cycle backward and forwards through all the pages you have been to within a certain tab with these buttons.

- **Collections** – This feature can be used to save web information such as images, text, or entire pages into one place so you can retain this information and refer back to it later. Edge used to have a similar feature called Set Aside Tabs that was replaced by Collections.

- **Personal Info** – You don't need to log into your Microsoft account in order to use Edge but if you are logged in then you can view and manage your profile settings from here.

- **Settings Button** – This is where you can configure and customize Edge to suit your needs. (I will be going over these settings later in the chapter.)

So now that you know what all the important buttons do, you can start browsing and searching to find exactly what you're looking for.

Microsoft is constantly changing\improving the Edge web browser so if things look a little different or something is not where it used to be, it's probably because they have made another one of their infamous changes which I think are just made for the sake of making changes!

Using Multiple Tabs
I can't stress enough how handy using the multiple tab feature is of any browser, and once you start using it you will find that you will have bunches of tabs open at one time. The cool thing is that you can set Edge to remember what tabs you had open so when you close your browser and reopen it you will be right where you

Chapter 8 – Microsoft Edge Web Browser

left off. To open a new tab simply click on the **+** symbol next to the rightmost open tab and it will open a new tab with a blank page (unless you change this setting, which I will show you how to do later in this chapter). To close out of a specific tab, simply click on the X on the tab itself and it will close yet leave your other tabs open.

You can have as many tabs open as you like but the more you have open, the harder it will be to find your tabs when you try to go back to them because it will start to show less and less of the webpage title to make room for the other open tabs.

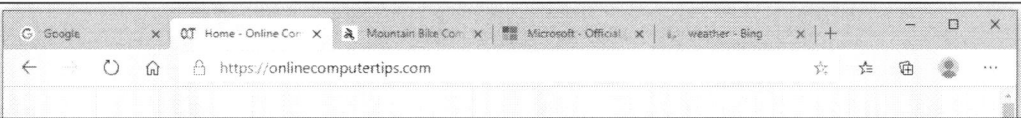

Figure 8.3

But once you figure out what websites you go to on a regular basis you will find that your open tabs will become more manageable because you will tend to only keep those tabs open and close the others to unclutter your open tab area.

Using Favorites
Favorites, or bookmarks, as they are also commonly called, are one of the most helpful tools you can use with your web browser because it makes it where you don't have to remember all of the website names or addresses that you like to go to on a regular basis.

To make a website page a favorite all you need to do is go to that page and then click on the favorite icon (the star). Then when the window pops up (as shown in figure 8.4) you can either keep the suggested name for the favorite or type in your own. Then in the *Folder* section, you can have it saved right in the default favorites folder or another folder that you have created within your favorites. After you make your choices, click the *Done* button and the page will be added to your favorites so you can easily get back to it later.

Chapter 8 – Microsoft Edge Web Browser

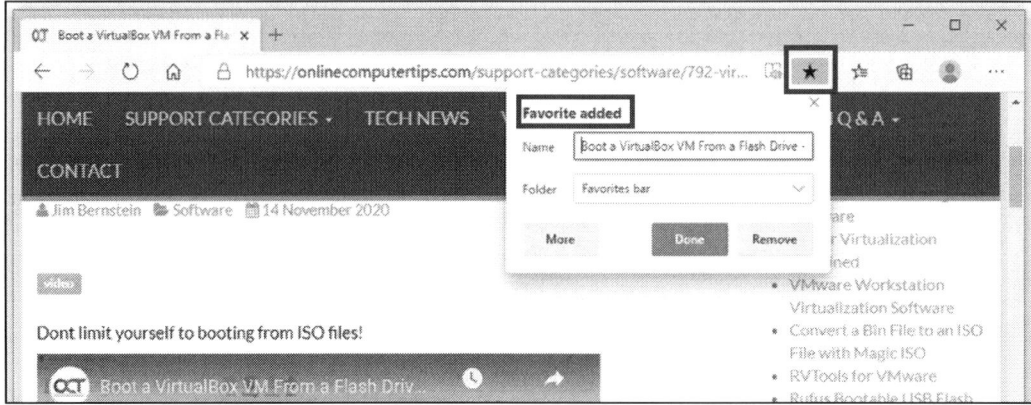

Figure 8.4

To edit your favorites and make new folders, click on the *View Favorites* button and from there you can edit, rename, delete, and sort your favorites by right clicking on them. You can also create new folders in that area if you want to organize your favorites.

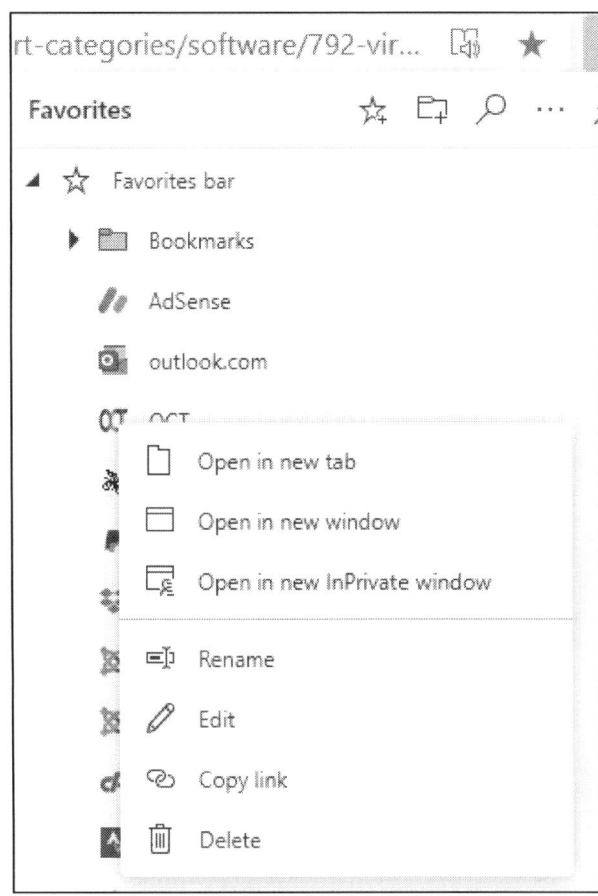

Figure 8.5

Chapter 8 – Microsoft Edge Web Browser

Customizing Edge Settings

Just like any other browser, Microsoft Edge has a bunch of settings that you can configure to make it work the way you want it to work since the defaults rarely work just fine for everyone. I'm going to go over some of the more important ones to give you an idea of how you can customize Edge to your liking.

To get to the Edge settings click on the ellipsis (…) at the top right corner of the window and click on *Settings*. Then you will see your profile options as shown in figure 8.6. You can then click the > next to any one of them to expand the options in that category.

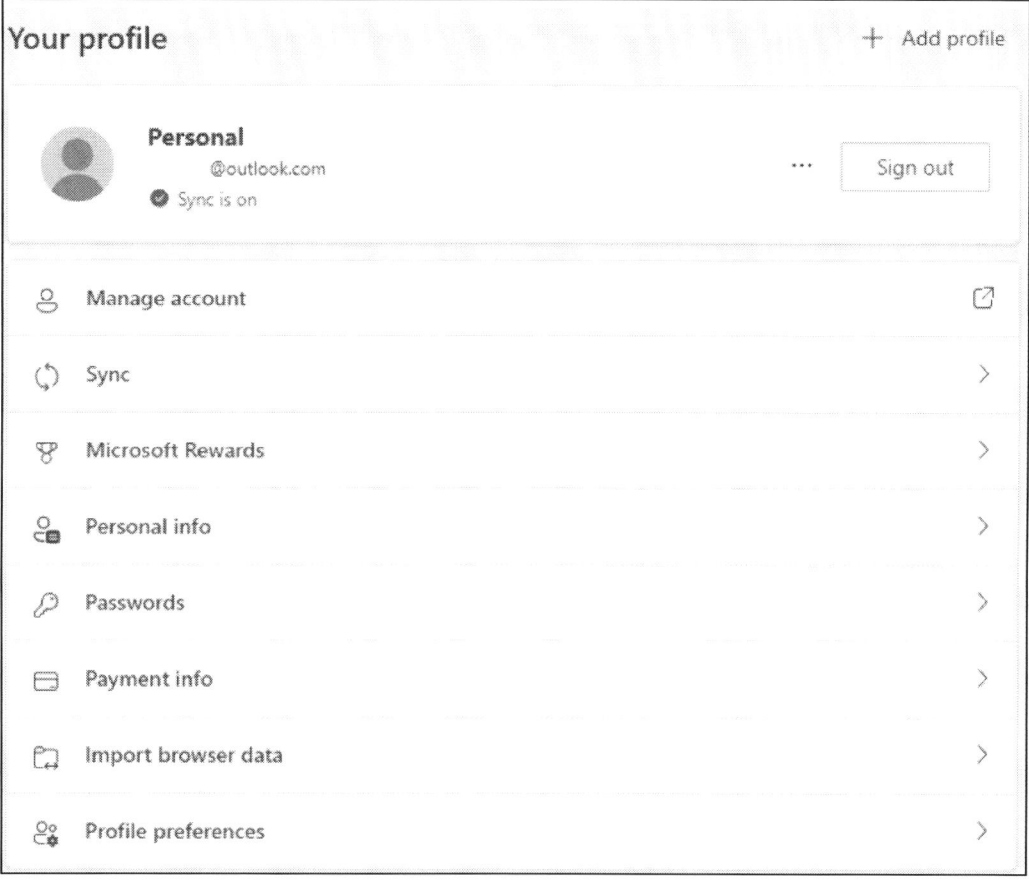

Figure 8.6

You can also click on the three horizontal lines next to Settings to bring up even more options as seen in figure 8.7 which I will be discussing as well.

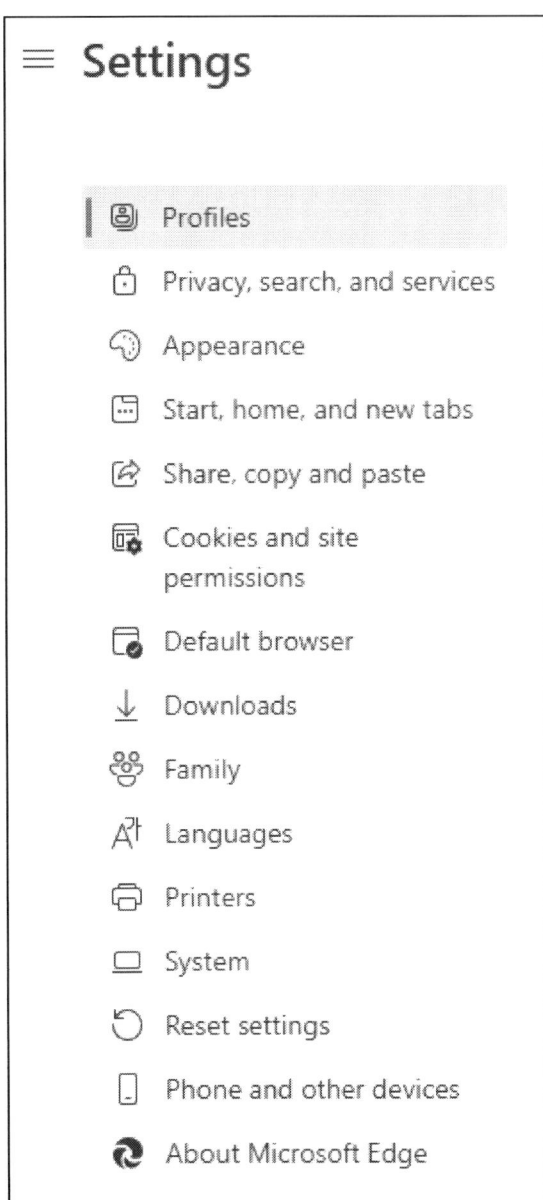

Figure 8.7

There is enough information here just on the Edge settings that I can write another book just on the settings themselves so I will now go over what I feel are the important options that you might actually want to configure. For the most part, many people don't change any of the options in their web browser except for maybe their default home page.

Chapter 8 – Microsoft Edge Web Browser

The *Sync* option as seen in figure 8.6 is one you might want to use if you have multiple computers or devices that you use Edge with so you can keep your browser experience the same between your devices. As you can see from figure 8.8, you can sync various items between your web browser on your devices such as your favorites, history and passwords. You can also enable or disable these choices or turn off the sync feature altogether from here.

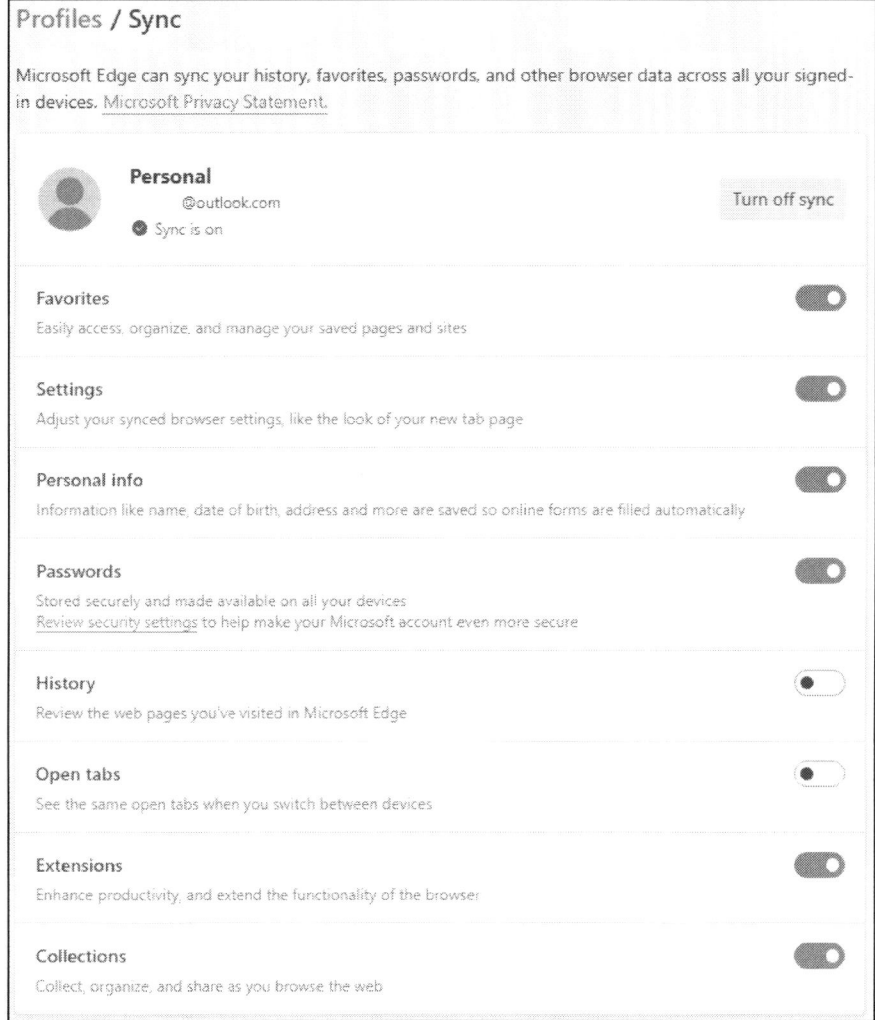

Figure 8.8

The *Passwords* setting section is an important one that you should be aware of. If you are the type who likes to save their website passwords within your browser so you don't need to remember them or type them in each time you go to that site, then you can manage any saved passwords from here. You can do things such as view, change or delete any saved passwords that you might have.

Never save any financial or banking information site passwords in your web browsers because it's too easy for hackers to get into your saved passwords and compromise your accounts!

The *Payment info* section from figure 8.6 is similar to the Password section except it will allow you to save credit card information so you can make your online purchases without having to break out your wallet and manually type in the credit card number into the website form. Once again, I don't recommend using this feature.

Most web browsers will allow you to save form information such as addresses and phone numbers, so you don't have to type them out each time you place an order online and need to enter the delivery address for example. By going to the *Addresses and more* section you can edit and delete any of this kind of information you might have saved in the past.

Finally, there is the *Import browser data* (figure 8.9) section which is used to import things such as favorites\bookmarks, passwords, history and so on from another browser into Edge. For example, if you were a previous Google Chrome user and have all of your information stored in Chrome and decided to start using Edge, you can import all of your data into Edge in one quick step. Of course you can always use more than one browser but at least this way you will have all of your settings each one. You can also choose to import your favorites from an HTML or CSV file that you exported from another computer.

Chapter 8 – Microsoft Edge Web Browser

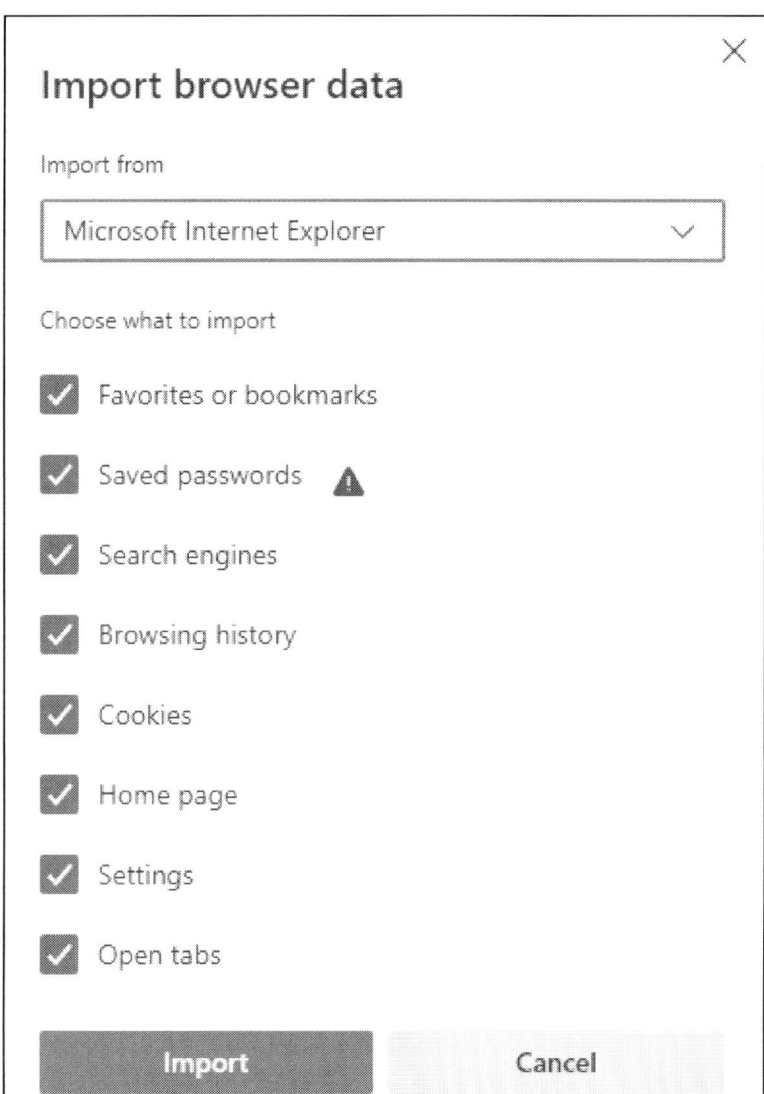

Figure 8.9

Going back to the other settings that I mentioned a few pages back, I would now like to go over these settings in case you feel like checking them out for yourself.

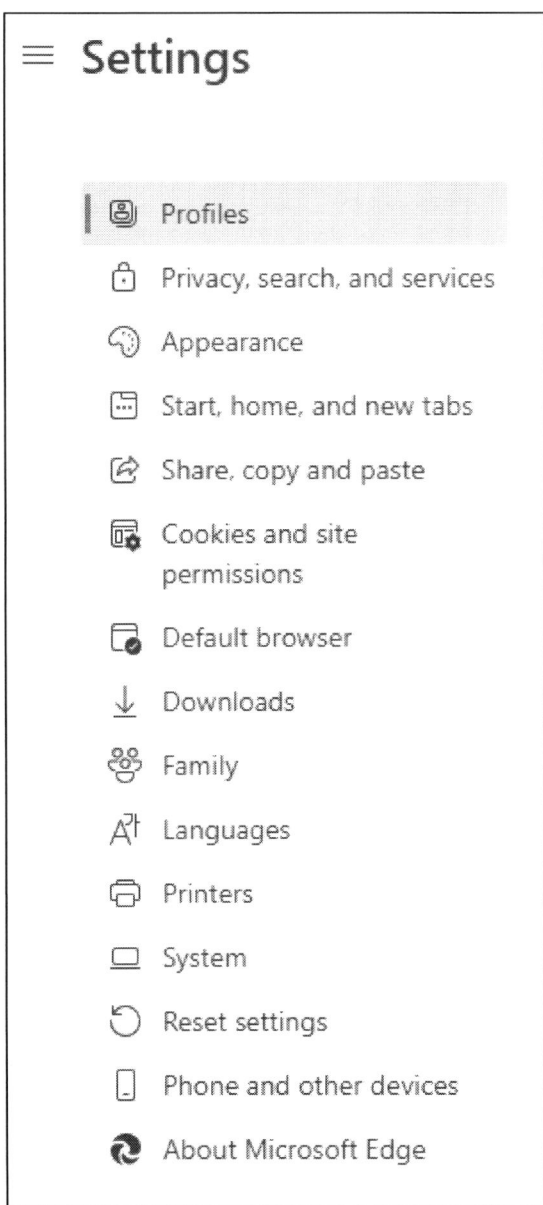

Figure 8.10

There is a good chance that you will never need to edit any of these settings, but I will touch on each one of them and spend more time on the settings I think are the most important to know about.

- **Profiles** – I just went into detail about all of the profile settings so we can skip this!

Chapter 8 – Microsoft Edge Web Browser

- **Privacy, search and services** – As you may or may not know, when you go online, websites are always trying to monitor what you do and what you click on in order to learn as much as they can about you for the sake of advertising products to try and get your hard earned cash. Here you can adjust what level of tracking Edge will allow to occur within the browser. You can also allow or block specific trackers as needed and view tracking history.

- **Appearance** – If you are the type that likes to customize the way things look then you can make some changes here such as what theme or fonts Edge uses as well as what buttons are shown, and which are hidden. Here is also where you can change the zoom level and font size to make things easier to see.

- **Start, home, and new tabs** – This is where you would go to change what website opens when you first open Edge and as well as the page that opens when you click the home button. If you want a certain tab or tabs to open every time you start Edge, then you can configure them here. You can also tell Edge to continue where you left off so if you close your browser with 20 tabs open, the next time you open Edge it will open those same 20 tabs again.

- **Share, copy and paste** – When you copy and paste an item in Edge you can specify if you want links etc. to be pasted or if you just want the text itself to be pasted from here.

- **Cookies and Permissions** – Since Edge is a Windows app, it can access many of your computer's components such as its camera, microphone and location. Here is where you can go to block or allow these types of permissions. As for cookies, you can come here to enable or block cookies as well as see what cookies are already on your computer.

- **Default Browser** – When you click on a link in a document or email etc., Windows will open that link with whatever browser is set to be your default. If you would like to make Edge your default browser, you can do so from here and you can also do this from the Windows settings.

- **Downloads** – When you download files from websites, they will go to whatever folder you have specified here. The default folder is your Downloads folder.

- **Family** – If you would like to set up things such as activity monitoring and website filtering for family members, you can do so from here.

- **Languages** – Here you can change what language Edge displays web pages in and also configure translation options for web pages that are not in your native language. This is also where you can come to enable or disable the built in spell checker which is enabled by default.

- **Printers** – This is just a shortcut to take you to the Windows printer management settings.

- **System** – This area contains a few settings related to background services and hardware acceleration that you will most likely never need to adjust.

- **Reset settings** – If you want to wipe out all of your customized settings and bring Edge back to the way it was right out of the box then you can do so from here.

- **Phone and other devices** – Edge allows you to sync your phone with your browser so you can sync things such as your favorites and passwords etc.

- **About Microsoft Edge** – This is where you would go to see what version of Edge you are currently running.

Chapter 9 – Windows 11 Settings

This will be a relatively short chapter because all I want to discuss are some of the more important aspects of the Windows 11 Settings since I have referred to them so much throughout the book. If you really want to do some custom configuration, then you should familiarize yourself with these settings and go check them out for yourself since that is the best way to learn how to use them.

Windows 11 Settings App
Starting with Windows 10, Microsoft had come up with new ways to accomplish common tasks while trying to make them easier to do at the same time. But for people who are used to doing things a certain way and like the way things used to work, this means they have to change their ways. Even though you can still get to most of the same configuration settings the old way in places like Control Panel, Windows 10 and 11 have their own interface that puts most of its settings for Windows in one place and also includes some new options that we didn't have before Windows 10. To access these settings, simply click on the Settings icon (that looks like a gear) from the Start button, or type in **settings** in the Cortana or search box and you will see the main Settings window with all its categories (figure 9.1).

Chapter 9 – Windows 11 Settings

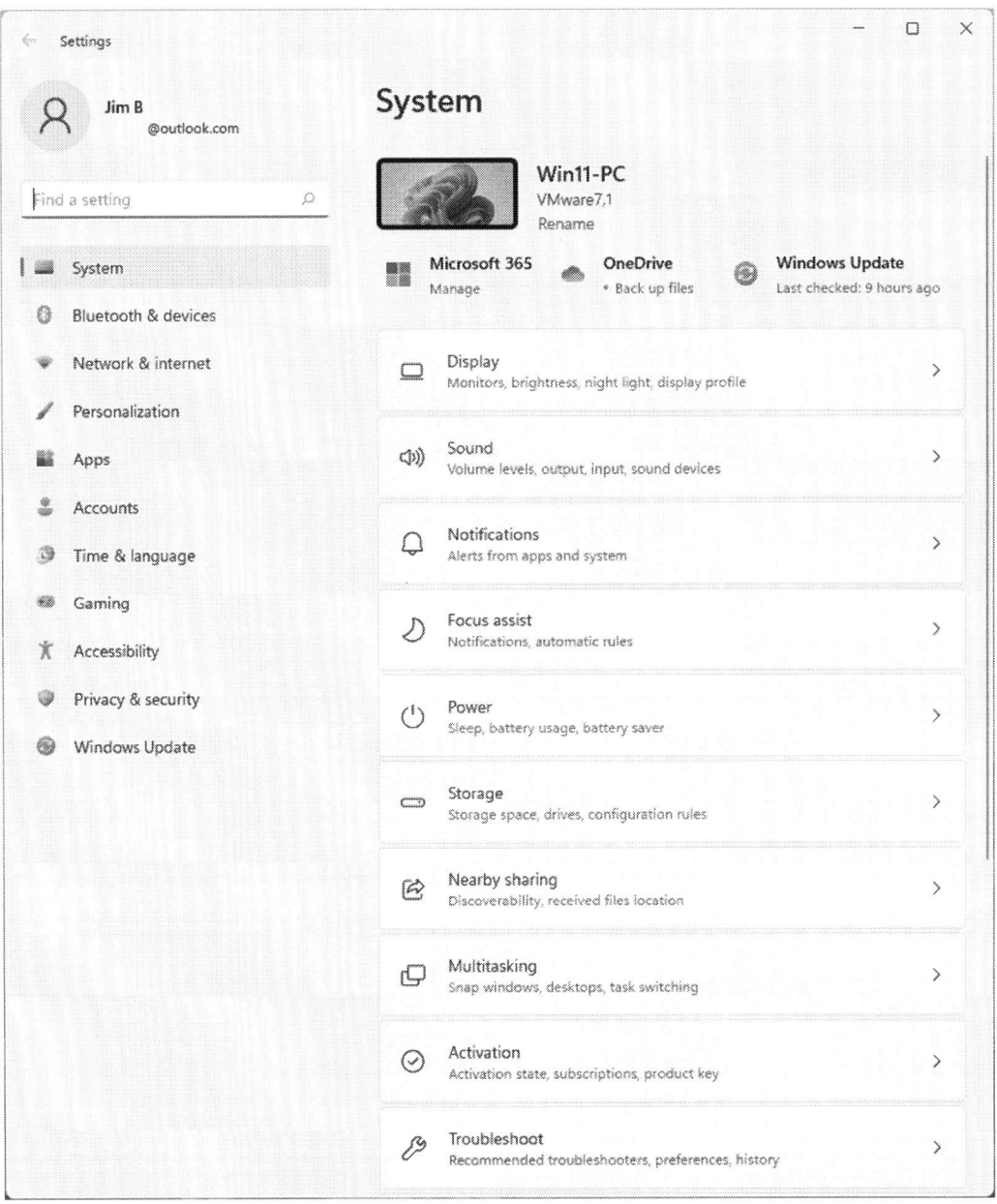

Figure 9.1

Commonly Used Settings

Let's go over what each settings category contains so you can get an idea of what type of settings you can configure in Windows 11. I won't go into a lot of detail but rather give you a summary of what each setting does and then you can check them out yourself to see exactly what you can do with each one.

Chapter 9 – Windows 11 Settings

System Settings

- **Display** – This is where you can change your screen resolution, text size, and configure multiple displays.

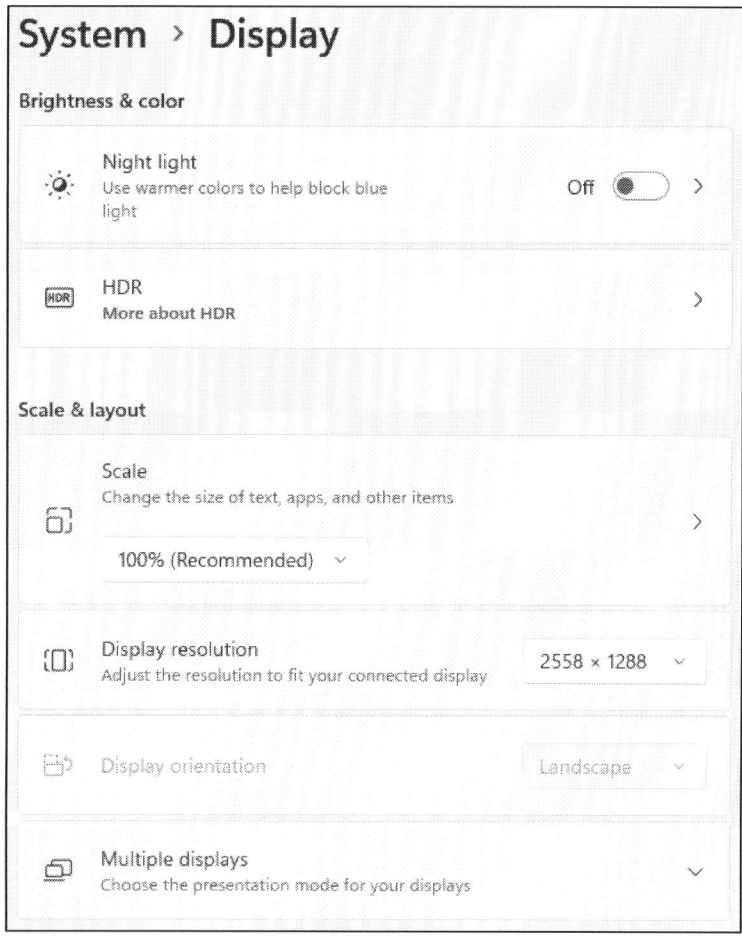

Figure 9.2

- **Sound** – Here you can do things like change volume levels, set input devices, test your microphone if you have one, and also run tests on your soundcard hardware.

Chapter 9 – Windows 11 Settings

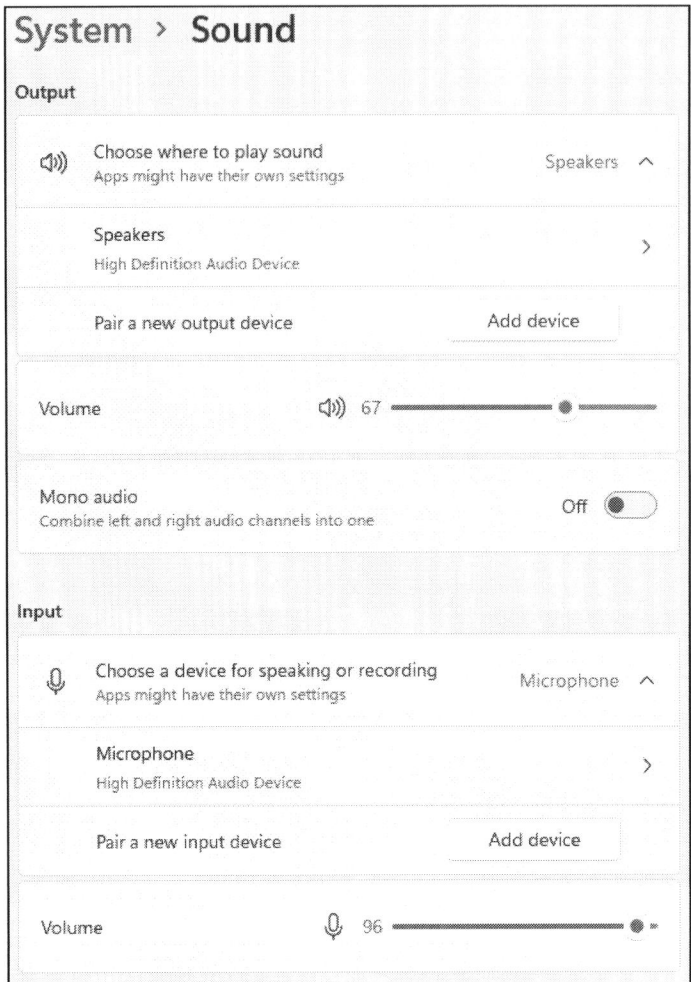

Figure 9.3

- **Notifications** – Lets you enable and disable notifications for things like apps, calls, and updates.

- **Focus Assist** – Here you can let Windows know what types of notifications you want to be shown and when you want to see them so you can make sure to stay "focused" on your work.

- **Power** – This allows you to configure settings for turning off your monitor and putting your PC to sleep, as well as other power settings.

- **Storage** – Lets you see your local storage drives and devices, free space, and what types of data are using up space on the specific device. You can also remove temporary files from here to free up disk space.

Chapter 9 – Windows 11 Settings

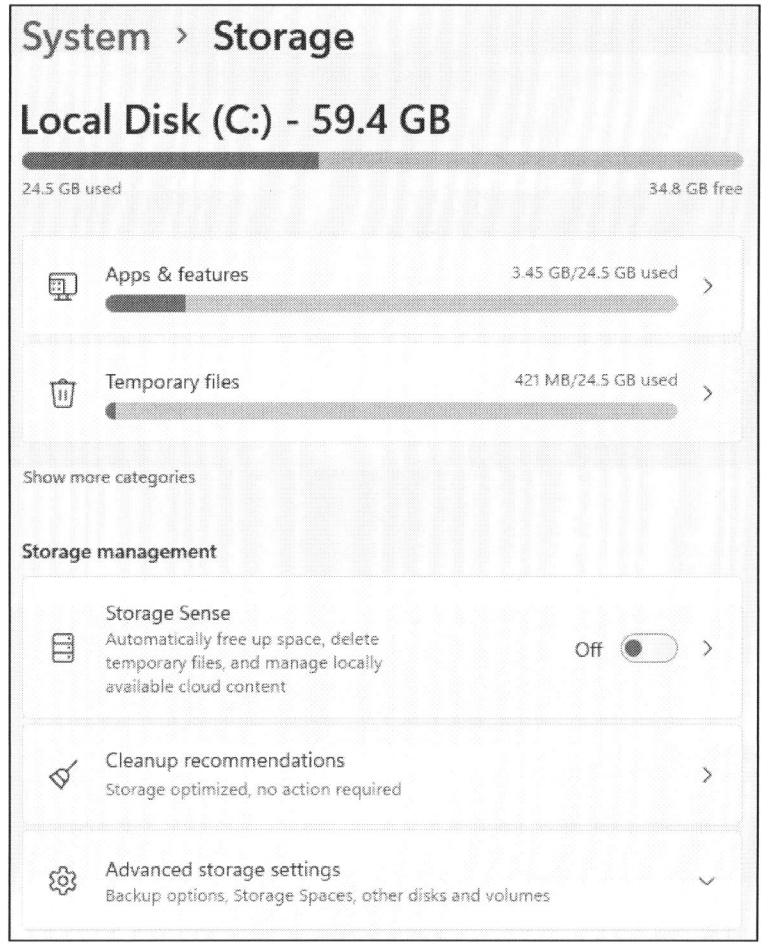

Figure 9.4

- **Nearby sharing** – If you plan on sharing files with family members or coworkers in the office, you can configure which of your devices will allow sharing and where files that are shared with you are stored.

- **Multitasking** – Here is where you can adjust settings for things such as working with multiple windows or even Windows Virtual Desktops.

- **Troubleshoot** – Windows has many built in troubleshooting tools to help you fix common problems such as your printer not working or sound issues etc. Many times, Windows will ask you if you want to run the troubleshooter when it senses a problem, but you can also come here and run one of the many troubleshooting tools manually.

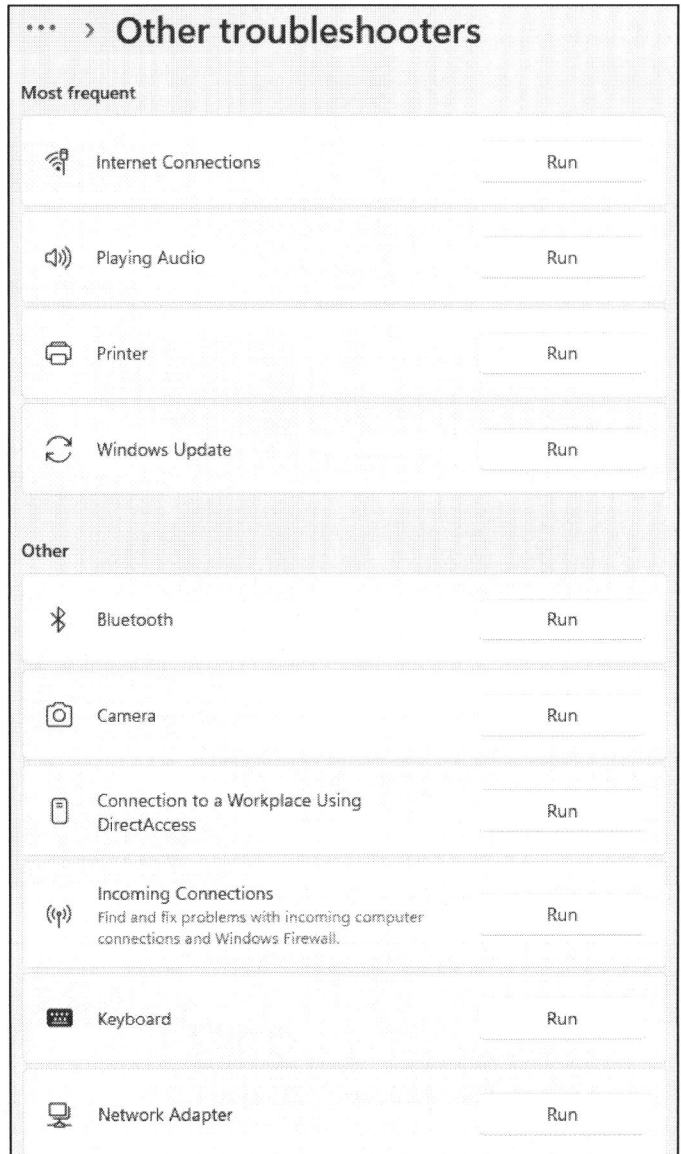
Figure 9.5

- **Recovery** – If your computer is not starting up correctly or having other issues such as constantly crashing or freezing up then you can come here to change things such as startup settings or even do a reset of your PC to reinstall Windows.

- **Projecting to this PC** – Depending on your computer's configuration, you might be able to use it as a projector screen for another computer or mobile device.

Chapter 9 – Windows 11 Settings

- **Remote Desktop** – This is where you can enable or disable Remote Desktop and assign users access to this feature. Remote Desktop allows you to remotely control a computer over the network, or even over the Internet.

- **Clipboard** – The Windows Clipboard is where items such as text and pictures are stored when you copy them so you can then paste them somewhere else as needed. Here you can configure sharing your clipboard data across devices and also the ability to have more than one item at a time be stored on the clipboard.

Bluetooth & Devices

- **Bluetooth** – Here you can enable or disable Bluetooth as needed.

- **Devices** - This is where you go to add devices such as printers, keyboards, displays etc.

- **Printers & scanners** – This shows you your installed printers and scanners and allows you to manage or remove them. You can also add a new printer and scanner from here.

- **Your phone** - Windows can connect to your smartphone allowing you to view things such as your pictures and text messages.

- **Cameras** - Here is where you can manage connected cameras such as webcams.

- **Mouse** – Shows configuration options for your mouse, such as the primary mouse button and wheel scrolling options.

- **Pen & Windows Ink** – Windows as a way for you to use an electronic pen or your finger to draw and do handwriting if your PC supports it. Here is where you can go to change these types of options.

- **AutoPlay** – Decides what Windows does by default when you do things like insert a removable drive, memory card, camera, CD, and so on.

- **USB** – You can't do much here except have Windows tell you when there is a problem with one of your USB devices.

Chapter 9 – Windows 11 Settings

Network & Internet

- **Ethernet** – This shows your Ethernet connection status and gives you another place to change adapter, sharing, and firewall settings.

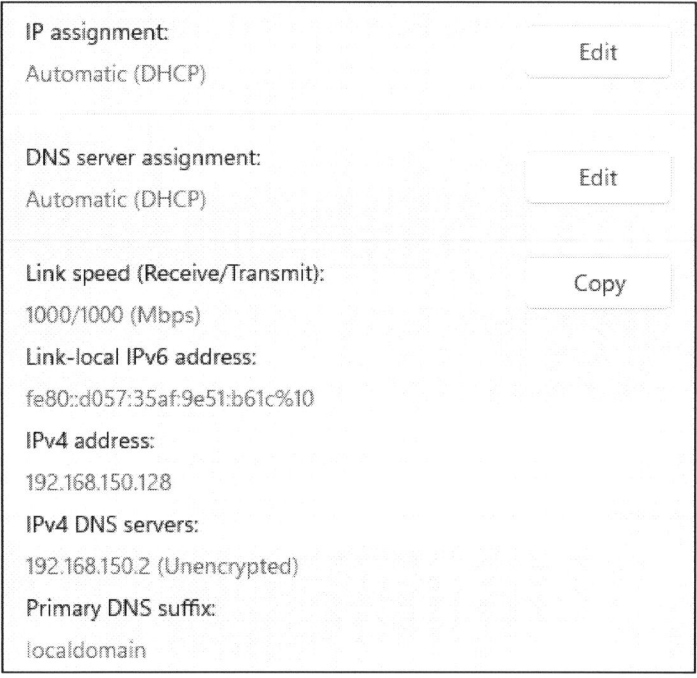

Figure 9.6

- **VPN** – Lets you add VPN (virtual private network) connections which is a secure connection between two computers over the Internet.

- **Mobile hotspot** – If you want to share your Internet connection with other devices, you can configure it here. This way your computer will act as a Wi-Fi hotspot.

Chapter 9 – Windows 11 Settings

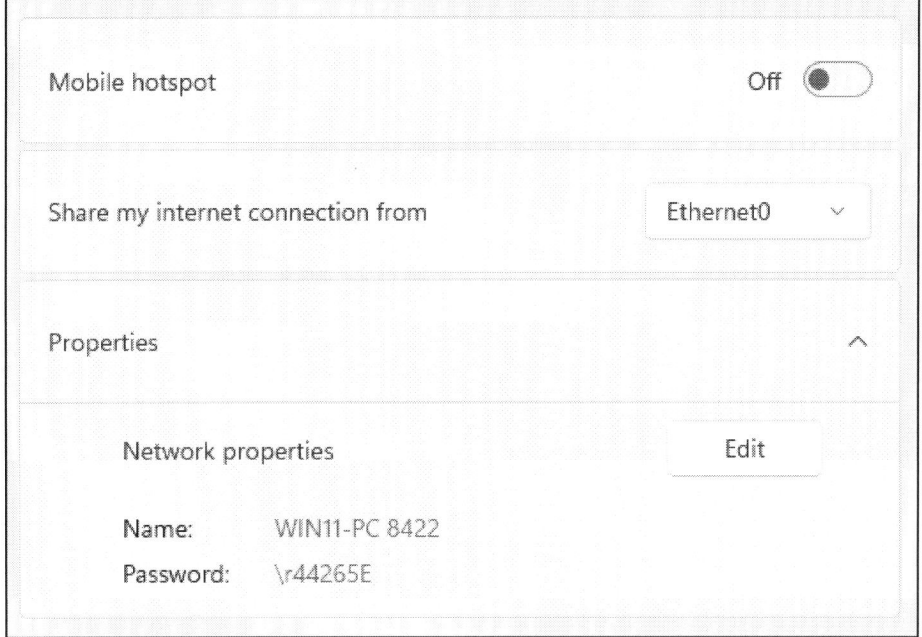

Figure 9.7

- **Airplane Mode** – If you are going to be traveling with your laptop and need to disable a configured cellular connection you can put it in Airplane Mode just like you can with your smartphone.

- **Proxy** – Proxies are not used too often these days but if you use a proxy server at the office for your Internet connection you can configure those settings from here.

- **Dial-up** – If you need to set up some type of legacy dial-up connection, you can configure that here assuming your computer has the right kind of hardware such as a modem to make this type of connection.

- **Advanced network settings** – Here you can disable various network adapters as well as see data usage for those individual connections.

Chapter 9 – Windows 11 Settings

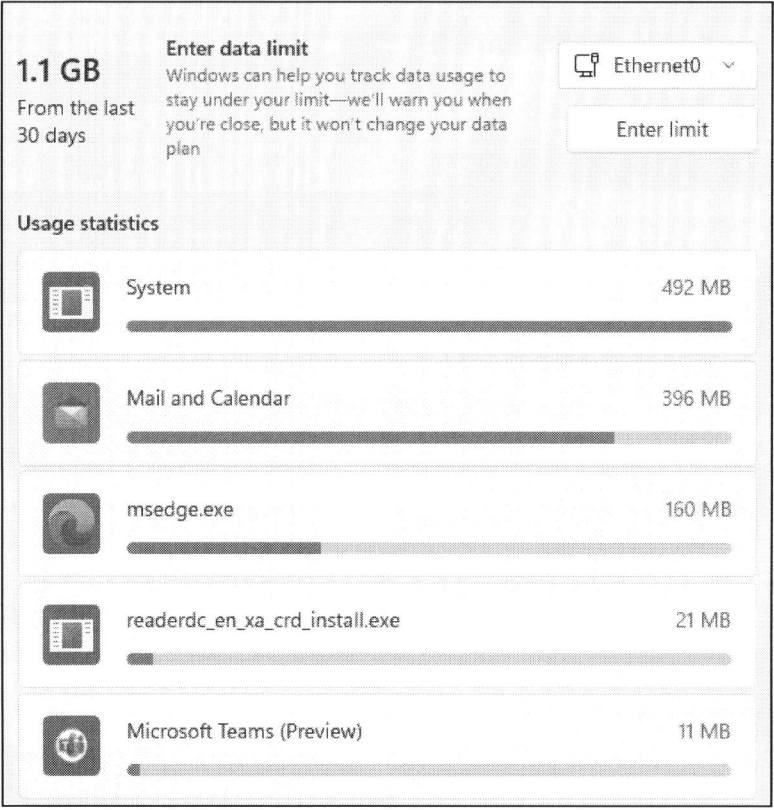

Figure 9.8

Personalization

- **Background** – Here you can change your desktop background wallpaper image or choose a solid color if you like.

- **Colors** – Here you can change accent colors for things like the Taskbar and window bars.

- **Themes** – Themes allow you to customize the look of Windows by using a preconfigured design for things such as the desktop background, color, mouse cursor, and system sounds.

- **Lock Screen** – If you set your computer to lock itself then you can still configure certain apps to show things like their status on your lock screen so you don't need to unlock your computer to get updates.

Chapter 9 – Windows 11 Settings

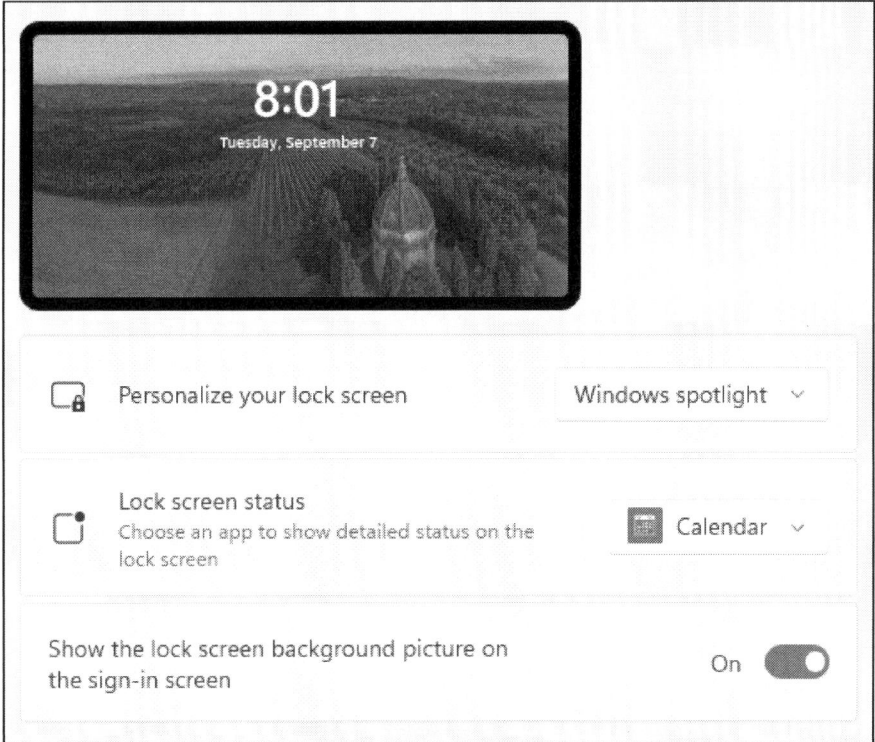

Figure 9.9

- **Start** – This section allows you to further customize the Start menu, such as pinning commonly used apps to the menu itself.

- **Taskbar** – This section allows you to further customize the Taskbar, which I went over in Chapter 3.

- **Fonts** – View your installed fonts (typestyles) and install more or uninstall ones you don't need.

- **Device usage** – Here is where you can tell Windows what you plan on using your computer for. Then Windows will use this information to show you related tips, ads and recommendations to help your user experience. I like to leave all of these disabled so I don't get bombarded with useless information.

Chapter 9 – Windows 11 Settings

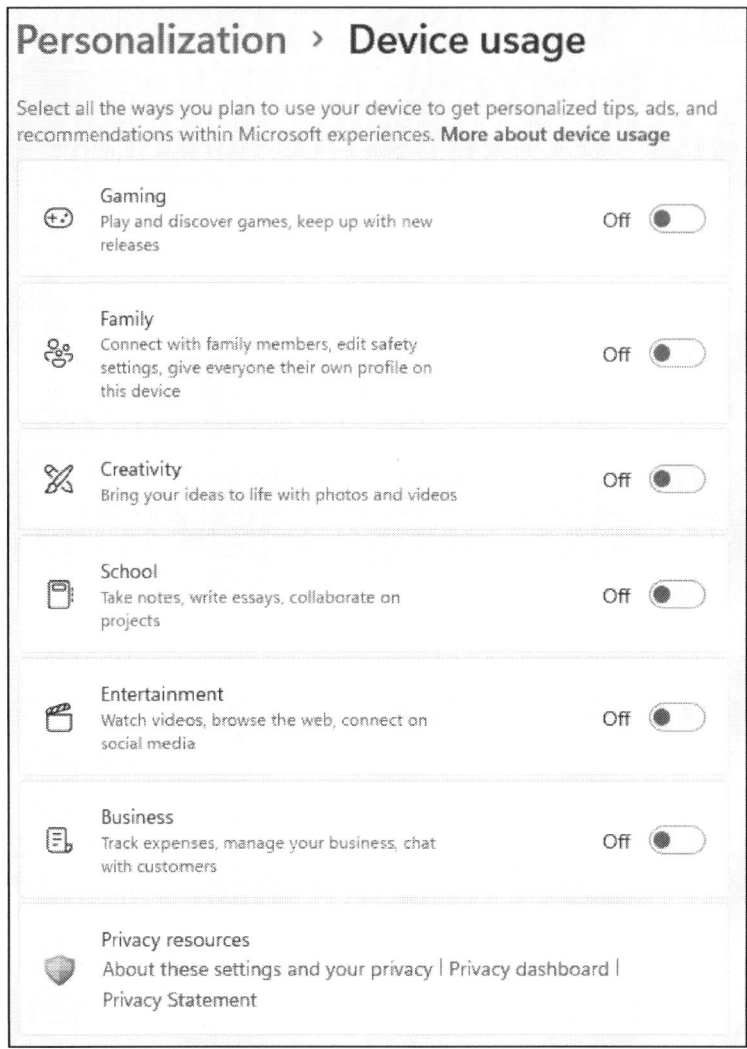

Figure 9.10

Apps

- **Apps & features** – In this section there are options to choose where you can get apps from, as well as a way to uninstall apps and other programs.

- **Default Apps** – Here you can tell Windows what programs or apps you want it to use for things such as email, music, photos, and your web browser.

- **Offline Maps** – Windows comes with a map app called Maps and if you would like to download maps offline in case you need to use them without an Internet connection then you can do so from here.

- **Optional features** – Here you can view, add and remove many additional features that Windows has to offer such as default apps like Notepad and Windows Media Player as well as custom regional fonts.

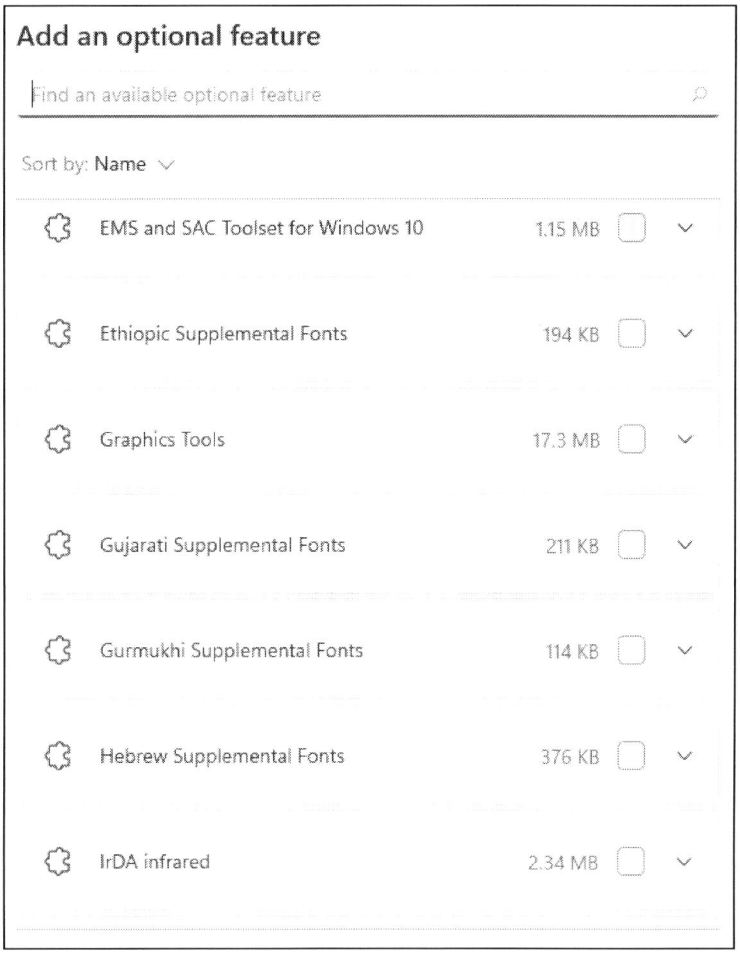

Figure 9.11

- **Apps for websites** – Here you can enable or disable certain apps from being opened by your web browser.

- **Video playback** – If you would like to change your video playback quality settings then you can do so here.

- **Startup** – This area is very useful because it shows what apps are set to start with your computer. You might find that a certain app is causing problems by running all of the time or using too many resources so you can disable (or enable) these apps from this area.

Chapter 9 – Windows 11 Settings

Figure 9.12

Accounts

- **Your info** – Shows you information about the currently logged in user and allows you to manage your account as well as add a picture.

- **Email & accounts** – Here you can manage various email and app accounts as well as calendar and contact information.

- **Sign-in options** – In this section, you can determine when Windows requires you to sign in again after a certain event like the computer going to sleep. You can also change your password or add a PIN if you would rather use that instead of a password.

- **Family & other users** – Here you can add another user account to your computer.

Chapter 9 – Windows 11 Settings

- **Windows backup** – If you want to back up your files to your OneDrive account or set up the syncing feature between your computers then you can do so from here.

Figure 9.13

- **Access work or school** – Here you can connect to your school account to sync things such as email and apps and connect to school resources assuming your school allows you to do so.

Time & Language

- **Date & time** – Provides a place to change the date, time, and time zone, as well as turn daylight savings settings on or off.

- **Language & Region** – Here you can change your region to get local content. Windows will display all text in your default language which you can change if required. You can also add additional languages to be used on your computer as well.

- **Typing** – Windows has some of the same spelling tools as you would see in Word where it can highlight or automatically correct misspelled words. It also has a feature where it will offer word suggestions as you type. If that is not something you are interested in using, then you can disable these features here.

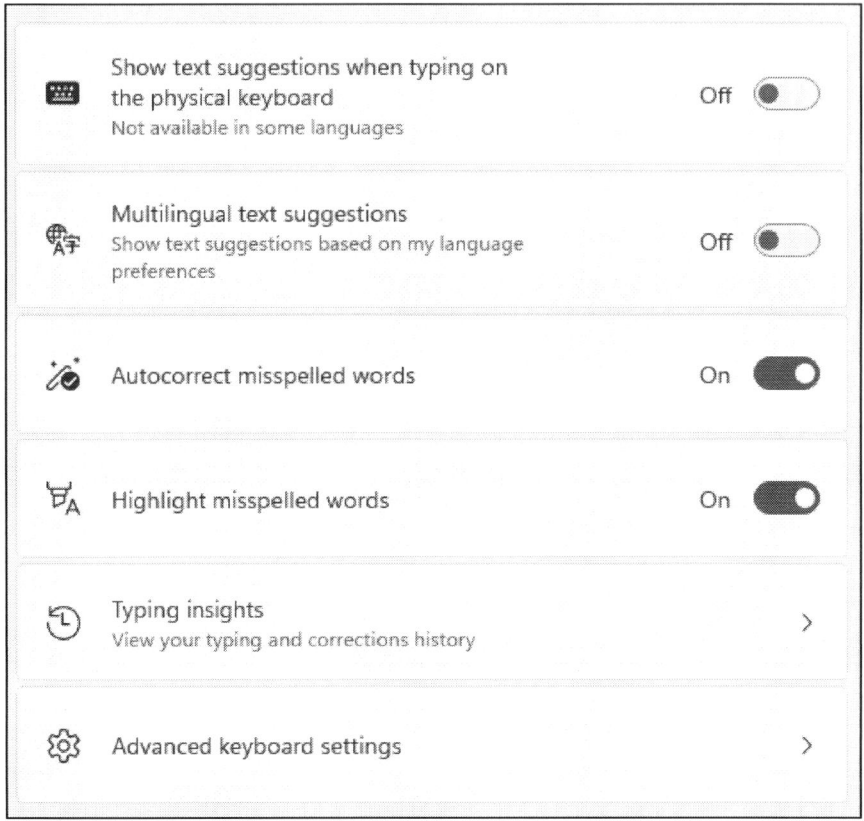

Figure 9.14

- **Speech** – Windows allows you to use a microphone to speak commands into your computer and to also do things such as translate speech to text. In this section, you can configure your microphone settings, language defaults and also what language is spoken when a Windows app speaks to you.

Gaming

- **Xbox Game bar** – Lets you record videos and screenshots while playing your favorite video games assuming you are playing them on a Microsoft Xbox.

- **Captures** – Determines where your game video captures and screenshots are saved.

- **Game Mode** – When this is enabled, Windows will optimize your display for video games.

Accessibility

- **Vision** – If you have trouble seeing things on your screen then you can come to this section and enable features such as the magnifying glass or increase the text size used in Windows etc.

- **Hearing** – Here you can enable settings for those who are hearing impaired such as setting up visual notifications or turning on the caption feature.

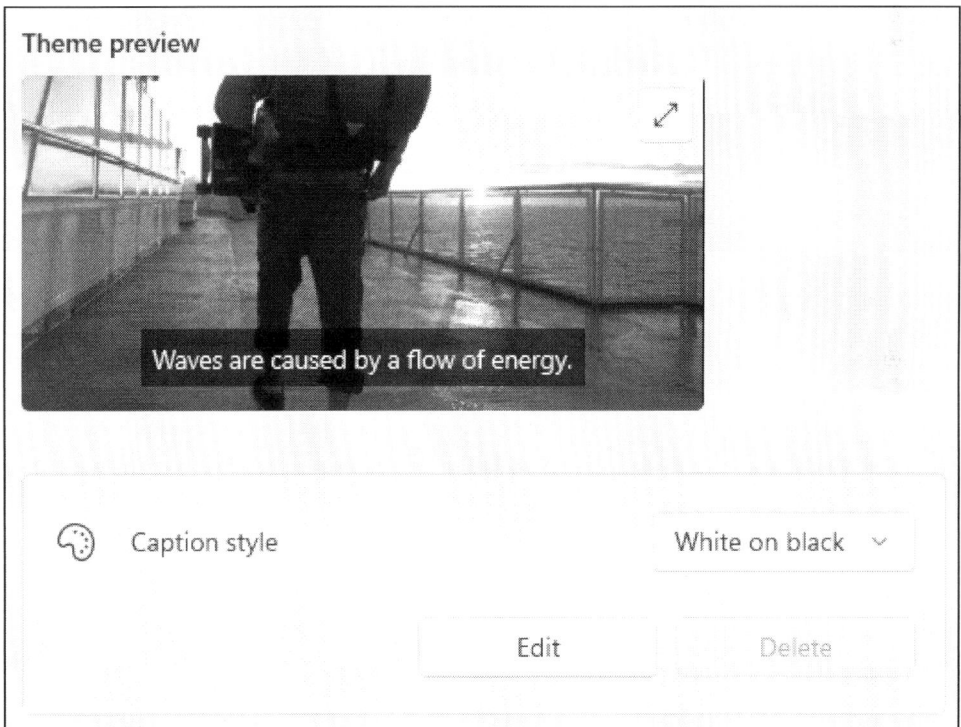

Figure 9.15

- **Interaction** – This section has options to help you interact with your computer such as adjusting how your mouse works or setting up voice recognition and text to speech.

Chapter 9 – Windows 11 Settings

Privacy & security

- **Security** – Here you can view and adjust Windows Firewall security as well as view the status of your antivirus software. If you are using a mobile device that has an internet connection, then you can locate it using the *Find my device* setting.

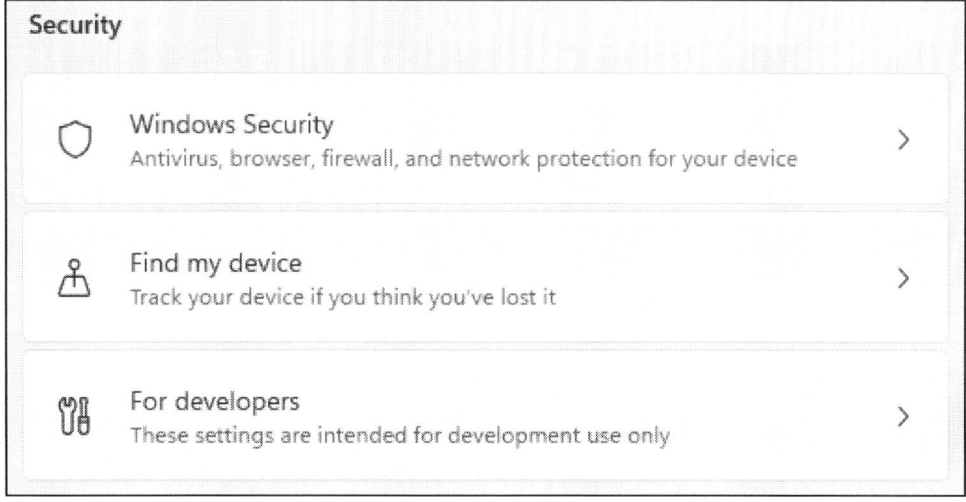

Figure 9.15

- **Windows permissions** – Windows will require your permission when it comes to giving certain features access to things such as advertisements, speech recognition, and keeping a log of the things you do on your computer. If you want to restrict what Windows is keeping track of then you can do so from here.

Chapter 9 – Windows 11 Settings

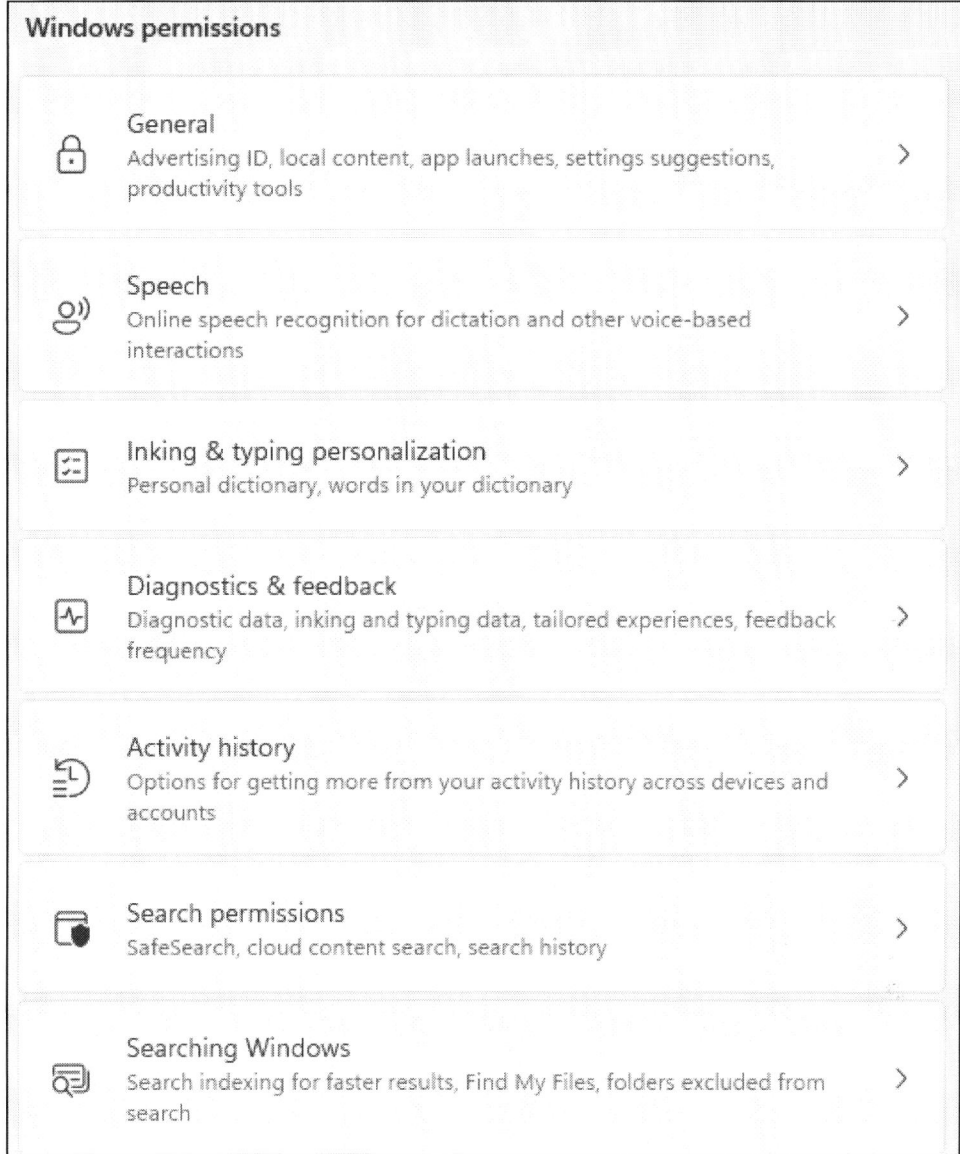

Figure 9.16

- **App permissions** – Since Windows comes with many built in apps and also allows you to install even more apps, you can come to this section to allow or block certain apps from doing things such as accessing your camera, location, contents and so on.

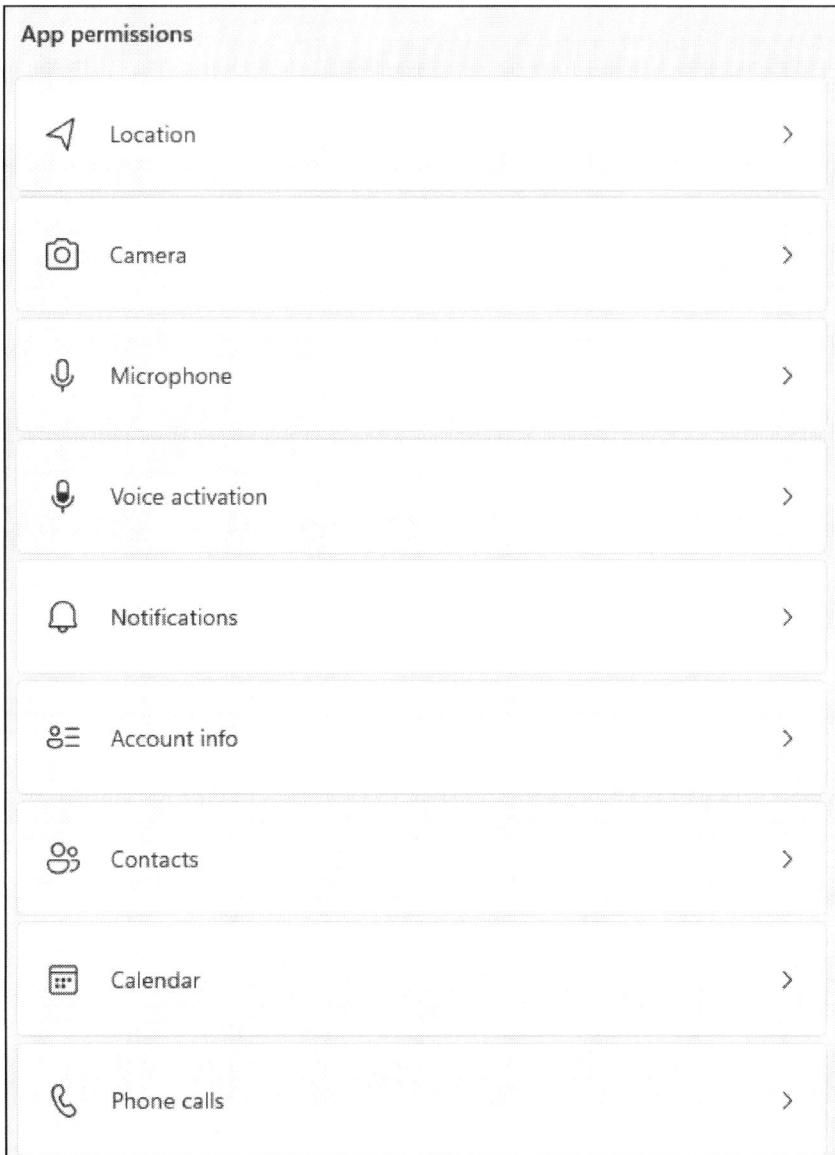

Figure 9.17

Windows Update

As you probably know, Microsoft releases updates for Windows (and other software) on a regular basis. Some of these updates are critical security updates while others are meant to add new features and functionality to Windows. With older versions of Windows, you were able to disable these updates but now they are mandatory and the only way to avoid them is to not be connected to the internet.

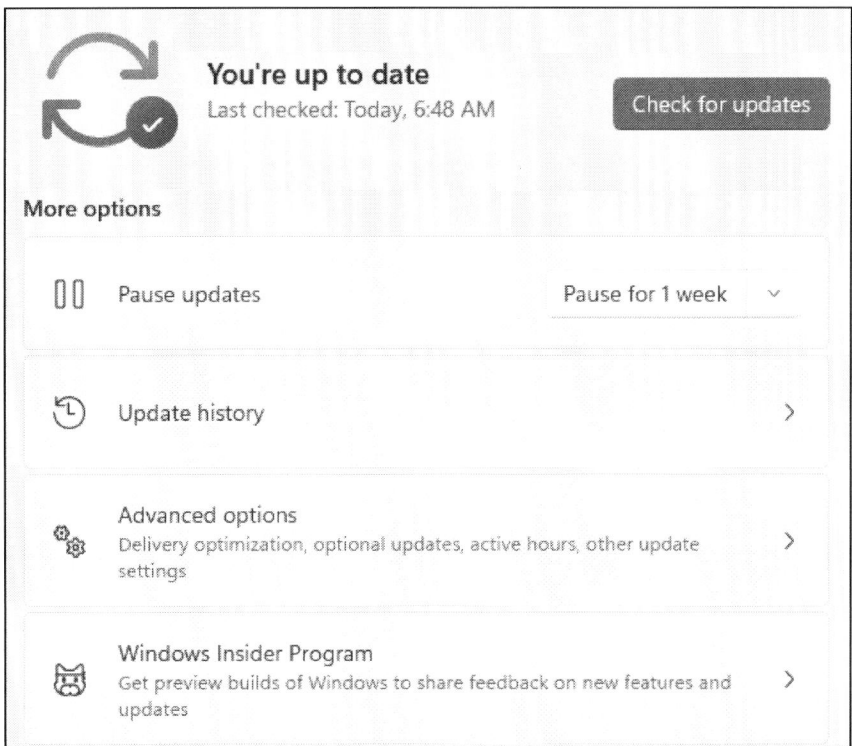

Figure 9.18

There are some adjustments you can do from the Windows Update section to tweak how updates are applied to your computer.

- **Pause updates** – If you need to pause the installation of updates to make sure they don't interfere with your software or just don't want to deal with them at the moment, you can pause them for up to 5 weeks.

- **Update history** – Here you can view the installed updates which can come in handy to diagnose any issues that might have been caused by a particular update.

Chapter 9 – Windows 11 Settings

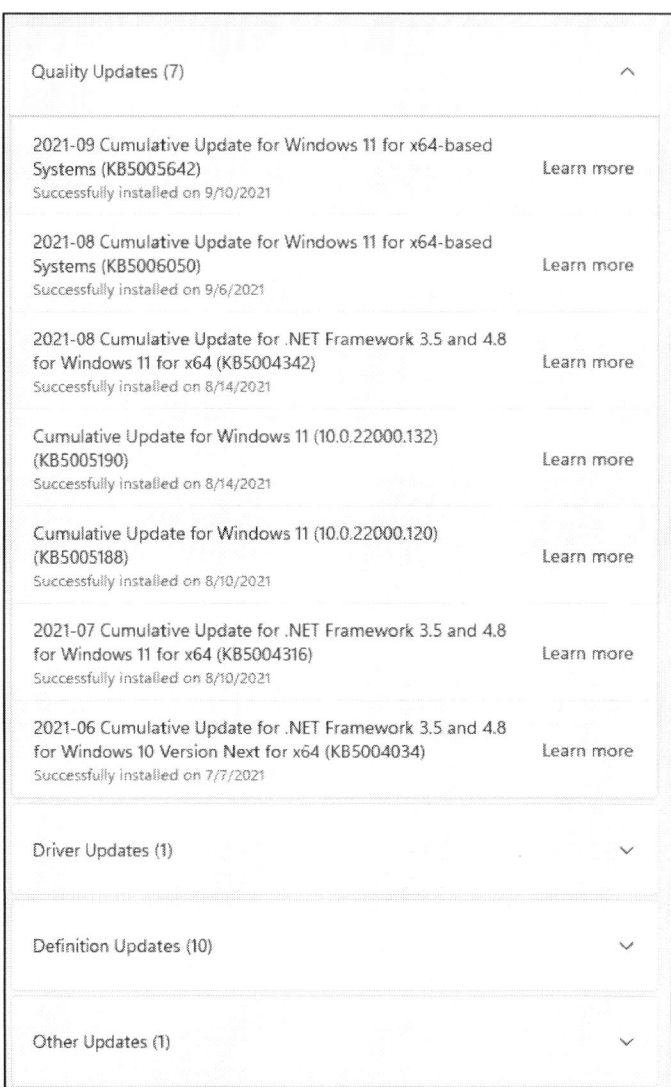

Figure 9.19

- **Advanced options** – There are several options here that will let you customize how Windows Update works such as allowing Windows Update to automatically update other software such as Microsoft Office. You can also set your "active hours" so that Windows won't try and install any updates during that time to avoid interrupting your work.

- **Windows Insider Program** - If you would like to receive updates and new features before they are officially released, you can join the Windows Insider Program to have these features installed on your computer. Just keep in mind that there is a chance they may cause problems since they are not officially ready to be rolled out to the general public.

Chapter 10 – Networking

Computer networks are everywhere these days, and everything seems to be connected to everything else, so it's important to know a little about basic networking to be able to connect your computer to things like other computers, wireless printers, etc. After all, the Internet is the world's biggest network, so without networking, we would all be just talking to ourselves... at least when it comes to our electronic gadgets.

Networking with Windows is not all that difficult if you are just setting up a basic home network or small office network. When you start dealing with domains (discussed next) and multiple sites and networks connected together, then things get a little more interesting. But if you just want to network a few computers together, then it's fairly easy to do. I'm not going to go through a step-by-step demonstration because there are too many variables that won't relate to your configuration, so I will just go over the basics.

Workgroups
In order for your computers to be able to communicate with each other on a network, they need to be in the same, let's say "club" if you will. For Windows, this club that your computers are a part of is called a Workgroup. These workgroup computers are all equal when it comes to who is in charge and no computer has any authority over another computer. The default workgroup name for Windows is actually called Workgroup, but you can change it to whatever you like as long as all the computers you want in the workgroup have the same workgroup name as well. All the computers have their own local user accounts, and if you want to access another computer from yours, then you need to have an account on that computer as well.

Domains
If you work at a company with a reasonable number of computers that run Windows, then you are most likely part of a Windows domain. In a domain, all

Chapter 10 – Networking

access and security is controlled by centralized servers called domain controllers. You log into your computer with your domain username and password and that determines what level of access you have to all network resources like file servers and printers. Using domains makes it easy for network administrators to control user accounts and permissions since it can all be done from one place and apply to the entire network.

To check your workgroup name or to see if you are a part of a domain you can go to the *System* settings and then the *About* section. Then you will see a link that says Domain or workgroup which you can then click on to take you to screen as seen in figure 10.2. Next to the word Workgroup will be the workgroup name. (In my example it's called WORKGROUP.) If your computer were joined to a domain, it would say *domain* rather than *Workgroup* in this section.

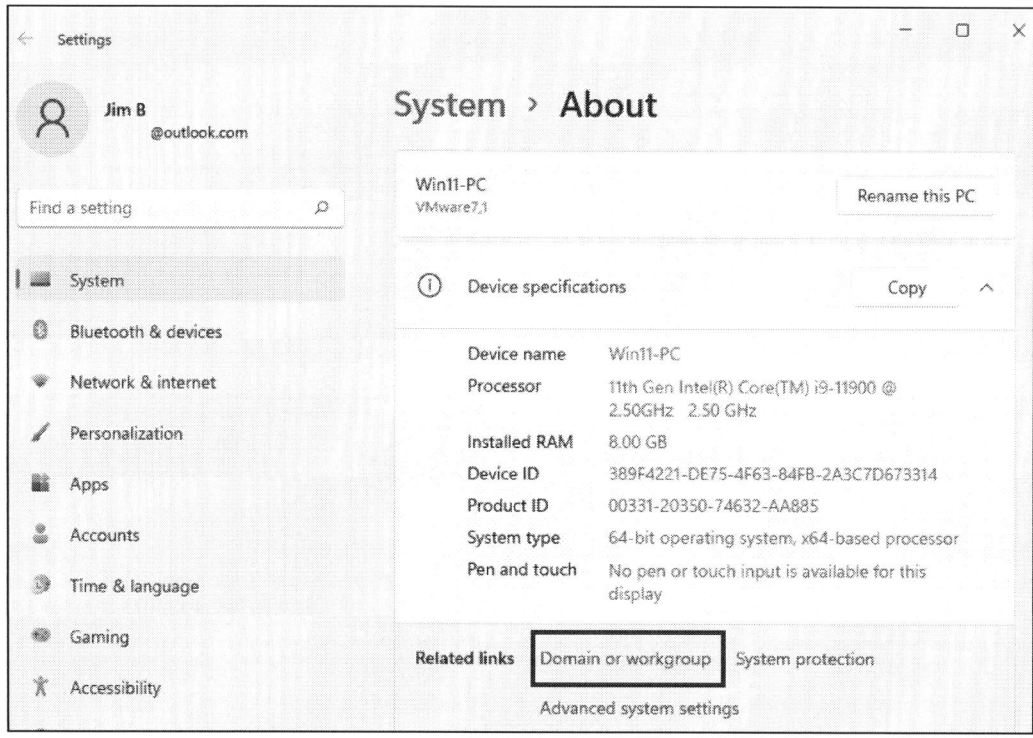

Figure 10.1

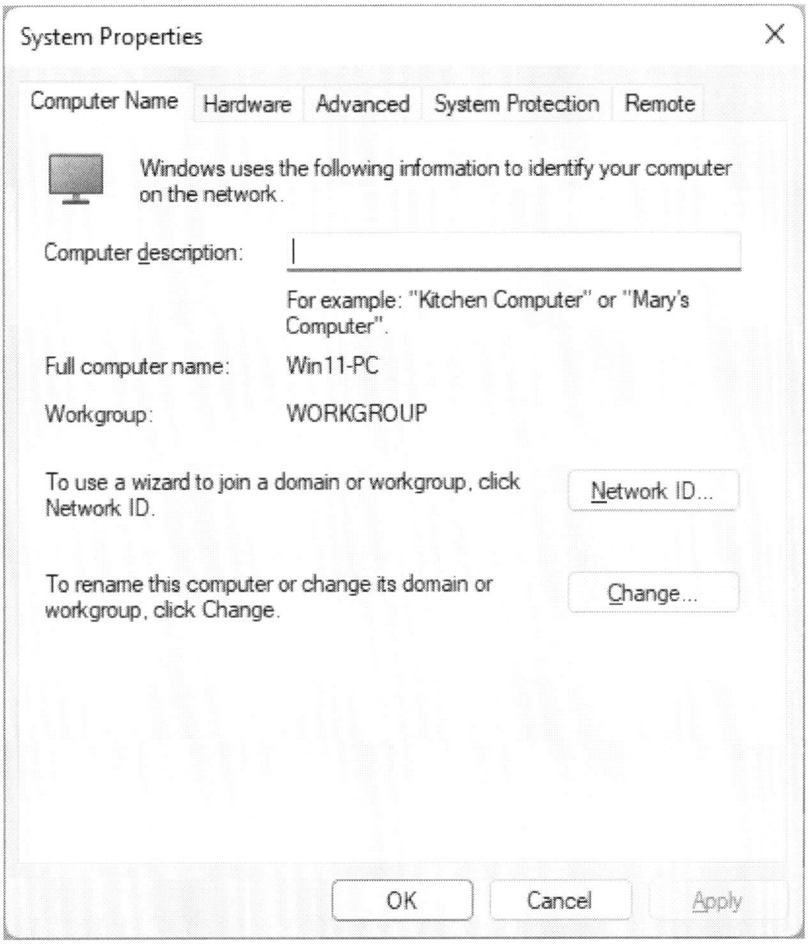

Chapter 10 – Networking

Figure 10.2

IP Addresses and Configuration

Computers and other devices on a network use IP addresses to communicate with each other. MAC (media access control) addresses are also used for network communication, but that's a story for another day!

An IP address is a number (for the sake of simplicity) that is assigned to a computer that is then used to communicate with other computers and devices that also have an IP address assigned to them. It consists of 4 sets of numbers (called octets) and looks something like this – 192.168.10.240. There are several types of address classes, and things can get really complicated, so I will just stick with the basics, so you have an understanding of how IP addresses are used.

When you want to connect to another computer on the network (or even to a website) you can type in its name and then a service called DNS (Domain Name

Chapter 10 – Networking

System) translates that computer or website name into the IP address of that computer or web server. That way you don't have to memorize IP addresses and only need to know the computer name or website name. On a network you can't have the same IP address assigned to two devices otherwise there will be a conflict.

There are also what are known as public and private IP addresses. Public IP addresses are used for things such as web servers and are unique to that server (meaning that IP address can't be used on any other public\Internet device in the world). Private IP addresses, on the other hand, can be used by anyone on their internal network and assigned to devices that only communicate with other internal devices. That doesn't mean these internal devices can't connect to the Internet or other public devices. To do this, the private IP address is translated to a public IP address through the process of NAT (Network Address Translation). This process is beyond the scope of this book, but feel free to look it up if you want to learn more about it.

So the bottom line is that your computer needs an IP address to communicate on the network and even to get on the Internet. There are a few ways to find the IP address of your computer, and I will now go over what I think is the easiest one. If you open a command prompt (which is a way to run text based commands on your computer as they did before Windows), you can type in a certain command to find your IP address information. To open a command prompt simply type in **cmd** from the search box or from Cortana and you will be shown a window with a black background and flashing cursor.

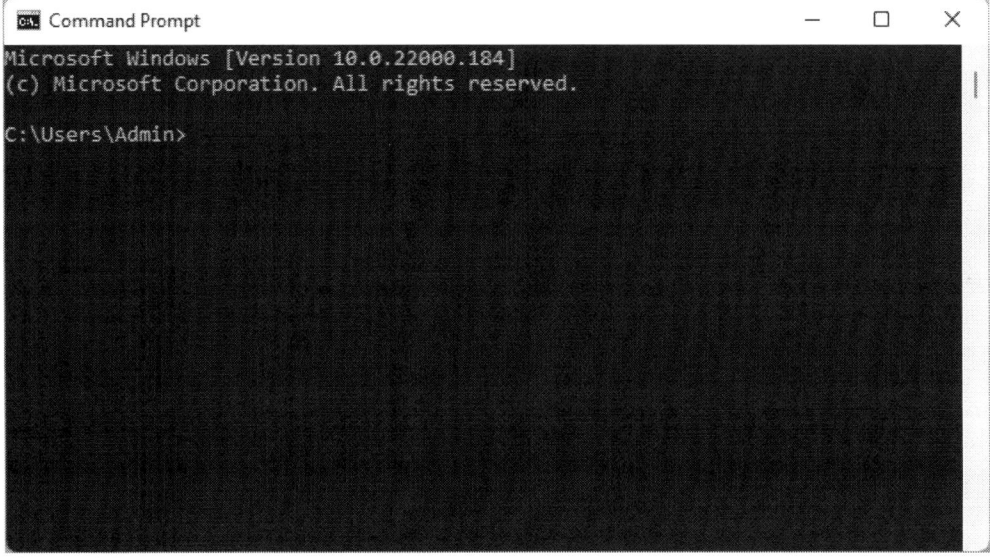

Figure 10.3

Chapter 10 – Networking

From this box, all you need to do is type in the command **ipconfig** to be shown the basic IP configuration of your computer (figure 10.4). Keep in mind that the information given here will vary from computer to computer based on how many network connections you have, such as wireless and Ethernet (plugged in), and so on.

```
C:\Windows\system32\cmd.exe                                    —    □    ×

Microsoft Windows [Version 10.0.19042.1165]
(c) Microsoft Corporation. All rights reserved.

C:\Windows\system32>ipconfig

Windows IP Configuration

Ethernet adapter Ethernet:

   Connection-specific DNS Suffix  . :
   Link-local IPv6 Address . . . . . : fe80::2472:73cf:552f:e8cf%3
   IPv4 Address. . . . . . . . . . . : 192.168.1.12
   Subnet Mask . . . . . . . . . . . : 255.255.255.0
   Default Gateway . . . . . . . . . : 192.168.1.1

Wireless LAN adapter Local Area Connection* 1:

   Media State . . . . . . . . . . . : Media disconnected
   Connection-specific DNS Suffix  . :
```

Figure 10.4

As you can see in my example, my IP address is **192.168.1.12**. For now, you only need to be concerned with the IPv4 address, but soon we will all be using IPv6 addresses since we are out of publicly available IPv4 addresses to assign to new public devices. You might also notice that I have a network connection for a Wireless LAN adapter but it's not in use so therefore it doesn't have an IP address. You need to know which network interface you are dealing with when running this command to get the information you need.

There is a more advanced version of the ipconfig command you can run to get a lot more detailed information about all your network connections. To run this command just type in **ipconfig /all**.

Chapter 10 – Networking

Dynamic and Static IP Addresses

One more thing I want to mention about IP addresses is the difference between a static IP address and a dynamic IP address. Each one has its place in networking, so it's important to know the basic difference between the two.

A static IP address is an address that does not change over time unless changed manually. It is used when you need the IP address or network location to remain the same consistently. A good example of this is for a web server. If you go to www.google.com you are really going to the IP address of 66.102.7.99. If this were to change suddenly, you would not be able to get to Google unless you knew the new IP address or until Google updated their DNS records. Most of the time your servers at work will use static IP addresses so you will always be able to access them and so that your network administrators will know how to get to them.

Dynamic IP addresses are what you will most likely be dealing with at home for your computer and other devices on your network. A dynamic IP address is an address that can change from time to time. It is mostly used when having a consistent IP address is not necessary. An example of this would be the IP address your modem or router you use for the internet assigns your computer when it boots up. When you reboot your computer, there is a chance that your computer will be assigned a different IP address based on how long the lease for that address was configured. This is process is done using DHCP. Your workstation at work most likely has a dynamic IP address since there is usually no need for it to have the same IP address all the time. Dynamic IP addresses are leased from the DHCP server for a period of time and then your computer will request a renewal or a new IP address when the lease expires.

DHCP

I want to mention DHCP really quickly since I was just talking about it in the last paragraph. DHCP (Dynamic Host Configuration Protocol) simplifies the management of IP address configuration by automating address configuration for network clients. In order for DHCP to work, you need to have a device acting as a DCHP server. This device can be a computer, router, or another type of network device. The DHCP server is configured with a range or ranges of IP addresses that can be used to give to clients that request one. It can also be configured with other network parameters. For a client to be able to obtain information from a DHCP server, it must be DHCP enabled. When it is configured this way, then it will look for a DHCP server when it starts up.

Chapter 10 – Networking

Wireless Setup
Nowadays people seem to use wireless (Wi-Fi) for their Internet connection rather than plugging into a modem with a cable. This makes sense because everything is wireless enabled and that way you don't have to be tied down by cables. With Windows 11 it's pretty easy to get your computer connected to your wireless connection and online. The first thing you need to check for is to make sure you actually have a wireless adapter in your computer and that it's enabled. To check your wireless adapter status, go to the Windows 11 Settings, then to Network & Internet, and then look for an entry for Wi-Fi.

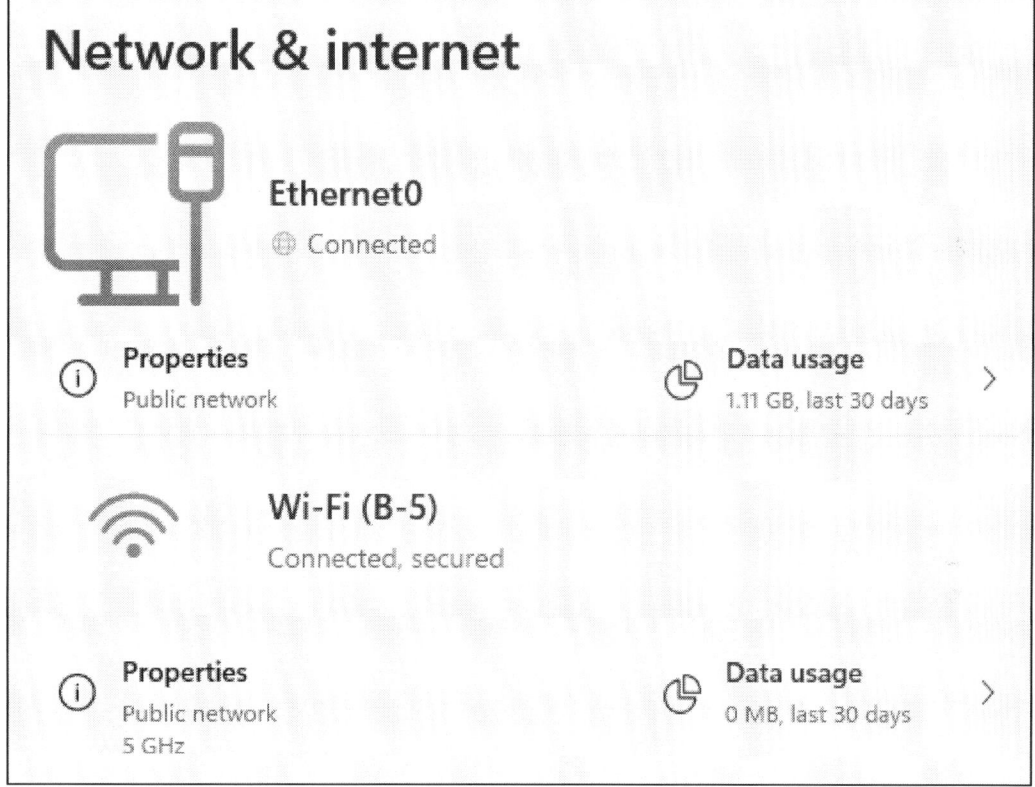

Figure 10.5

If your wireless adapter is not enabled, then you can click on the network icon down by the clock in the taskbar and enable your adapter by clicking on the wireless symbol as seen in figure 10.6.

Clicking on the right arrow will show you the available Wi-Fi networks that are in range of your computer and their signal strength (figure 10.7). Then you will be able to connect to one of the networks in range assuming you have permission to do so, because most of the time they are password protected and if they aren't,

Chapter 10 – Networking

then it's probably not a good idea to connect (it might be a trap from someone looking to hack into your computer). If it's somewhere like a Starbucks that offers free Wi-Fi with no password, then you are usually okay to connect to it. Notice how all of the connections in figure 10.7 have a padlock symbol? That means that they are all password protected so you won't be able to connect to any of them unless you know the password.

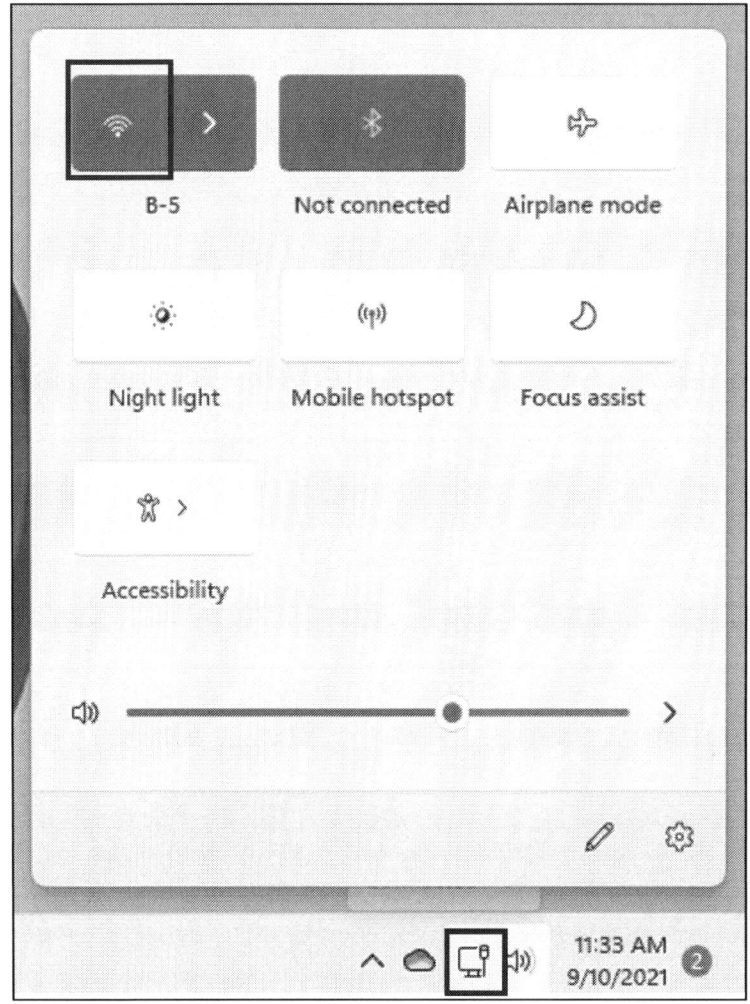

Figure 10.6

If you've ever heard the term SSID used when talking or reading about wireless connections, it is referring to the name of the connection itself. SSID stands for service set identifier, and this name can be customized within your modem or router to make it easy to identify your network when adding a device to connect to it. In figures 10.6 and 10.7, I am connected to the B-5 network and B-5 is the

Chapter 10 – Networking

SSID and was configured in the wireless router settings. If you know how to get into your wireless router settings, then you can change this name.

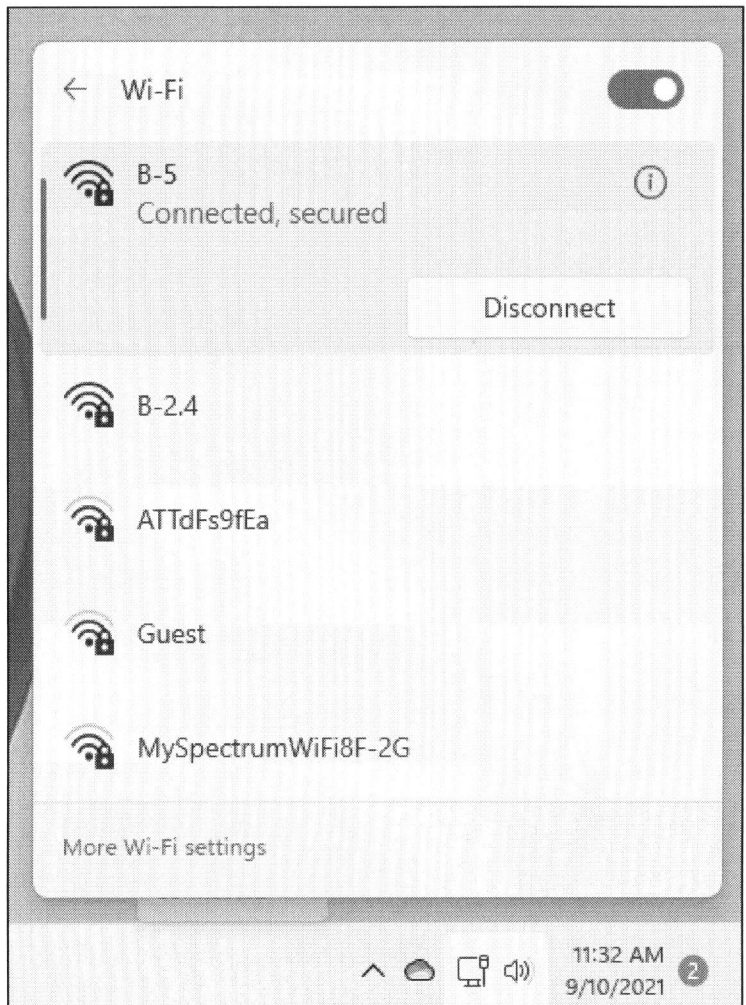

Figure 10.7

 Even though today's modern wireless adapters boast speeds that are higher than what most people have for their broadband connection, don't expect to have as fast of a connection compared to using a cable.

Chapter 11 – Basic Troubleshooting

Just like everything else in life, nothing works perfectly all the time, and that goes for computers and Windows as well. But if you learn some basic troubleshooting skills, you can fix a lot of the common problems you may encounter as you use your computer on a regular basis. In this chapter, I will discuss many common Windows issues and tell you what you can do to attempt to fix these issues. Some of the content in this chapter may be a little advanced for some people, but it can be helpful if you want to take your troubleshooting skills to the next level.

Printer Troubleshooting
Printers have their share of issues and tend to not work properly when you need them the most, but there are several things you can do to get your printer back online if you know what to look for. Printer issues can consist of things such as blank pages printing out, no pages printing out, strange characters on the page, and so on. Here are some fixes you can try for certain types of printer issues:

Nothing printing at all

- Make sure the printer is turned on.

- Make sure the USB cable is connected if that method is being used.

- Check your wireless connection on your computer and printer if using a wireless connection.

- Click the printer queue icon by the clock in the Taskbar and see if there are any failed or backed-up jobs causing your print job not to go through. Clear out any backed-up jobs and try again.

- Look for error messages on your printer screen if it has one.

- See if your printer is listed as "offline" in Devices and Printers.

- Restart the Print Spooler service.

- Look in Device Manager for errors.

Chapter 11 – Basic Troubleshooting

- Turn the printer off and on and maybe reboot the computer as well.

- Print to a different printer (if you have one) to see if the issue is computer or printer specific.

Printing blank pages

- Check the ink levels in the software if it's supported.

- Take the inkjet cartridge out and shake it to see if there appears to be ink in it.

- If you are printing something like black text, try changing it to red to see if it actually prints. (This way you will know it's your black ink cartridge that's causing the problem.)

- Install a new cartridge temporarily (if you have one) to see if it fixes the problem.

- Clean the print heads for inkjet printers using the printer software.

- Take the inkjet cartridges out and clean the tip where the ink comes out with a tissue.

- Take the laser printer toner cartridge out and shake it, then put it back in and try again.

- Make sure you are printing a page with something on it and not a blank page.

Paper jams

- Make sure the paper is properly aligned in the paper tray.

- Try a different paper tray or manual feed tray (if you have one).

- Make sure the paper is not curled or warped.

- Make sure you are not using paper not designed to run through your printer.

- Check the rollers for the paper trays and feeder for excessive wear or try cleaning them.

- Laser printers require periodic cleaning to function at their best.

Strange characters (gibberish) being printed on the page

- Check your printer property settings under the Advanced tab to make sure the right driver is being used.

- Download and install a new driver.

- If you recently installed a new driver or did some type of printer update, see if you can roll back to the old driver.

Wireless and Internet Troubleshooting

When it comes to problems, wireless Internet connections will be more troublesome than wired connections because there is more involved with making a successful wireless connection compared to a wired connection. There is usually more hardware and software configuration with wireless connections that leaves more areas for things to go wrong.

The first step in troubleshooting wireless connections is to see if your computer is connected to your wireless router\access point. The first place you should look is at your wireless connection, and the easiest way to do that is to click on your wireless connection icon in your system tray down by the clock (as shown in figure 11.1). This will tell you if your computer is connected to your access point, and if not, then the first thing you need to do is reconnect it. If it doesn't want to connect, then there is an issue with your access point or the wireless device on your computer. You can try to reboot\reset your access point and see if that fixes it, or try to connect to your access point with a different device such as your smartphone or tablet. If other devices connect successfully, then you know it's the computer that has the problem.

Chapter 11 – Basic Troubleshooting

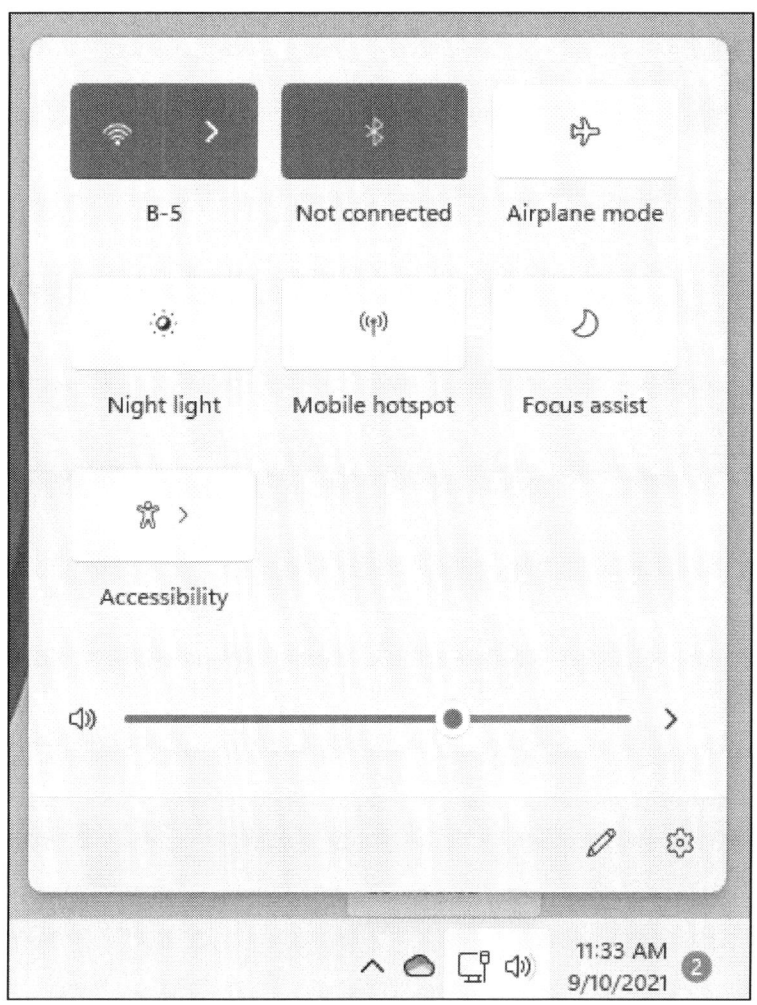
11.1

Another place you can look to see connectivity status is the Network & Internet section in the Windows settings. Here you will be able to see what wireless network your computer is connected to (SSID connection name) as well seeing if the connection is secure or not. Clicking on *Properties* will show you details about your IP address, DNS speed, link speed etc. (figure 11.3).

Chapter 11 – Basic Troubleshooting

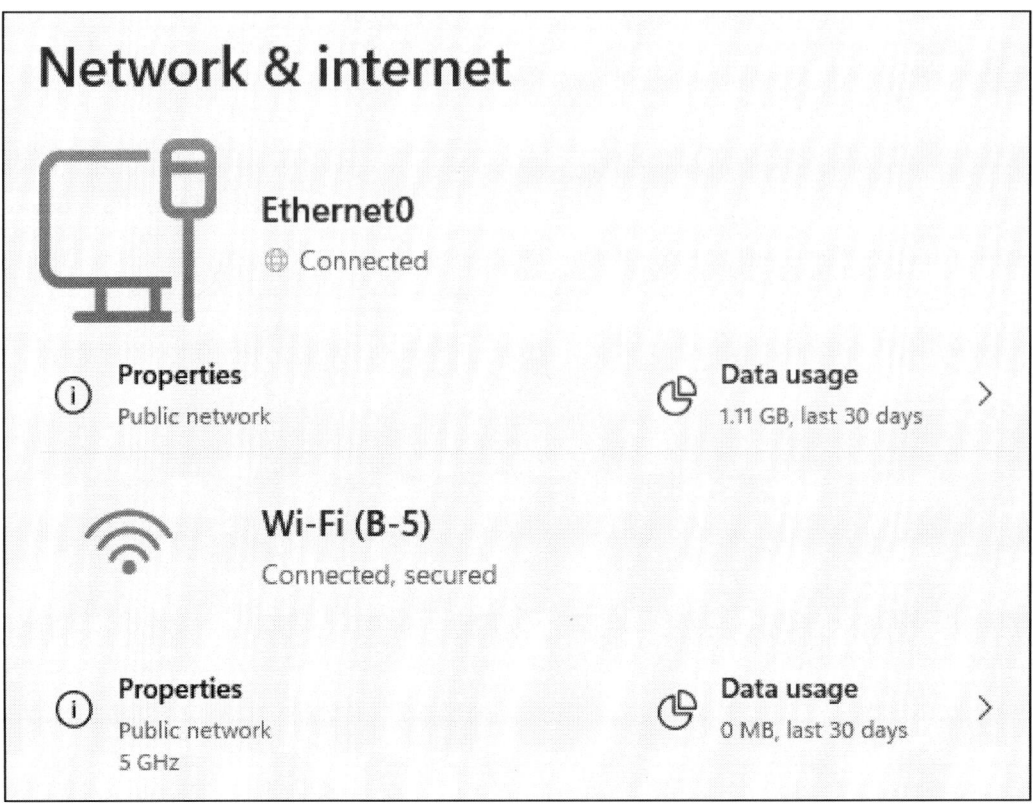

11.2

Chapter 11 – Basic Troubleshooting

IP assignment: Automatic (DHCP)	Edit
DNS server assignment: Automatic (DHCP)	Edit
Link speed (Receive/Transmit): 1000/1000 (Mbps)	Copy
Link-local IPv6 address: fe80::d057:35af:9e51:b61c%10	
IPv4 address: 192.168.150.128	
IPv4 DNS servers: 192.168.150.2 (Unencrypted)	
Primary DNS suffix: localdomain	

11.3

If you are into doing things the old school way, then you can still manage your network settings from the *Network and Sharing Center* which can be found in the Windows Control Panel.

Chapter 11 – Basic Troubleshooting

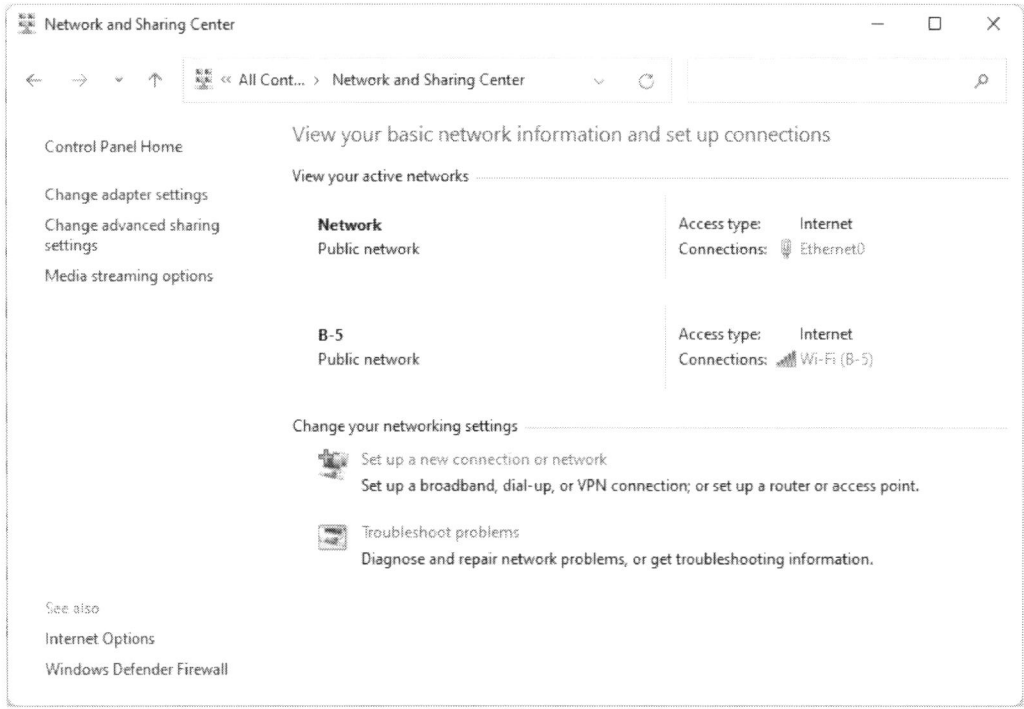

11.4

One important thing to keep in mind with wireless connections is that just because your computer can connect to your router\modem\access point doesn't mean you will have a connection to the Internet. If your router itself doesn't have an Internet connection, then your computer won't either. The devices that you use to make your wireless connection to the Internet rely on each other for their connection. Let's say you have your modem from your ISP connected to your wireless router and then you connect your computer to your router. The modem gets its Internet connection\IP address settings from the ISP, then the router gets its settings from the modem, and finally your computer gets its settings from the router. If one of the devices in the chain is not working correctly, then you will not be getting on the Internet. One method you can try is to turn everything off (or unplug the device if there is no power button) and then turn on the modem first and wait until it's fully started. Then turn on the router and wait until it's started, and finally turn your computer back on. For the modem and router, I would wait a few minutes for each one before assuming they are completely started up.

If your connection to your access point is working, then you will want to see if your computer has an IP address, subnet mask, and default gateway. All of these are needed to make a successful connection to the Internet or any other type of network. You can get this information using the ipconfig command that I discussed

Chapter 11 – Basic Troubleshooting

in Chapter 10. Open a command prompt by typing **cmd** from the run box or Cortana search box and then type **ipconfig**. Then press enter, and it will show you similar information to figure 11.5.

```
Select Command Prompt

Microsoft Windows [Version 10.0.22000.184]
(c) Microsoft Corporation. All rights reserved.

C:\Users\Admin>ipconfig

Windows IP Configuration

Ethernet adapter Ethernet0:

   Connection-specific DNS Suffix  . : localdomain
   Link-local IPv6 Address . . . . . : fe80::d057:35af:9e51:b61c%10
   IPv4 Address. . . . . . . . . . . : 192.168.150.128
   Subnet Mask . . . . . . . . . . . : 255.255.255.0
   Default Gateway . . . . . . . . . : 192.168.150.2

Wireless LAN adapter Local Area Connection* 9:

   Media State . . . . . . . . . . . : Media disconnected
   Connection-specific DNS Suffix  . :

Wireless LAN adapter Local Area Connection* 10:

   Media State . . . . . . . . . . . : Media disconnected
   Connection-specific DNS Suffix  . :

Wireless LAN adapter Wi-Fi:

   Connection-specific DNS Suffix  . :
   Link-local IPv6 Address . . . . . : fe80::1481:1c01:f3ea:3542%26
   IPv4 Address. . . . . . . . . . . : 192.168.1.13
   Subnet Mask . . . . . . . . . . . : 255.255.255.0
   Default Gateway . . . . . . . . . : 192.168.1.1
```
11.5

If you are missing any of this information, then you are not getting the correct IP settings from your DHCP server (which will be your modem or router). If you are getting an IP address that starts with **169.254** then that means your computer can't contact a valid DHCP server and is using what is called an APIPA address, which is when Windows gives itself an IP address. The main problem is that APIPA addresses can't be used to get to the Internet.

Many times, a software or spyware issue can prevent your web browser from accessing web pages properly, so it will look as though your Internet connection is not working when it's really just a browser problem, so run some spyware and virus scans and see if they find anything.

Another test you can run is to see if your email client is working for sending and receiving emails. If so, then that proves you have an Internet connection and that there is just something wrong with your web browser. This only applies to locally

Chapter 11 – Basic Troubleshooting

installed email clients and not for webmail accounts, since they are accessed via web pages.

If you have more than one web browser, then you should try and use a different one to see if that allows you to access the Internet. If so, then you know the problem lies within your other web browser and may be a case of a configuration change or spyware infection that has altered its settings. If you only have one web browser, you can try to download another one from a different computer, put it on a flash drive, and then install it on your computer and test it out to see if it works.

Error Messages, Crashes, and Freezing Issues
There are many reasons why a computer can crash, freeze, reboot itself, and so on. Sometimes it's easy to figure out the problem, and sometimes it is very difficult. Poorly written software can cause crashes because of conflicts with other programs, shared files, and compatibility issues with Windows itself. Hardware can cause crashes as well, mostly because of buggy device drivers which the software used to allow the hardware to work with Windows.

The computer's hardware itself can cause issues because if there is a problem with essential hardware (such as the processor or RAM), then Windows will not run properly, if at all. Even something as simple as your processor getting hot can cause issues and crashes. Computer hardware doesn't last forever, even though it seems that if it's going to go bad it will happen sooner rather than later.

Error Types
There are many types of errors you can receive on your computer, which makes it even harder to narrow down the cause sometimes. We will now go over some of the more common error types and what they mean.

- **Application errors** – These can be caused by faulty software in regard to how it was created\programmed. They can also happen because of an unexplained glitch in the software, a compatibility error with other software, or with Windows itself.

- **System errors** – When you see these you can assume it's related to a Windows problem, or maybe even a hardware or driver issue. Many times a reboot will clear up these types of errors.

Chapter 11 – Basic Troubleshooting

- **Stop errors** – These are usually caused by faulty hardware such as bad RAM or a bad sector on your hard drive. When you see these errors, you are usually looking at the famous Blue Screen of Death (discussed next) message on your monitor.

- **POST errors** – POST (Power on Self Test) errors can be caused by faulty hardware or BIOS\motherboard misconfigurations. You usually hear a beep sequence on boot up, and then you can research the beep pattern to help narrow down the problem.

- **Runtime errors** – These are usually caused by corrupt application executables or system files that cause certain programs to shut themselves down, or not even open to begin with. Sometimes they can even cause your computer to freeze up.

Windows Blue Screen of Death (BSOD)
If you have been using Microsoft Windows for a while, there is most likely a chance you have encountered a blue screen of death error. This is where the computer will simply crash in the middle of whatever you are doing, and the screen will be a blue background with white text (figure 11.6) showing the error and some suggestions as to what the cause can be. Many times you can look up the hex values that say something similar to 0xF73120AE to get an idea of the cause. If you are lucky, you can reboot and carry on, but sometimes the BSOD will occur again right after you reboot. BSOD errors are usually caused by faulty hardware or poorly written device driver software and can be very difficult to diagnose.

```
***STOP: 0x000000D1 (0x00000000, 0xF73120AE, 0xC0000008, 0xC0000000)

A problem has been detected and Windows has been shut down to prevent damage
to your computer

DRIVER_IRQL_NOT_LESS_OR_EQUAL

If this is the first time you've seen this Stop error screen, restart your
computer. If this screen appears again, follow these steps:

Check to make sure any new hardware or software is properly installed. If this is a
new installation, ask your hardware or software manufacturer for any windows updates
you might need.

If problems continue, disable or remove any newly installed hardware or software.
Disable BIOS memory options such as caching or shadowing. If you need to use Safe
Mode to remove or disable components, restart your computer, press F8 to select
Advanced Startup Options, and then select Safe Mode.

**** ABCD.SYS - Address F73120AE base at C0000000, DateStamp 36B072A3

Kernel Debugger Using: COM2 (Port 0x2F8, Baud Rate 19200)
Beginning dump of physical memory
Physical memory dump complete. Contact your system administrator or
technical support group.
```

11.6

Chapter 11 – Basic Troubleshooting

Using Task Manager and Ctrl-Alt-Del
One of the tools you will become familiar with when learning how to troubleshoot your computer is called *Task Manager*. This tool is used for a variety of different things, from monitoring performance to killing unresponsive programs.

To open Task Manager, you can do a search for it, or you can press *Ctrl-Alt-Del* on your keyboard and then choose Task Manager from the menu items. Many times, if your computer is not responding to mouse input, you have to use the Ctrl-Alt-Del method. The purpose of Ctrl-Alt-Del is to be sure that you are typing your password into a real login form and not some other fake process trying to steal your password and to also restart the computer if needed. Once you have Task Manager open, you can click on More details at the lower left of the window and then you will see a window with multiple tabs such as Process, Performance and App history.

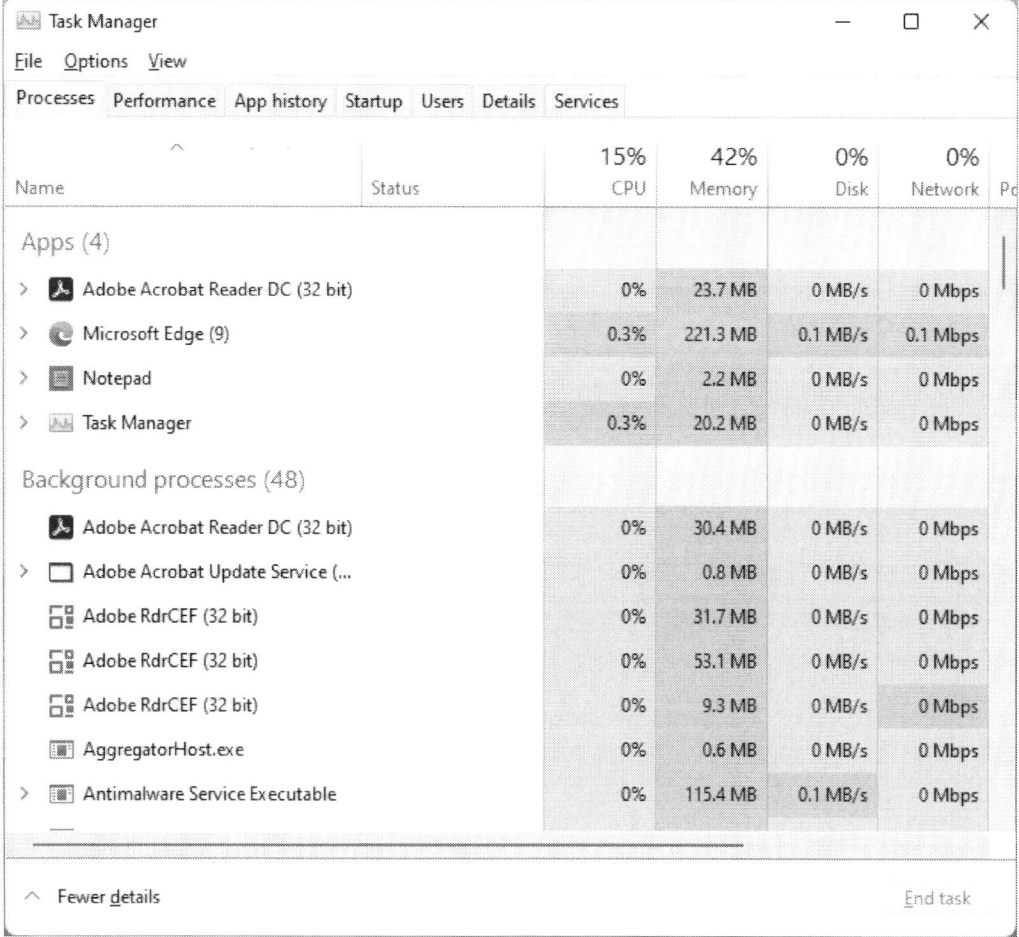

11.7

Chapter 11 – Basic Troubleshooting

Now I will briefly go over what all the tabs in Task Manager are used for so you have a basic understanding of what you can do with it.

- **Processes** – Shows the running processes on the computer and what percentage of CPU, memory, disk, etc. is being used by that process. Processes are instances of an executable (.exe) used to run programs. If you have a program that is not responding, you can highlight it and then click the "End task" button to force close the program. You can also right click the program and go to the actual location of the running executable file.

- **Performance** – This tab shows the CPU, memory, disk, Ethernet, Bluetooth, Wi-Fi, and GPU total usage. You can click on each one and get real time usage graphs as well.

- **App history** – Here you can see what apps were recently used and what resources they have consumed.

- **Startup** – This tab shows you what programs are set to run every time you start your computer. (This topic will be discussed further when we get to the MSconfig tool in the next section.)

- **Users** – If you have multiple users logged on to your computer, then you can get information about what resources and programs they are using from here. You can also disconnect remote users from here.

- **Details** – Here you will find information such as the process ID, status, CPU usage, and memory for running programs. You can also see what user account is running the program, as well as a description of the process.

- **Services** – This tab shows you all the installed services running on your computer and their running state. You can also start or stop services from here.

System Configuration Utility (MSconfig)
The Windows System Configuration utility (also commonly known as MSconfig since that's what most people type in the search or run box to open it) has been around for many years and is still a valuable tool for troubleshooting. It especially comes in handy when you have a virus or spyware issue since they like to set malicious programs to start with your computer. It's also a useful tool to use to increase the performance of your computer, which we will get to in a bit.

Chapter 11 – Basic Troubleshooting

When you open the System Configuration utility, you will notice that it has several tabs just like Task Manager does. Once again, we will go over what each tab does so you can get an idea of how the System Configuration utility can help you manage and troubleshoot your computer. The easiest way to open this tool is to type **msconfig** in the search box.

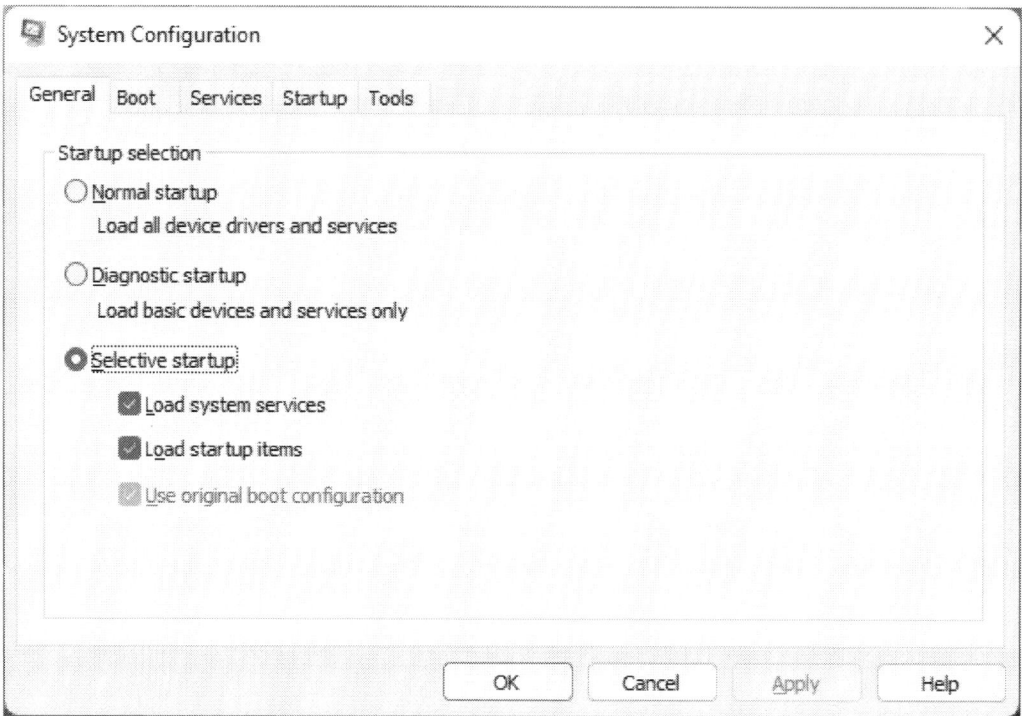
11.8

- **General** – Here you can choose how you want your computer to start up when it comes to device drivers and services. *Normal* will load all drivers and services, *diagnostic* will load only the basic drivers and services, and *selective* will let you choose what services and startup items are loaded. The default is Normal, but the Normal startup option changes to Selective startup if you select any of the options in the Advanced Troubleshooting Settings dialog box.

- **Boot** – This tab lets you decide what operating system to load if you have more than one installed on your computer. The Boot options section lets you choose how your computer boots. So, if you want to do some diagnostics or testing, you can choose *Safe boot* and choose what options to load with it. Safe boot is the same thing as booting into Safe Mode, where you would press F8 on startup to load a basic configuration of Windows. Just be sure to change it back to normal after you are done so it won't go into Safe Mode on your next reboot. You can also change the timeout setting from the default of thirty

- seconds so it will load the default operating system faster if you have more than one.

- **Services** – Just like Task Manager, MSconfig has a Services tab, but here you can enable and disable services, so they start or don't start with Windows. This comes in handy for diagnosing issues, and if you have some services that don't need to start every time with Windows, you can disable them to improve your computer's performance. (Just be sure that you know what the service does before you enable or disable it.)

- **Startup** – In older versions of Windows, this would be where you would see what programs are set to run when Windows starts, but in Windows 10 it just shows a link to open Task Manager, and it will take you to the Startup tab there. This is one of the most commonly used areas because it allows you to prevent software from starting up that doesn't need to run every time you boot your computer, saving you resources and also allowing the computer to start faster. Virus and spyware infections love to put items in your startup section so they will load every time you start your computer. So, if you are having a virus or spyware issue, this should be one of the first places you check to see if there is anything set to run that shouldn't be running, and then you can disable it.

- **Tools** – This tab will let you run a variety of common tools all from one location. Some of these tools include Task Manager, System Restore, and Event Viewer. You can open all these tools from their default location, but it's nice to be able to see them all in one place. Plus, you may even discover a tool you didn't know existed.

S

Booting with the Windows DVD to Run Repair Utilities
When things really go bad with Windows, you might find yourself resorting to the repair and recovery options available on the Windows DVD. To use these tools, you will need to boot from the DVD and run the setup as shown back in Chapter 2, but instead of going through with the installation, you would choose the option to *Repair your computer* instead of clicking on the Install button (figure 11.9).

Chapter 11 – Basic Troubleshooting

11.9

The way Microsoft changes the recovery\repair process changes so much that you might find your options vary from what I have here but hopefully they are close enough so you can follow along if needed!

After clicking on Repair, your computer will be given a list of options to choose from as shown in figure 11.10.

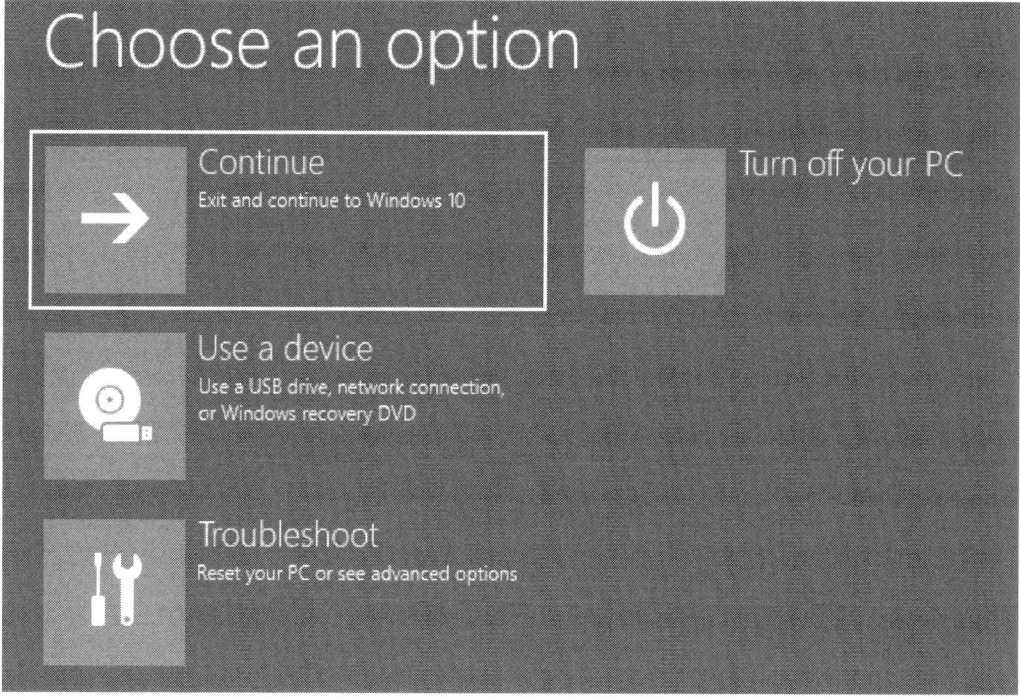

11.10

If you choose the *Continue* option, then the repair process will exit and continue booting into Windows, or at least try to. Choosing the *Turn off your PC* will obviously just shut your computer down and you would only use this if you decided you don't want to try any of the repair options at the moment. So that leaves us with the *Use a device* and *Troubleshoot* options.

The Use a device option will show you devices such as CDROMs, USB drives and network adapters that you have connected to your computer that you might be able to use to boot from in order to run repair utilities.

Chapter 11 – Basic Troubleshooting

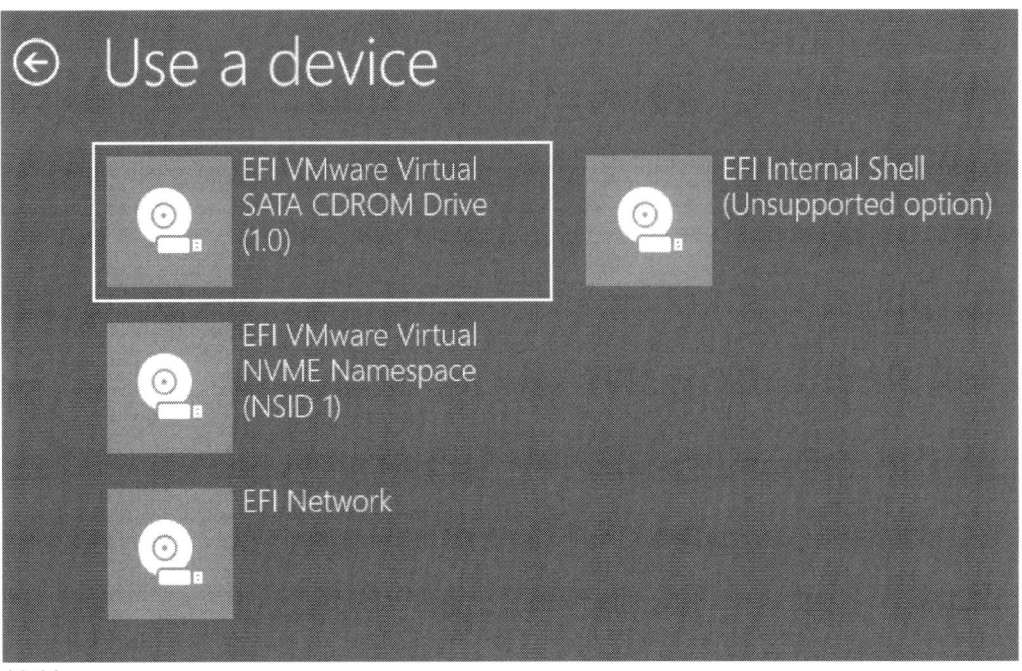
11.11

You will most likely have better luck getting your computer up and running if you use one of the tools from the Troubleshooting section.

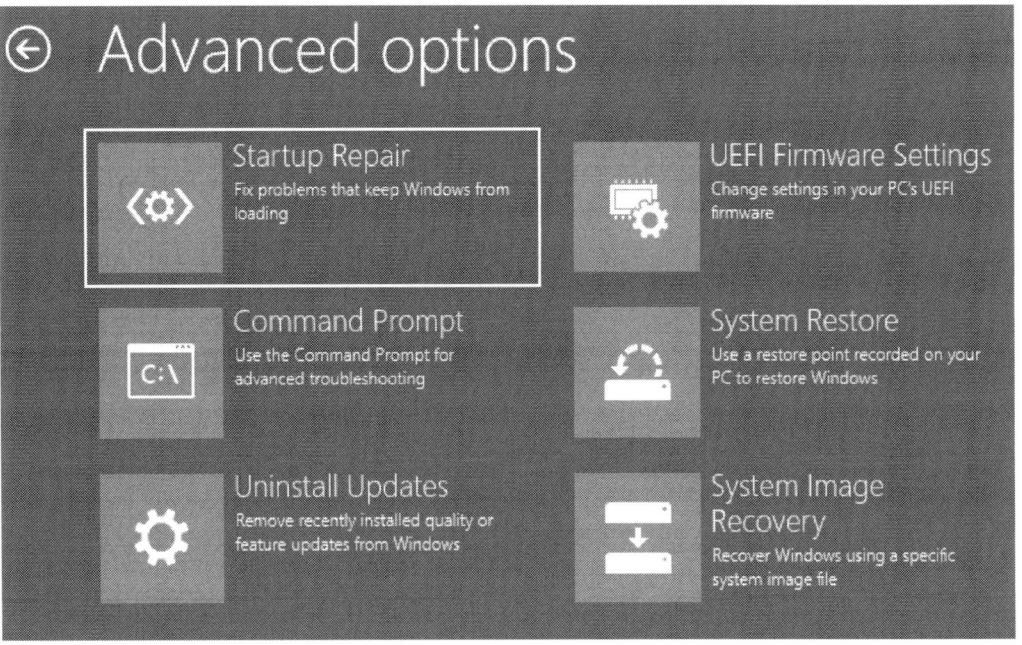
11.12

Here is what each of these tools can do.

- **Startup Repair** – When you run the Startup Repair, Windows will reboot itself and run some diagnostics to see if it can figure out why your computer will not boot into Windows.

- **Command Prompt** – Many times there are specific tools that you can use for troubleshooting that can only be run from a command prompt. Use this option to open a command prompt to run those types of commands.

- **Uninstall Updates** – If you think a certain Windows update is responsible for your computer not starting up properly then you can try this option to uninstall any updates that were installed right before the problem started.

- **UEFI Firmware Settings** – This will boot your computer into its UEFI settings to allow you to correct any changes that might have been made to your bootup settings.

- **System Restore** – This will restore your computer's system configuration back to a point in time of your choosing. However, the catch is that there had to be a restore point made at that time. By restoring your system, you are putting Windows back to the way it was at that time, but it won't affect any of your personal files that were created since the restore point was made.

- **System Image Recovery** – If you, by chance, made a system recovery disk before you had any problems, you can use this option to restore Windows back to the way it was when you created the image. (The image creation is done from the Windows Backup utility.)

You might encounter a situation where nothing you do will get Windows running again, and you are stuck formatting and starting from scratch. If that's the case, and you need to recover your files, try booting with a live Linux CD and then copy them to a USB drive (assuming your drive is ok).

Troubleshooting Windows can be a difficult task and even the so called experts often have trouble figuring out the problem and end up starting over but that is the price we pay I suppose!

What's Next?

Now that you have read through this book and taken your Windows 11 skills to the next level, you might be wondering what you should do next. Well, that depends on where you want to go. Are you happy with what you have learned, or do you want to further your knowledge or maybe get into a career in the IT (information technology) field?

If you do want to expand your knowledge on other computer-related topics, you should look at subject-specific books such as networking, storage, virtualization, etc. Focus on one subject at a time, then apply what you have learned to the next subject. You can also check my other books that cover a wider range of topics mentioned above and then some.

There are many great video resources as well, such as Pluralsight or CBT Nuggets, which offer online subscriptions to training videos of every type imaginable. YouTube is also a great source for training videos if you know what to search for.

If you are content in being a standalone power user that knows more than your friends, then just keep on reading up on the technologies you want to learn, and you will soon become your friends and family's go-to computer person, which may or may not be something you want!

Thanks for reading **Windows 11 Made Easy**. You can also check out the other books in the Made Easy series for additional computer related information and training. You can get more information on my other books on my Computers Made Easy Book Series website.

https://www.madeeasybookseries.com/

What's Next?

You should also check out my computer tips website, as well as follow it on Facebook to find more information on all kinds of computer topics.

www.onlinecomputertips.com
https://www.facebook.com/OnlineComputerTips/

About the Author

James Bernstein has been working with various companies in the IT field for over 20 years, managing technologies such as SAN and NAS storage, VMware, backups, Windows Servers, Active Directory, DNS, DHCP, Networking, Microsoft Office, Exchange, and more.

He has obtained certifications from Microsoft, VMware, CompTIA, ShoreTel, and SNIA, and continues to strive to learn new technologies to further his knowledge on a variety of subjects.

He is also the founder of the website onlinecomputertips.com, which offers its readers valuable information on topics such as Windows, networking, hardware, software, and troubleshooting. James writes much of the content himself and adds new content on a regular basis. The site was started in 2005 and is still going strong today.

Printed in Great Britain
by Amazon